Mostly in the Line of Duty

"I had been for thirty years a happy librarian, first inside my country and later outside. . . ."

Photograph by Chase Studios, Ltd., taken on the occasion of the author's farewell speech as president of the International Federation of Library Associations on 23 November 1974 in Washington, D.C.

Mostly in the Line of Duty

THIRTY YEARS WITH BOOKS

by

HERMAN LIEBAERS

1980

MARTINUS NIJHOFF PUBLISHERS

THE HAGUE / BOSTON / LONDON

Distributors:

for the United States and Canada

Kluwer Boston, Inc.
160 Old Derby Street
Hingham, MA 02043
USA

for all other countries

Kluwer Academic Publishers Group
Distribution Center
P.O. Box 322
3300 AH Dordrecht
The Netherlands

Library of Congress Cataloging in Publication Data   CIP

Liebaers, Herman.
    Mostly in the line of duty.

    Includes index.
    1. Libraries. 2. Books. 3. Liebaers, Herman. 4. Librarians-Belgium-Biography.
I. Title.
Z674.L49   020'.92'4 [B]   79-23942

ISBN 90-247-2228-4

PRINTED IN BELGIUM

Contents

Preface

IT ALL STARTED with the American Library Association (ALA) which wanted to celebrate its centenary in 1976 at its headquarters in Chicago. With five American librarians and non-librarians I was invited to give a centennial paper. I declined the flattering offer because I had left the profession and had no time to do any research. I added innocently, however, that I would be delighted to speak out of personal experience, for instance on the importance of American librarianship in my professional life. This proposal was accepted; I delivered the lecture and my text was printed in *Libraries and the Life of the Mind*.

Before I had read my paper in Chicago I received a request from the International Federation of Library Associations (IFLA) to contribute with *Recollections of a President* to the fiftieth anniversary volume of IFLA (1927-1977). For reasons with which I agreed IFLA did not publish my paper in full, such as it is given here as chapter 10. I am confident that no one will compare the two versions in order to try to find out what has been left out in the earlier printing. Two other papers have appeared in German Festschrifts, one for Kurt Köster from Frankfurt-a/M (chapter 7) and one for Gerhard Liebers from Münster (chapter 5) the former being focussed to accord with the interest of the recipient on medieval Dutch manuscripts, the latter, for similar reasons, on library buildings.

The tone set by the ALA paper and kept by the other requested articles and the chapters which I added on my own initiative shows clearly that this book is half-way between an autobiography and a collection of professional papers. It is a blend, like most of my life has been. The word which I would prefer to use for blend or mixture would be "*bastarda*." It is not listed in the dictionary though it exists with a very specific meaning: the handwriting of the Burgundian manuscripts. All I would like to do is to broaden its meaning slightly and use it as a type of blend applied solely to the people living in what is today called Belgium. For thirty years I have not missed one opportunity to look with love at the Burgundian *bastarda* used in all those princely manuscripts which still represent the rich core of the Royal Library in Brussels. This calligraphic handwriting, a mixture of Gothic and Roman, and blending the qualities of both, has been used to write impressive chronicles of England and of France, also some historical fiction to prove that Philip the Good descended straight from Alexander the Great, with from time to time a sly wink of the eye towards God, as in the glorious *Vita Christi* written in Brussels in 1461 where the *bastarda* matches the exquisite miniatures from the hand of Loyset Liedet.

The very conception of the various chapters excluded a chronological sequence. The book can be read backwards, except for the preface which I wrote last. It can also be read piecemeal, which would certainly be to my advantage because not much consistency went into these pages. Foreign readers are advised to skip chapter 2, as being too heavy with domestic flavour which could be dull from a distance. The situations to which it refers do not travel too well.

The danger of duplication has been my constant worry. The manner in which I spread the material over the various chapters led unavoidably to factual repetitions, but I was careful to limit any detailed treatment to the chapter which seemed most relevant to me. So I leave Brussels several times for my first trip to the United States, but I dealt with it only at some length in chapter 2. There are numerous other examples because I had the feeling that so many activities occurred simultaneously in my life which I, at least, felt worthwhile recording.

The bastard character of this publication lies not always in the way the subject matter has been dealt with but also in the choice of the language. All chapters but one were originally written in English. *Of Men and Books* was written in French because it was published in a Brussels Miscellanea where all contributions had to be in the language of the smaller half of the Belgian population and also of some people outside Belgium. Although I am a poorly trained linguist the language phenomenon remains always with me, more from a sociological than from a philological point of view. At the family level I am living in Dutch, at social events I speak mostly French, and when it comes to professional experience, English comes readily to my mind. Hence it was quite natural for me to write down these recollections in a foreign language. It was, however, awful to rewrite *Of Men and Books* from French into English and I am afraid the result will again give a pejorative meaning to that lovely bastard feeling.

Clark Stillman corrected most of my mistakes, except in those sentences where he felt that I was exaggerating his exceptional qualities and qualifications. Since I started from scratch, without the slightest note because all that counted for me was the event of the next day, there were innumerable gaps in my draft, relating mainly to dates and titles, sometimes to more important factual omissions. Erna Jacobs, a former colleague at the Royal Library and once my international secretary, not only filled them in but also corrected those which I thought I had remembered rightly. Anne Thienpont, whose English is poorer than mine but who reads my handwriting better than I do, typed all chapters several times. She was kind enough to tell me that it improved her English. I am grateful to the Rockefeller Foundation which allowed me to finish the manuscript at its International Study and Conference Centre at Bellagio, Italy.

It has been fun to write this book. I thank all those who induced me to start with it. They forced me, for the first time, to take a hindsight look. This also turned out to be a reason for gratitude. It all happened at an appropriate moment, just when I was about to turn over a new leaf. Indeed the story ends rather abruptly with my resignation from the Council on Library Resources in Washington after the King of the Belgians asked me to work for him. My doubts about my ability to meet his expectations were numerous, but the King waved them off airily: "You only have to cross the street from the Library to the Palace." I was soon to realize that I needed more than a topographical knowledge of Brussels to understand what he meant.

H.L.
July 1979

Acknowledgements

THE PUBLISHERS OF the following original versions of papers kindly granted permission to use them here:

"The Impact of American and European Librarianship upon Each Other" in *Libraries and the Life of the Mind in America* (Chicago, ALA, 1977).

"Anekdotisches zu Kurt Köster und zur Erwerbung mittelniederländischer Handschriften für die Königliche Bibliothek Albert I. Brüssel" in *Bibliothek-Buch-Geschichte: Kurt Köster zum 65. Geburtstag* (Frankfurt am Main, Vittorio Klostermann, 1977). A Dutch version "Jan Deschamps en de Middelnederlandse handschriften in de Koninklijke Bibliotheek" in *Dietsche Warande & Belfort* (mei 1979).

"Personal Recollections of IFLA" in *IFLA's First Fifty Years* (München, Verlag Dokumentation, 1977).

"A New Library in Old Europe" in Festschrift Gerhard Liebers: *Das Buch und sein Haus* (Wiesbaden, L. Reichert Verlag, 1979).

"Des livres et des hommes" in *Liber Amicorum Léo Moulin* (Bruxelles, Elsevier-Sequoia, 1979)

All these papers have been revised and/or extended.

1. Some Irrelevant Personalia

ALTHOUGH ONE OF THE LATEST papal decisions regarding saints killed off Nicholas, he remains in my part of the world the children's best friend. On the eve of 6 December he and his black assistant Piet drop loads of toys, sweets and presents through the chimney of every house, where the kids discover their new wealth in the morning because they had put a lot of food for the Saint's donkey exactly where all the goods were supposed to land. This is a beautiful story and the whole of Brussels' youth should blame the Bollandists, those Jesuits who have been writing the *Acta Sanctorum* in Brussels since 1778, for not having saved our friendly Saint from the Roman rigours.

The story did, however, not reach my parents' house. My father lived by principles, the first one being that I had to share them. So he had decided when I was about six years old, I guess, that the Saint Nicholas' legend was nonsensical and that he was going to tell me the truth. One day I heard the brutal reality that the Saint did not exist, that my father was buying the toys and that after all he was actually Nicholas. Next morning at school it was not long before I wanted to spread out my newly acquired knowledge and I said casually to some of my classmates "I am the son of Santa Claus." Since nobody apparently wanted to believe me it ended with a serious fight which I was doomed to lose. One against all.

Later on, elliptic thinking has played other tricks on me.

Another principle of my father was that no schoolmaster should touch a hair of my head since he himself never did. He repeated it so many times, that I was anxiously waiting for a teacher to spank me. This supposedly happened some time when I was ten or eleven years old. The sweetest of my teachers, Mr. De Keghel, whom I liked very much, and who liked me similarly, had lost his temper at my misbehaviour and had made a threatening gesture in my direction from which I had concluded, in bad faith, that he had tried to hit me. During lunchtime at home – because in Belgium we went home for lunch and most people still do – I gave my version of the story to my father, who apparently was also waiting eagerly and decided to accompany me to school in order to find out what kind of a wild animal had dared to touch his beloved son. On our way to school we passed by the world-famous convent of the Scheutists, who had tried to convert China to Christianity and who all had in fact fallen in love with their country of adoption. Later in life I met quite a lot of them in South East Asia, as they had been forced out of mainland China, but were still reading communist papers coming from the place where their hearts lingered. They were in all respects wonderful people, and one of the most out-standing of them was Jesuit Father Fernand Verbiest (1623-1688) who had become the Imperial Astronomer and whose manu-scripts and books are kept in the Brussels Royal Library, while his observatory can still be seen in Peking, at least from a distance.

When we passed before the convent, my father still angry and I already ashamed, neither of us cared about the good fathers and their missionary vocation. Just beyond the silent walls was the school and in no time we found ourselves in the director's office where my father made a great fuss about my mishandling. The puzzled director called in the teacher who did not guess what was ahead of him. Neither did I. After he had listened to my father's elaborate complaints, while staring at me in growing bewilder-ment, he finaly said: "Herman, will you please repeat on my head what I did to yours." Extremely shameful I slightly touched him at his right or left temple with my right forefinger and that was it. My father looked at me for one or two seconds and gave me such a heavy blow on the right cheek that I fell on the floor, where I would have preferred to stay for the rest of my life. I do not remember how it all ended, but knowing the kindheartedness of the schoolmaster, I suppose that he brought me back to the school-room consoling me for the harm he had done to me. Because he was a wise man we remained good friends and he took me out regularly on private bicycle tours. Once he suggested a major one because I had just received a new bike. Ten minutes after we had left home I made a false movement, badly injured my knee and we had to return to my mother immediately. In later years I met him from time to time with his clear blue eyes and blond hair, growing younger the more I grew older.

That is about all I remember from my grammar school days.

According to my father's rather newly acquired political credo I was to become a manual worker, not an ordinary one of course but a kind of foreman in mechanical or electrical equipment. Belgium was fortunate to have in this field a school of European reputation, founded early in the century, the Labour University *(Université du Travail)*, in the old industrial city of Charleroi, where van Gogh started his preaching career. Among its former pupils it proudly recalls Chou-En-lai and the school is still going strong today. In view of this peculiar schooling I went first, after leaving grammar school, for two years to a "fourth grade school" which has a purely manual training programme and I finished it with honours in carpentry. Instead of going afterwards straight to the Labour University my father was advised by its director to send me first for three years to a high school in my home town and then to enter me in that University at the age of seventeen or eighteen. The jump from fourth grade to high school was awful and I was tentatively accepted, although I knew nothing of what had been taught there during the two previous years. My position improved over the years and instead of leaving high school after three years I finished it and went to a regular university.

From high school days I keep happy memories of schoolmates and teachers. The school was my heaven of friendliness after my parents' household had gone to pieces. School laws were in a transition period – it has been my experience that they are always in a transition period, at least in my country. I would even venture to say that education exists solely to be reformed – and I had two teachers of mathematics, one using Dutch and the other French. They were both outstanding characters, had little in common and were good musicians and friends. The older one was Father Lagae and the younger Jacques Mueller. Father Lagae was no Father at all, but his son Arthur was our classmate and so all of us called him Father Lagae. I remember that one of his courses was descriptive geometry, while Jacques Mueller was teaching analytical geometry. Arthur, who was not a brilliant mathematician, had always the best answers to the assigned tasks in analytic geometry and every week Mueller's comments were the same: "Arthur, tell your father that his son is a mathematical genius." What struck me also every week was that Father Lagae's answers were always three or four times shorter than ours. At that time my doubts about mathematical rigours began to take shape.

It was reported to me that Mueller told a pleasant story on the occasion of his retirement. Among his former pupils he had had many good mathematicians and most of them had become clever engineers. Unfortunately five of the better ones took the wrong road: Jacques Ledoux who became the director of the national film archives; Maurice Huisman who, after a brilliant masters in chemistry, became director of the National Opera; André Vandernoot who was to be a leading orchestra conductor; a fourth one whose name escapes me; and myself as number five, who became a librarian, which was worst of all from Mueller's point of view since the others were at least in a more pronounced artistic profession. Like many mathematicians he was very close to all forms of artistic expression, fortunately I would say, because the mathematicians who lack this interest are the most conceited people on earth.

With Mueller behind me and with a mathematical background I decided to try physics at the university. Today I am still not sure that it was a mistake, but at the time I had a highly persuasive girl friend who convinced me that it was one, and that I had to study Germanic philology because she was going to do so. With the academic regulations in force this was not an easy transition because I first had to pass an examination before a central jury to prove that my knowledge of Latin and Greek, of which I had had none in high school, was satisfactory. Instead of physics I studied Latin and Greek for one solid year, from early morning until late at night. Without really knowing these languages, they remained dead for me indeed, I miraculously passed the examinations. Nearly every other student flunked mathematics, but I was exempted. By the time I was ready to start Germanic philology my girl friend and I had quarrelled and I went without her to Ghent University.

Since I was living alone with my mother, my father took me on a yearly vacation, which he liked very much. I remember that in 1937 or so we spent a few days together in the French Vosges and we travelled on his newly acquired motorcycle, I sitting in the back. It started rather strangely. Fifty miles south of Brussels he needed to refill his gas tank and he drove to the pump in such an elegant way that both of us ended up on the gravel. The first day he wanted to reach Metz, which we barely did after nightfall. He found a nice place to put up our tent and we were not yet lying down when we heard one loud motor noise after another and it lasted for hours. Next morning when we awoke we were surrounded by an armed police force because we had put our tent up at the very end of the runway of a military airport.

We finally reached the beautiful Vosges and more particularly the Ballon d'Alsace. Unfortunately we were aiming for the top when from the opposite side the *Tour de France* poured down upon us. My dear father, rather stubbornly, wanted to drive against the Tour. After some time he said to me "you are too heavy at my back and I suggest that you walk to the top while I serpentine upwards". I was the most happy man in the world and walked with my knapsack through the woods, crossed the roads and the crowds, convinced that I would never meet my father again in the Vosges. My grief was great when he and I met exactly at the upper milestone and I silently jumped on the back to be driven by a happy father to the lower regions of this world. Since that time I have been keen on the *Tour de France* and in later years I have always hoped to cover it with a literary reportage. It never materialized but others have done it much better than I could have dreamed of. It is really the pacifist epic of the twentieth century, whatever commercial interests may be involved.

At the University I had two peace years and two war years. I started as a very poor student. As is well known, Belgium is one of the easiest countries in the world in which to be admitted to a university, but to finish it is another story. I was careless, did not attend the lectures but was very prompt at all basketball games, had a good time with my two roommates who were no better students than I (who actually had already decided to leave the University after one more year of fun). I was very popular at the fraternity meetings. Actually I did everything except study. I owe it to a classmate, Isa Hereng, whom I was to marry five years later, that I passed my first examinations. My qualification as a serious student improved gradually over the years.

If I had to blame someone, except myself, for the fact that I wrongly used my freedom of living alone in Ghent it should be my mother, my sweet and gentle mother. During the five preceding years, when we were left to ourselves, I was her god, and I was spoiled to the roots. I was too young to understand that the best thing my parents could do was to separate. They had nothing in common. My mother was modesty and kindness personified, living for the others, perfect in the household, but with no wide horizon beyond. Sensitive and with a lot of common sense, she had everything to make a normal and reasonable husband happy. But my father was not a normal and reasonable man. He had an extremely strong personality and made everybody whom he met unhappy after a while, my mother first, then me and all the others. He was admired by many but it never lasted long.

When I said earlier that he was a man of principles, I should rather have said a man of *idées fixes* for a fixed period of time. He turned socialist during the first world war and immediately became an active propagandist since he was convinced that everybody had to become socialist with him. He was one of the earliest Belgian travellers to the USSR. He was also one of the first to break with the Soviet Union. He did it together with the Dutch poetess Henriëtte Roland Holst van der Schalk, on whom I was to write my thesis later. It is said that, as a child, I met Trotsky at home, but I do not know if it is true. I remember, however, many German Jews sharing our table, who had fled from their home country after Hitler came to power.

My father was a public figure who had his hour of fame as a pacifist and anti-fascist leader in the years before World War II. Nowadays, students regularly ask me questions about him when they have to prepare a paper on pre-war Belgian politics. I generally cannot answer their questions because I have practically no archival material, although he wrote and published a lot. Most of his life he earned his living as a union leader, and one of his employees told me a story which is rather characteristic of him, I would say. They went together to London and neither of them knew one word of English. Upon arrival, before going to the hotel or the meeting, my father wanted to see Karl Marx's tomb. I cannot imagine his conversation with the London bobbies but for sure he finally landed at the tomb. My father is responsible for the fact that I made two solemn promises to myself, one to stay out of politics and two, not to get married. I kept the first one. I probably owe to him the international dimension which was soon going to appear in my work. He was, however, an ideological internationalist; I was to become a purely geographical one, locally as uncommitted as possible.

The last prewar trip with my father took us to Sweden. He had some professional meeting and I wanted to see the *Codex Argenteus* at the University of Uppsala. I never reached Uppsala because I was held up in Stockholm by the outbreak of the war, actually by the beginning of *la drôle de guerre* period. [1] Everybody was panic-stricken and I was so scared that I even knew Swedish for one day. I read the newspaper to my father in order to have some information about what was happening around us. My father was rightly afraid to go home via Germany and he decided to fly. I was taking the return trip as planned by train from Stockholm to Trelleborg, from Trelleborg to Sassnitz by boat and again by train from Sassnitz to Brussels via Cologne.

On the boat, in the middle of the night and in a complete black-out, I ran into someone. I apologized and from the voice which answered me I heard it was a woman and the language was German. We went on talking for a couple of hours and I wondered how she looked and whether she was old or young. When daylight came up faintly on a smooth Baltic sea I gradually discovered a beautiful, young, blond German woman. The conversation went on very easily and my German must have been better than usual. She was going to Cologne too and we spent at least twelve hours standing in the corridors of an overcrowded train, the seats being reserved for the soldiers who were joining their units. From time to time we fell asleep on one another's shoulders, but time passed quickly and when we separated we decided to exchange letters, she writing in French and I in German. We were never to meet again but we remained in correspondence for some time. One day she came to my house in the uniform of a *Kriegsmädel*. I was not at home and my mother kicked her out furiously, because such a visit under German occupation was enough to compromise our reputation. Apparently she did not know, and neither did I, that I was on a blacklist of the Germans and that in turn such a visit was compromising for her too.

In the train from Cologne to Brussels I was a witness to appalling scenes. At the border Jewish families, among the last ones to try to flee from Nazi Germany, were torn violently from the train which halted over a ditch where many of them were discovered hiding

---

[1] Finally I was to see the *Codex* thirty-eight years later when I went to Sweden as a member of the suite of Ilya Prigogine who was going to collect his Nobel prize.

under the carriages. I myself was so exhausted that I passed through Brussels twice before I awoke. When I finally arrived home my mother was mad at me and asked me why I had not decided to stay in Sweden? I did not have the courage to answer that I had come home for her.

The last journey I took with my father was in May 1940 when we fled to France for the German invasion. In fact we left separately. He went by car and I took the road by bicycle with a friend. The worst thing which happened to me during this flight occurred less than one hour after we had left Brussels. The road full of refugees was attacked by Stukas and the two of us dived off the road and landed with our faces in the midst of a bunch of nettles. In the hell of the north of France we were pushing our bicycles when suddenly someone blew the horn and there was my father. My friend and I put our bicycles against the trunk of a tree and we stepped into the car, on our way to Poitiers. There, my father was assigned to Dijon to look after Belgian refugees and we joined him on the eastward journey. I worked on a farm for two weeks. It was heavy work but I earned my first salary. My father lived, of all places, at Gevrey-Chambertin, although he was a teetotaler and I had not yet discovered the qualities of the high ranking Burgundian wine produced on the spot. One Sunday my friend and I decided to pay a visit to my father by hiking to Gevrey-Chambertin. An old Citroën with two officers picked us up. In the back we spoke Dutch and in the front French was used by the officers to convince each other that we were German spies and that they were not going to deliver us at the Cathedral of Dijon, where my friend wanted to attend mass, but straight to prison. We looked at one another and did not protest. Arriving at the police station it was not difficult to prove that we were simple Belgian refugees and it all ended with a cheerful farewell. When leaving the room my friend and I again commented on the whole scene in Dutch, and we were interrupted by a little old man who looked like a farmer to us. "Are you Flemish?" he asked us. Since we were, he told us that he had been sitting in the room for two days because they thought he was a German, and that he could not explain to them that he was one of the *Flandriens* who had been coming for thirty years to Burgundy to weed the beets. We volunteered as interpreters, went back to our police friends and got him out in no time. Apocryphal or no, Charles V was right when he said that a man with two languages is worth two men. Still in Burgundy, I registered with the University of Dijon, but before I could take courses the Germans approached the city and we had to flee again, landing this time in Périgord. Once more I worked on a farm and I even became rather good at collecting truffles under the guidance of an old sow.

My friend went farther southwards, while my father and I, together with one or two of his colleagues decided, like most Belgians, to go home soon after the Germans had stopped at the Loire river. Petrol for the car was one of the major problems and when we reached the river the rumour spread that, on the other side, the Germans distributed it generously to civilians. I was the youngest of the group and was sent across the river with a jerry can. This was still a new gadget which had entered our lives with the beginning of the war. There was not too much water and I began to walk confidently until I reached the middle with water up to my neck. It was running fast and I began to swim with one hand, keeping the jerry can afloat with the other. After half an hour I had the feeling that I was being driven westwards and that the middle of the river was not very far behind me. I was exhausted and thought the situation over. I probably was going to die unheroically in front of a peaceful German line. I decided to inhale deeply, to let me sink to the bottom of the river and to rest in the meantime. To my surprise I hit the bottom so quickly that I hurt my toes. I got on my feet and barely had water above my knees, I looked around and blushed. I met the first German soldiers on the riverbank. They filled my jerry can and I walked back through the river without telling anyone what had happened to me when I was on my way to the enemy.

Back home I finished the University in two years, which were years as dull as the preceding ones had been pleasant. The professors and the student body were divided into two groups, a minority which was pro-German and a majority which was anti. I belonged to the latter group. I have always tried to agree with the majority, to take the middle of the road, to match the average. I have not always been successful, but that was not my fault. In retrospect I must confess that I was never compelled to make a choice in my life. All major decisions which affected the course of my existence were taken by others. I am not even sure that my reactions to these decisions were purely mine.

I went practically straight from my Flemish University to a

German concentration camp located, however, in my beloved Flanders. This happened in 1943. I am not going to dwell upon this period of my youth. So much has already been written on the subject of totalitarian temptation and in addition it commands a tone which is not exactly the one I have decided to use throughout this book. My experience has been that of the more lucky prisoners, since I am still alive. The camp, Breendonck, was not an extermination camp, as Auschwitz for instance. Though quite a number of the inmates did not survive torture and hardship, most of them were sent to other camps. That was my case and I ended in the Citadel of Huy, in the French-speaking part of Belgium. This being said, both Breendonck and Huy were psychologically situated in Germany, the first one in SS land, the second one in the land of the armed forces'. This implied some difference.

One day someone knocked at the door at 5 AM and it was not the milkman, as Winston Churchill would have said. I was arrested by mistake and now I would say it was a good one. The Gestapo thought they had laid hands on my father, and thanks to the fact that I knew some German I was able to send them off on the wrong track, which was not too difficult, I must admit.

My questioning started with a few kicks and slaps before one word was said. Then I had to sit next to someone who fortunately proved to be an ass in uniform. He had a list of questions typed out before him and he was supposed to fill in my answers, while a beautiful lady interpreter was sitting in front of us. When they discovered that I knew some German – more at that time than today – she awarded herself half an hour off to smoke a cigarette while looking at other prisoners who had not yet reached the talking stage. A quick glance at the list of questions showed clearly that they had mistaken me for my father, and I was wondering how I could explain that my arrest was an error without involving him. When I was blamed for having set up a communist cell in 1920 it was rather easy to convince my stupid examiner that I was one year old at the time, but I felt that I came pretty close to my father. I saved him and myself because I could see a misspelling of my name. You should have heard my arguments, one more pseudo-scientific than the other. My fresh graduation as a philologist was a tremendous asset. I pretended that I got excited by the fact that the end of my name was spelled -*aers*, while on his sheet it was erroneously written -*aert*. And didn't my Teutonic judge know that -*aers* meant that my family came from the eastern part of the country, actually close to the German border, while -*aert* was used only in the western part? All this proved that there was not the slightest relation between me and the criminal he was looking for. Had I known at the time that in the western part of the country, actually in my university town Ghent, a Liebaert was living who would join the government soon after the war, I would have been more cautious. Anyhow, Minister Liebaert also survived the war.

Notwithstanding the false track on which I put my examiner, I was still afraid during the following days that I would discover my father among the newcomers. Finally the war ended without my father being caught and that is the reason why the error of my imprisonment was a good one, because it was easier to survive at my age than at his. I must admit shamefully that I nearly sent him to jail myself. After I was transferred to the second prison it became possible to communicate with the outside world and when a prisoner who looked trustworthy to me was released, I asked him to warn my father that the Germans were after him. I certainly am not a good psychologist because all he did was to send an open postcard to my father telling him to hide. When I myself was liberated I learned that my father had blundered as much as I did. The day after I was arrested he went to the Gestapo headquarters in Brussels, just before they were brilliantly attacked by an RAF fighter, the pilot of which was the Belgian Jean de Selys Longchamps. In a lift, he was face to face with a German officer and when my father protested my innocence, the officer asked "But is there no other Liebaers?" At that time, everything at once became clear. My father had had some difficulty in being allowed to enter the Gestapo headquarters, but he felt relieved that he could leave it after all as a free man.

The most original part of my life in prison was my liberation. I was *Zugführer*, that means responsible for the forty-odd prisoners who slept and ate in the same room. One morning I was standing in front of my group and had to report, as usual, the exact number of inmates. That day I was supposed to say forty-two and I said forty. And then everything happened as in a poor movie. The commander, followed by half a dozen officers descending gradually in rank, walked by until from the last one the news reached the commander that two were missing. He stopped, came back to me and shouted "How many?" My answer must have been a whispered "Forty!" He was furious and ordered my arrest and I said to myself "Now I am a prisoner in the second degree!" I was thrown in a dark cell and I do not remember how often I received a piece of bread and a cup of water. After some time, which seemed endless to me, I was called to the commander's office and I knew that this meant a concentration camp in Germany. To my surprise he asked me to sit down in front of his desk, which I knew well because I had been assigned earlier to the cleaning of his office. He looked at me and I looked at him and there was a long, strange silence. "Did you know that two of the prisoners, for whom you were responsible had decided to flee?" "No" was my lie, which he knew as such very well, but which I did not know he knew so well. At the time of the explanation I was completely ignorant of what had happened to the two fellow prisoners.

The night before their flight the two prisoners, who were French, came to see me and told me an incredible story. For two months they had been making ropes with all the fabrics they could collect in such a strange place as the one in which we were living. They asked me abruptly "Do you want to try it with the two of us?" "How much time do you give me to think it over?" "Two hours" was the answer. These were two long hours during which I reviewed as well as I could all aspects of the adventure. Finally I said "Thank you for your proposal, but I shall stay here and I wish you good luck." My main argument to stay was that they had been condemned to death and that I had not gone beyond the stage of questioning. What made me hesitant, however, was the fear of being killed, with all the other prisoners, if the Germans had to quit the camp on the approach of the allied forces. They went and were successful in their difficult nighttime escape gliding down along the cliffs, but were stupidly killed by French customs officers when they tried to cross the Belgian-French border.

"Here I have an order from Brussels" the commander went on, "to inform me that I can liberate you." Another endless silence. And while he was carelessly holding the order with one corner and balancing it between us, he added: "Since you are being punished, I have the authority to tear it to pieces and moreover, while you were cleaning my office, you listened to Radio London." The following silence was ominous to me. Finally he said "I listen to Radio London too, and you should have spared yourself the trouble of turning the knob around when leaving the office. You may go." I could have kissed him but I did not move. I could have answered him but I remained silent. I slowly went down the slope of the Citadel with the last guard assigned to me. He was from Schleswig-Holstein and the allies were going to be there before him. From the gate of the Citadel I walked, all by myself, to the railroad station.

At the station I sat on my empty cane suitcase and waited for the train to Brussels. After a couple of hours the train was announced and, at the moment of boarding the carriage, I took one of the most important decisions of my life, and one of which I am still proud today. I let the train go without me.

I was a free man and could take a personal decision. Nobody expected me at home, so I waited patiently for the next train and sat for many hours – not many trains during the war – on my cane suitcase again. Probably, the most beautiful hours of my life. I reviewed carefully what had happened to me since the university. I did it all with a boundless generosity, with that feeling of being the winner and being sorry for the losers.

During those hours of quiet meditation I took two decisions for the future. The first one was that trivialities would never again upset me. If I missed the streetcar, I would take the next one. If things did not go exactly as I expected them to go, I would adapt myself to the situation. In my excitement I even said to myself "You entered prison as a pessimist and you are leaving it as an optimist." I have, of course, cursed the streetcar which I missed, but all in all I have not done too badly in this respect.

I do not know if the second decision was more serious but it certainly was more difficult to apply. Henceforth I was going to live superficially, *vivre à la surface des choses*. It meant something at the opposite pole of what the Germans call *"warum einfach wenn es kompliziert auch geht?"* why make it simple when you can make it complicated? Life is not simple and with the assistance of the great authors one can try to understand some of its roots. Why did the Gestapo kill innocent people? Why did they hate people who loved their country, with a love as pure as their avowed allegiance was dirty? Such a quest, which like other students I had started at the University, would inevitably lead to a disbelief in mankind. After having spent too much time too close to death, I eagerly wanted to enjoy a rediscovered sense of being alive. Henceforth, I would avoid unanswerable questions, I would ignore the existence of enemies, I would deny the presence of the negative sides of life. I would try to escape dramatic issues. And I was prepared to pay the price: the simplification of reality, the acceptance of others' deceits, the control over feelings, and, when it comes to admitting the naked truth, I am reluctantly prepared to confess a leaning towards egoism. I have however tried to live as honestly as possible by this deliberate attitude. This has not proved to be too difficult over the years. I would venture as an explanation that most of my strongest relations have always been with groups of people, with institutions, with collective issues. Exceptions were however unavoidable and when it came to deeper involvement with individuals, I tried to explain the basis on which I had been living and I backed out. Such an explanation was never easy, and writing it down drew me away from what I considered a page or so ago the most happy hours of my life. [2]

These hours on the cane suitcase in Huy were filled with the wildest ideas, forgetting where I was and who I was. I do not remember much but I went several times over the scene of my release in the commander's office. What would have happened if I had not remained silent? For instance, if I had said, when he blamed me for listening to Radio London, that on the other hand every week since I had been under his custody I had read *Das Reich*. He might have thought that I was kidding, and that would have been the end with a German officer. Actually I regularly read Goebbels' *Reich* and since I had nothing else to do I read it carefully, I read it aloud to the other prisoners, I translated most of it into French; in one word, I read exactly between the lines of what Goebbels wrote. Believe me it was not so different from Radio London. What the speakers simply called "a victory on the front" was translated by Goebbels in German as "faithfully executed

---

[2] All these memories and some other strange reminiscences came back to my mind in vivid detail when not so long ago, more than thirty years after the events, I inaugurated a monument to the victims of the Huy Citadel, not listening too carefully to the patriotic speeches. This return to the past was immediately followed by another. I had carefully avoided visiting again the camp at Breendonck, which had been turned into a national monument. I was not a member of the association of former prisoners. But when President and Mrs. Heinemann had expressed the wish to deposit a wreath at the gallows of the camp during their official visit to Belgium, I was assigned to them. After more than thirty years I went back for the first time to the hideous place and closed my eyes, seeing myself mounting the gallows.

withdrawal according to a pre-established plan." I admired his journalistic quality very much and I understand that in the meanwhile a lot of university theses have been written on this and similar linguistic phenomena. The younger students of totalitarian language do not risk their lives by listening to Radio London, and in fact I should not have done it either.

When I finally arrived home my mother told me that I had better try to disappear again because the Germans were sending people of my age to forced-labour camps in Germany. A forced-labour camp was not exactly what I had dreamt of upon my release from prison. I discovered, however, that civil servants were exempt from forced labour and so I decided to become a civil servant while waiting quietly for the end of the war, in order to start real life in peace. I looked up my main professor at Ghent University, who sent me to a colleague who had heard from a friend that there was a vacancy at the Royal Library in Brussels. I went to see the director who told me he wanted a philologist trained in Germanic languages, who was not pro-Nazi. I was his man and happily I entered the Library a few months before the end of the war, firmly decided to look for a more lively job when peace should be restored. I stayed in the Library for thirty years, with a couple of escapes, I must admit.

The very first thing I did when I entered the Library was to ask for a day off to get married. I was not proud at all of doing so but the date had been fixed weeks before I knew that I was going to work at the Royal Library. During the war the wedding ceremony was reduced, unavoidably, to its simpliest version. My wife to be and I, however, found a cart and a couple of horses to take us to the city hall and my parents-in-law were rather good at securing some food, allowing us to have, with some relatives and friends, a dinner far above the allowed average. It is strange how a group of people can forget, for a while, the worst misery in the midst of which it is doomed to live for a prolonged period.

At the end of the dinner my father wanted to make a speech. Making speeches was a major part of his life, although not exactly on occasions like weddings. He was a born politician and so he always wanted to impress his audience. According to his tone the distance was a short one between my wedding party and a party reunion. It took him half an hour to show to a rather dozing audience how exceptional the fact was that he and his son were both born on the 1st of February. And proudly he sat down. My father-in-law was a completely different person. Modest and shy, going through life as unobtrusively as possible. He felt however compelled to say a few words also, which he hated to do. He rose and said, "My daughter and I were also born on the same day of the same month, the 16th of March." And he sat down, while the whole effect of my father's speech was killed in a few seconds.

No honeymoon trip during the war. Marriage being customarily celebrated on a Saturday, I joined my basket-ball team the next day and played a regular game, offering afterwards a poor drink, because there was no other available, to my teammates on the occasion of my wedding. On Monday morning I resumed my work in the Library.

In retrospect I would add that my whole share of life's misery fell upon me before my marriage. Firstly, the complete failure of my parents' wedded life marked me deeply – so much so that I decided never to get married in order to avoid inflicting upon another woman what my father did to my mother. Circumstances however decided otherwise. Secondly, the war and the German occupation took the better sides of life away. I did not really suffer from hunger but it was the doubts about the human race, the inescapable evil which was always present. And finally the concentration camp, living permanently with death as the closest neighbour and, even worse, with the constant fear of being tortured. There are no degrees in the dehumanizing aims of concentration camps, as there is no liberalization in totalitarian regimes.

Reaching the end of this introductory chapter, which has already been unavoidably too personal, I guess I should add here that my fellow citizens probably do not consider me as a typical Belgian. I was born on the linguistic border, I lived all my life in Brussels, the hot meeting point of the two national communities, and I have already prepared, some time ago, my retirement at a third place on the demarcation line. I further belong to a double minority in Brussels because I am a non-Catholic Fleming. It is however pleasant to confess that I feel fully at ease in the nation's capital and among Catholic friends.

This last paragraph was needed, I thought, to round off the preceding abstract of what happened to me before I started real life. I tried to do it in such a way that it may explain later professional and nonprofessional attitudes and activities.

2. A Librarian by Accident

MY FIRST ASSIGNMENT in the Library was to translate the subject catalogue from French into Dutch. No less, no more and fortunately I knew nothing about catalogues. I was seated at a small desk with my back towards the readers, close to the Aa-drawer. And faithfully I began to translate the main entries. Luckily the first couple of hours it was only "A" to be translated by "A". It raised, however, the first doubt about the usefulness of my work. I do not remember exactly but by the end of the day I may have reached "Aux" and I was disgusted forever with the catalogue. I went home with the idea of resigning next day. Next morning an elderly librarian, Franz Schauwers, waited for me and told me that he had been absent the day before and so he had not been able to give me a welcoming introduction as he usually did with newcomers. Franz Schauwers was a bachelor and was married to the Library.

When he wanted to start with the foundation date of the Library I interrupted him and said that he would be wasting his time because I was going to quit anyhow. I did not quit and he explained to me why such a ridiculous assignment had been forced upon me. In Belgium the Flemish majority of the population was only a quantitative phenomenon and that is the reason why the American historian Shephard Clough, an expert on minority problems, was so excited when he discovered after World War I an oppressed majority in Belgium. He was so eager to understand that he ended up in jail and afterwards wrote his book *The Flemish Question*. At the time I did not know the story, but during my first trip to the United States, Marnix Gijsen, director of the Belgian information service in New York and a leading Flemish novelist, told it to me and introduced me to Shephard Clough, who did not complain about his unpleasant experience during his youth in Belgium; on the contrary, it allowed him to work in quietness.

To make a long story short, the social elite of Belgium had not yet felt the necessity, at the outbreak of World War II, to use the two national languages – French and Dutch – on an equal footing in public institutions and among many other outcomes of this situation there was only a French subject catalogue in the National Library. Some Flemish nationalists made the mistake of using the German occupation powers to impose fair answers to their complaints. This is what happened in the Library and it explains also why the director wanted a philologist in Germanic languages who was not a pro-Nazi. My instructions were clear: I had to pretend to translate the catalogue and to do as little as possible while waiting for the end of the war.

It did not take long to realize that the translation of a catalogue with a few million entries was pure nonsense and I forgot about it. Instead I tried to understand the place where I was working and my attention turned to general problems. This was encouraged by an in-service training which was compulsory and which opened all major library aspects to me. There was and there still is no formal library training at the University level in Belgium. Later I was to discover that this in-service training happened in an awfully old-fashioned way.

I remember that I had to spend most of my time in the cataloguing division, where endless discussions took place among the dozen or so cataloguers because the decisions on nearly each entry came close to a philosophical issue. The senior cataloguer had only one enemy: the cataloguing rule. To try to apply rules was a proof of intellectual poverty. This having been going on for two generations at least, it is not difficult to imagine what kind of a catalogue was available to the reading public. I was appalled but happy too because I was going to stay away from these sterile discussions. It could never have occurred to me at the time that some fifteen years later, at the very end of the year, I was going to close the subject catalogue and open the next day, exactly on 1 January 1960, two new subject catalogues: a French one and a Dutch one.

The building in which the Library operated was the visual symbol of its obsolescence. As in so many European cities it was an old princely palace. In the Brussels case it had more or less been adapted to library use over a period which lasted more than a century. When I discovered it the reading room reminded me of the former ball room, the rare books were close to the wine cellar, the staff was housed in the attics, the readers had to queue to find a seat and had to wait hours to get a book. In every corner books were piled up. In the stacks the books were so tightly pressed that when a journalist looked at them he said that his professor of engineering cited pressed books to explain the idea of pre-stressed concrete. In our case it was post-stressed with books forced between books beyond any reasonable limit. Upon my first acquaintance with the Library a ten-year-old project existed to erect a new building and I of course did not realize that the implementing of the plans was going to be one of the major tasks of my professional life.

When, in my part of the world, war came to an end I was drafted into the army. The few months I spent in uniform represent the vaudevillesque episode in my life. Everything was in a mess and, if I remember correctly, the government had decreed six conditions for being granted early leave from the army. I fulfilled five of them. The one I could not claim was that agriculture needed me, but all the others were there: civil servant, married, political prisoner, etc. In retrospect I would say that this short passage in the army may explain why I did not leave the Library at the end of the war as had been my intention from the very beginning. It was a kind of transition between war and peace. I had no specific vocation, except that I had been playing with the idea of becoming a journalist. Local and family circumstances having temporarily forced my wife into journalism, I thought that one was enough. (In fact she stayed for more than thirty years with the same newspaper.) I must confess that I had taken a kind of liking to the odd place, as I probably would have for any place where destiny had dropped me. So, I decided to stay somewhat longer and see what would happen. I did not yet know myself and did not realize that nothing would happen.

For half a dozen years I tried to strike a balance between a daily cleaning of my desk of routine work and a systematic effort to understand what libraries meant to society in this postwar era. My evenings and my week-ends were filled with the preparation of a doctorate. It took me more than ten years to obtain my degree. In the Library I worked half-time at the Rare Books Department and

the other half at the Readers Service. Though I had "little Latin
and less Greek" I enjoyed my work very much and was initiated
into incunabula and early printing by Franz Schauwers. Rather
quickly I discovered the first lay printer in Brussels, Thomas van
der Noot (± 1475 - ± 1525) and he appeared to me such a pleasant
fellow and an interesting character – besides printer, he also was a
publisher, a translator and a poet – that I decided to write a book
on him. I still would like to do it, unless a younger staff member of
the Rare Books Department decides to do it in the meanwhile. One
of the reasons why I did not write it is because I gradually left the
Rare Books Department to spend all my time in Readers Service.
Interest in the history of the book, more particularly of the printed
book remained, however, with me for the rest of my life. I owe it to
Franz Schauwers. He was a shy man who did not publish but knew
much more than many authors writing in scholarly journals. He
was however always ready to communicate orally his knowledge
and wisdom, and several Belgian book historians are indebted to
him. When he retired from the Library I organized an exhibition
in his honour and as an introduction to the catalogue I wrote a
none-too-critical portrait of him.

My transfer from Rare Books to Readers Service was a move
from heart to reason. The gap I was supposed to fill was so
enormous that at moments of low mood I wondered if the Service
really existed. My older colleagues were living in an ivory tower or
rather in the time when the library was built, the late eighteenth
and early nineteenth century. When I asked for a telephone in my
office – if one could call the six square meters stolen from the
stacks an office – the rumour spread immediately in the Library
that I was an ambitious revolutionary. I dropped the idea of
securing the assistance of a secretary. (When I came back after my
first trip to the United States, which lasted for six months, I found
all the mail addressed to me piled upon my desk. I must admit that
quite a large proportion of the letters no longer required an
answer.) Peace brought back American and British literature from
which we had been severed for many years. The more I read about
Anglo-Saxon libraries the more miserable I felt in my own place.
In Belgium itself the Library was an isolated institution. The
university libraries were no better, although a couple of progressive librarians tried to do their best. In Brussels nothing had
changed since the good old days of the nineteenth century, except

for the period during which Victor Tourneur, 1929-1943, had been director. There were still epic fights between protagonists and detractors of the Universal Decimal Classification, and not much rationality went into the arguments on both sides. The language used sounded very military to me: camps, offensive, defensive, traitors, spearhead, etc. I counted the *coups*.

One of my few pleasant recollections of that period starts at six o'clock in the morning. I was sound asleep at home when the bell rang and a young excited man wanted to see me immediately. It took me a long time before I understood what he expected from me. Finally he made it clear that his first child had just been born and that he wanted to christen her Mireio, which had been refused by the civil authorities. Why knock on my door so early in the morning? At the town hall of one of the suburbs of Brussels, where he had to register the name he had been insisting on so much, a sympathetic officer told him that, if he could bring proof that such a name existed, the authorities could not maintain their refusal. He went straight to the Library, where he arrived a few minutes before closing time and where a messenger boy gave him my name, and he came so early the next morning to make sure that I would start my day with his problem, which I did. Being well on my way to becoming an uncommitted civil servant, I simply wrote down: "I, undersigned, hereby declare that the name Mireio is the title of a book by Frederic Mistral (1859)." It worked so well, that a couple of days later I received another request, and then they followed one after another. What happened is that the maternity hospital where that first child was born was one of the best known in town, where actually half of the Brussels children are born, and at the town hall they knew no other staff member of the Royal Library than me, because I had signed the first statement. It became such a routine job that I had a form printed in advance, saying that the name was mentioned in a *Dictionary of Given Names* by Flora Haines Longhead. I had a good chance of finding the chosen names because the book contained more than three thousand entries. Once or twice I refused to cooperate. The proposed name was so ridiculous that I thought of the child who was going to bear it. I regret that I do not remember these names. When I refused I was badly insulted, when it worked I was regularly offered a tip.

One day I was absent and the new father insisted so much that he got to my boss, who refused flatly and blamed me next day for having signed so many illegal documents without his knowledge. When I showed him my non-committing formula he mumbled something and went back to his favourite author. Surprising as it may sound, my boss, Etienne Vauthier, is another of my better recollections. I would not say that the Library was his prime interest. He was lecturing on Spanish and comparative literature at Brussels University and this presupposed quite a lot of reading and of linguistic and literary analysis. He was a very fine critic and his lectures were well-received masterpieces. I listened a lot to his wide literary knowledge, which he gathered while I was doing, with pleasure, his and my routine work. One day I was mad at him. We left the Library together and I was exhausted after one of those awful days where everything turns out wrong and where the readers are unbearable. While shaking hands he said to me with a feeling of relief: "and now my day begins."

I do not think that I shall tell the story of my appointment as director of the Library, but I would like to recall the rather unusual fact that Etienne Vauthier and I were candidates, he being nearly twenty years my senior. This situation did not bear at all on our good relations and once he called me into his office to tell me that he would withdraw. I asked him why and he answered "Because I have come to the conclusion that you would do a better job." Once again we agreed.

These pleasant memories should however not detract from the fact that I was at odds with my professional environment. I would not say that I was unhappy, because I had decided not so long before that I would never be unhappy. Gradually the desire to go to the United States grew in me and became nearly an obsession. In 1949 I applied for a Fulbright fellowship and at the end of the next year I sailed to Hoboken. I should add New Jersey because the original Hoboken is in my country near Antwerp. I am not going to describe my wonderful journey through the United States, from coast to coast, because it will be spread in its different aspects over most of these pages and there will also be a chapter devoted to my American experience as a whole. I only would like to mention that, in the first line of the first article that I wrote when I was back home, I stated with some juvenile emphasis that America was a happy country because there was no ministry of education. I forgot to mention earlier that the Royal Library fell under the

Belgian ministry of education. After 1968 it fell under two ministers of education, a French-speaking and a Dutch-speaking one,
which made the relations more than two times worse than they
used to be.

This trip to the United States was a turning point in my life. It
did not make things easier upon my return to the Library. I
promised myself never to compare any given situation with the
United States, actually never to mention America. Not long after
my return I was involved in a discussion about the number of
hours that the Library would be open to the public. I said that the
existing system certainly went back to the time of the gas light.
Some baiting colleague asked if it were better in the United States
and I made the unforgivable mistake of answering yes. I was a
traitor to the good old European civilization. But I liked my job,
did what was expected from me and a couple of other things too.

A new director was appointed in 1953 and that was the end. He
was a sweet, old, distinguished numismatist, Marcel Hoc, whom
everybody liked and respected in the Library as long as he remained among his coins. But as soon as he had overall responsibility he lost everybody's sympathy. He was a real pre-figuration of
the Peter principle, which had not yet been coined. My mood was
very low. I do not remember how he acted or forgot to act, but the
result was that he constantly prevented me from working and I
began thinking seriously of leaving the Library. On 1 January
1954 a solution *deus ex machina* offered itself. Among the season's
greetings which I received were two unexpected offers for a job.
The first one was to become temporary librarian of the European
Council of Nuclear Research in Geneva and the second one to
become assistant-secretary of the Belgian American Educational
Foundation with headquarters in New York and an office in Brussels. I accepted both. About the six months I spent in Geneva I
shall have an opportunity to say a few words elsewhere.

In the middle of 1954 I went back for two months to New York
to familiarize myself with the procedures of the Belgian American
Educational Foundation. It became the beginning of my lifelong
friendship with Clark Stillman, the secretary and a few years later
the president of the Foundation. I have two non-professional
recollections of this period of initiation in a small but effective
philanthropic foundation. At the initiative of a young Belgian
diplomat, my wife and I were invited to explore New York by

helicopter, Manhattan being the ideal place for a three dimensional visit. It was postponed several times due to poor weather conditions. Finally we left from the roof of a downtown skyscraper and we had a wonderful time. We even paid a visit to Clark Stillman at his office on the 23rd floor. When we left a couple of weeks later for Europe by ship, the pilot, who was a Canadian, named Chevalier, came to bid us farewell and nearly landed on deck. When we arrived home we learned that he had stupidly killed himself. On a take-off from the roof one of the wheelbelts was still fastened and the helicopter tipped over and fell onto the street.

The other recollection is quite different. Perrin Galpin, the president of the Foundation, and Clark Stillman wanted to introduce me to the honorary president, former President Hoover. We went up to his apartment in the Waldorf-Astoria and for one solid hour he insulted me. I was the symbol of all the Europeans ungrateful towards America. If America wanted a friendly newspaper it had to pay for it. And all Europeans had read Karl Marx (which was true in my case, at least partly), etc., etc. When the courtesy call was over, during which I had not said one word, and we were in the lift, Clark Stillman said "I think we can stand a double whisky." Later I met President Hoover a second time when he was President Eisenhower's envoy to the American Day at the Brussels Fair in 1958. He was pleasant to everybody, me included. I had arranged with Perrin Galpin – no relation whatsoever with the Galpin Society – to have President Hoover bring to Brussels for the Royal Library an inscribed copy of his translation of the *De re metallica* of Agricola. President Hoover was no bookman and certainly had nothing in common, as seen from this angle, with the friend of his younger days, Chester Beatty, with whom he started in the mining business. Today the Chester Beatty Library is worth a trip to Dublin, as the *Guide Michelin* would say.

My association with the Belgian American Educational Foundation was a pleasant one and was supposed to last for much longer than it actually did. I had left the Library with an idea of no return. Back in Brussels I did routine work for the Foundation and I continued to run its art seminar, which is the subject of a separate chapter. I also had the opportunity to spend more time on my doctorate than I could in the Library. Actually the time I spent with the Foundation allowed me to finish my thesis. After a few months my life took an unexpected turn. I received the visit of a delegation of former colleagues from the Library who asked me to put in my name as a candidate for the post of director. It came as a complete surprise to me. I even thought that it was a joke, but they were serious. They of course knew as well as I did that according to tradition I was much too young with my thirty-five years of age, and that when I had left the Library I was still at the bottom of the hierarchy. Their arguments were that I was no longer in the Library and that due to war casualties the new director would either be too old or too young. They wanted to sponsor the latter solution. I thought it over, asked advice from various sides and put in my name. It took the government nine months to make up its mind and on 29 February 1956 I learned that I had been appointed two days before. Obviously 1 January 1954 was a second turning point in my life.

I look back with mixed feelings on the eighteen years during which I tried to run the Library to the best of my ability. Though I shall put the stress on the more positive aspects, I shall not be able to avoid the explanation of my gradual involvement in professional activities outside the country and finally of my early departure from the Library.

Friendly relations with a fair number of staff members of all grades remain a rewarding memory. A few days after my appointment I brought the whole staff together – such a thing had never been heard of in the history of the Library – and I told them what I expected from them and what they could expect from me. And I remember that I summarized my whole philosophy in one sentence: *donc deux poids et deux mesures, s'il le faut trois poids et trois mesures*, not double, but if required triple standards of judging. This expression was used whimsically, because it is common to say, at least in French, that a proof of equity is to avoid applying two different standards in judging persons. What I wanted to say was simply that those who worked seriously would be judged in one way and those who were poor at their job would be judged in another way: the former would have a free hand and the latter would be put under strict control. The fact was that everybody understood me very well, but that hardly anybody crossed the border line which separated the two groups.

Nobody could have been more careful than I was in bringing changes about. I have forgotten the name of the French philosopher who said: *d'abord continuer et puis commencer*, first continue and then begin. That is exactly what I did. (Speaking about languages I must admit that my English seems to fade away the closer I come to local situations. I really do hope that in my struggle with Caxton's language I shall not lose too many nuances in what I want to convey. I have to make this confession, because no reader would understand me if I suddenly reverted, for a few pages, to Dutch, like David Gascoyne breaks into French in his *Paris Journal*, but for other reasons.)

The staff I inherited comprised four groups, at least according to my criteria. Some very few elderly staff members, such as my former boss, Etienne Vauthier, and one or two others of whom I thought very highly. I was extremely cautious with them and I went on considering myself as their junior colleague. I take pleasure here in mentioning Louis Lebeer, although we shall meet him again later. He ran the Print Room for more than thirty years and I was fortunate to benefit for a dozen years from his scholarly and artistic wisdom. Without any sizeable budget he expanded the collections in an impressive way. The only times that we disagreed were when I encouraged him to buy a good item and he refused because it was too expensive. One such example I still remember was an interesting volume of drawings by the Liège artist Lambert Lombard (1505-1566) from the renowned Arenberg collection. I was right because after his refusal the volume was bought by a provincial museum which paid a higher price than the one which had been quoted to us.

Along the same line I should recall his worst such attitude. When he was about to retire I looked, together with his potential successor, for an outstanding farewell acquisition. We found an exquisite drawing of an *Old Woman* by Felicien Rops, one of his favourite artists. When I showed it to him he was enchanted and I refrained from mentioning the price. A few days later he came to my office and asked if he could light a cigarette and sit down for a few moments. His silence was long enough to allow me to sense that something was wrong. Well, after all, he would prefer not to accept the drawing. Wasn't it good? Oh no, it was superb. "But you see the dealer, Paul van der Perre, and I are old friends and he told me the price, although you had instructed him not to do so." When Louis Lebeer left the Library he became lifelong secretary of the Royal Academy (one of our seven Royal Academies, because we

have many more than the British, but this is another story). At the
Academy he met again the best artists, with whom and for whom
he had already been working as a curator. The wide span of his
interest was one of his major qualities. He could easily move from
scholarly papers on Bosch, Brueghel, Rubens, etc. to sensitive
introductions to the work of living graphic artists of the country
such as Frans Masereel, Oscar Jespers, Lismonde, Marc Severin,
etc. To round off this portrait I should not omit the large amount
of time he gave to teaching, at both the universities of Ghent and
Liège, and the technical work related to cataloguing, preservation
and even administration.

The second group was somewhat larger and its members were
also elderly gentlemen. They did not like me and my response was
undoubtedly on the cool side. They had spent decades in an
institution for which they did not care, they had never discovered
the difference between a library and a bank, between a book and a
file, they had been living like bored bureaucrats. The only thing I
could do about them was to wait impatiently for their retirement
and to replace them by good young people. The process was slow
but effective.

I have the profile in mind of specifically such a representative of
this category of staff member, who unsuccessfully tried to avoid
the Library. I forget his name, but even if I remembered it I would
not quote it. He arrived late every morning. This reminds me of
the wonderful story of the excellent Dutch poet, Jacques Bloem,
who was starving during the war and out of pity was taken into civil
service. After a few months his director called him to his office and
said, "Mr. Bloem, you arrive so late every morning," and the poet
gave this beautiful answer "I oppose to that, Mr. Director, the fact
that every afternoon I leave so early." I would have been happy
with such an answer if my staff member had been writing good
poetry when he was not in the Library (or even in the Library). But
he wrote nothing, although he had been a brilliant student at the
university. He is partly responsible for the fact that in my opinion
knowledge does not rank very high among the values which make
life worth living. Character tempered by wisdom has to be put at
the top.

For such a staff member, with whom I had to live according to
civil service rules, there was only one way out: *la voie de garage*, a
nice jargon expression referring to the old railroad carriage which

was no good any more and which was put on a side track. How saintly, in opposition appears the portrait of my good friend Louis Bakelants, who never became a regular staff member but who rendered enormous services to the Library. He had been teaching Latin and Greek to high school students. Although he was an outstanding teacher, he actually was underemployed at high school level and this was my chance. He became an expert on sixteenth century humanism, and soon of wide repute. His doctoral dissertation on Gislain Bulteel of Ypres (1555-1611) commanded admiration in the circle of students of humanism in the Low Countries. His knowledge of the period and its many authors, together with his inborn modesty, made of him an irreplaceable contributor to the *Bibliotheca Belgica*, the old bibliographic enterprise which started in 1880 at the Library of Ghent University and was transferred to the Royal Library in 1933. Louis Bakelants died suddenly, fifty years old, the very day he was supposed to give his inaugural lecture at Brussels University where he was going to teach the course of the history of Christianity during the Renaissance in northern Europe. It might be worth while to note here that Brussels University is an avowed agnostic university, while the neighbouring one at Louvain, as everyone knows, is a Catholic university.

The *Bibliotheca Belgica* allows me to introduce the third group of staff members, those with whom I could put again the Royal Library on the map of national libraries. Incidentally, shortly before I took over, *Library Trends* had published a double issue on national libraries of the world. The Belgian national library was sadly missing and when I saw this omission I made a promise to myself to change this. A contributor to the *Bibliotheca Belgica* from the staff was Joseph De Reuck, who had written a splendid bibliographic article on Erasmus' *Querela Pacis*.

He was nearly twenty years older than I and from the very first day I was in the Library I took him as my mentor, as the example to follow. This was not an easy choice – I hardly had any choice – because our characters were quite different. Actually we had only one point in common: we highly respected one another. When he retired from the Library he read a farewell paper in which he mildly blamed me for lacking respect for the old structures of the Library and for having given him key responsibilities in destroying them. I published his paper as an introduction to the annual report.

The *Bibliotheca Belgica* is indeed a convenient introduction because it allows me to quote another name from the third group,
Marie-Thérèse Lenger. When she took over the general editor-
ship she realized that the newly developed reprint techniques
would allow her to get rid of the nineteenth century in-duodecimo
loose leaves on which the *Bibliotheca Belgica* was traditionally issued
and which created problems to private as well as to public subscrib-
ers. She transformed the twenty-four thousand loose leaves into a
handsome six in-quarto volumes set. At once it became possible to
add a general index and Joseph De Reuck, after he had retired
from the Library, published it as a seventh volume, realizing Louis
Bakelants' old dream.

The third group was not a very large one, but since each individual member was dedicated to his task, it did wonders, the most
important among which was to blow some life into the fourth and
largest group. In all institutions of a certain size, whether public or
private, a fair proportion of the staff is neutral, not basically
interested in its work but not without a potential amount of good
will. It is one of the management problems to get the most out of
these people. It has been my experience that the boss, way off
behind a heavy door, is the last one to achieve some positive results
in this direction. He has to trust good people in the different ranks
of the hierarchy. Good and poor people, I would add incidentally,
are spread in the same proportion over all ranks. I shall never
forget the elderly stack attendant who told me, a few days after I
entered the Library, that when a newcomer arrived, he asked him
to pile up a few books. The way he piled them up was enough for
him to judge the fellow. I bear witness to the fact that his judge-
ment was always right and I have *mutatis mutandis* systematically
and symbolically asked incoming librarians to pile up some books.
It was a useful indication but my conclusions have not always been
right.

I have left Frans de Vrieze as the last one, not knowing exactly to
which group he belonged. For the first group he was not old
enough, but a bit too old for the third one. The links between us
were not exclusively professional. We had both studied Germanic
philology, he at Louvain and I at Ghent. We both were Dutch-
speaking, though he felt much more oppressed than I in our
French-speaking environment. When I needed some wise advice I
always called on him, while he returned my confidence by behav-

ing as if he felt better when I was on his side. He meant a lot to me, both when I entered the Library as an inexperienced beginner and later when I was put in charge. After a certain time he took over nearly all the inside problems, leaving me enough time to handle the outside relations. He was acting director when I was away from the Library. When my absences became more frequent and when I began to think of leaving the Library, I asked him what he thought about a successor. He cited names but not his own and demurred when I mentioned him. It was a wise decision because he was too gentlemanly to take over the difficult relations with our socio-bureaucracies.

So much for the inventory of human resources available to try to make of the Royal Library a twentieth-century institution.

While working on the new building I constantly had the other vital problems of collections and staff in mind. The danger which I feared most, which actually kept me awake too many nights, was the poor quality of the contents of the Library as opposed to an expensive new building, an empty shell which threatened to mar the Brussels skyline. The fight was actually on three fronts: with the architects to come as close as possible to the ideal library building; with the administration to obtain acquisition budgets; and with the administration, again, to expand the staff.

I separated the development of the collection into two distinct parts: current material and museum items. The latter was so exciting that I gave too much time to it. After a few years' efforts I obtained two different budgets on the ground that even a biased manuscript curator would prefer to buy one thousand current publications in his field instead of one medieval manuscript, if he were compelled to make a choice. I wanted to protect him against this difficult decision, which had to be taken more at an ethical than at a technical level. The result was that we developed quite an ambitious programme in the field of patrimonial acquisitions, as it was officially called. At the dedication of the new building, the construction of which lasted fifteen years, we proudly opened an exhibition of fifteen years of major acquisitions, showing that bricks had not overtaken books. Here again I would refer for the details of this pleasant story to another chapter. It begins to look to me as if only the unpleasant memories will be left over here. These will refer indeed to the battles with the Belgian bureaucracy, which I lost.

In the field of current acquisitions the Library had a fairly solid tradition. Belgium being a small country, there never had existed such a thing as Belgian science, which means that for a research library the collection had to be international in scope. If I compare Belgium with our neighbours, I would say that science in Germany was German until World War I or French in France, which was never the case in Belgium. Another aspect related to the size of the country is the acquisition of a proportionally large number of scholarly journals as compared to monographs. Buying journals, as all librarians know, is a difficult way to spend one's money, and it is even more difficult when it comes to foreign serial publications. I have never been able to find out exactly how many journals we subscribed to, but I know that it was more than enough to use a large part of the allocation and to give headaches to quite a number of staff members, but also to establish a fairly good reputation in this field. When reprint publishers were pouring tons of publicity on our poor heads for long runs of reprinted leading journals in all fields from all industrial countries, we found out that we had nearly all of them. These clever publishers did not make much easy money on us.

This brings back to my mind that Kraus Reprints offered to reprint the national bibliography *Bibliographie de Belgique – Belgische Bibliographie*. I was surprized at that offer and I told H.P. Kraus that we had quite a substantial number of back issues in our cellars. His answer was both simple and convincing: "I cannot sell the original issues, but I can easily sell sets of bound volumes of reprints." And actually he did, and we even received as royalties two or three sets of the one hundred odd volumes of the bibliography. It must have been during that initial conversation that H.P. Kraus told me that he was earning his money with his reprints, while the manuscripts and rare books which he sold for thousands of dollars were actually gifts to the libraries. Neither of us believed this story.

The reference to the national bibliography allows me to deal briefly with the legal deposit system in Belgium. It was one of the few industrialized countries where no legal deposit law existed although the national bibliography was not a trade publication as in Holland, but a government document. All current Belgian books, on which the bibliography was based, were purchased. All attempts to establish a legal deposit system as those in France, the

United Kingdom or the Federal Republic of Germany had failed. Once we had a minister, Jules Destrée, who was considered by the librarians as a potential supporter of a legal deposit system, since he was the author of the first public library law in Belgium (1921). When asked he flatly refused: "I do not see why you should stop at publishers and not obtain from a shoe factory the deposit of a pair of shoes for each model." This was my starting point and I also realized that all previous attempts had failed because of the hostility of the publishers.

Instead of following normal bureaucratic channels, I began to talk to publishers and we found out rather easily that we were speaking the same language. Having the historical development of the local book trade in mind, I used as my main argument that publishing in Belgium had reached a level of maturity which it had never attained before and that not only acceptance, but full cooperation with a modern legal deposit system would be proof of this maturity. I was fortunate to have as opposite number a broadminded and able chairman of the publishers' association, Jean-Jacques Schellens. We worked hand in hand, each of us backed by a good team, and the draft of the legal deposit law was a joint enterprise in which the share of the publishers was larger than that of the librarians. The publishers and ourselves worked directly with the State Council and the legislative branch. The law passed in Parliament in 1965 and began to work on 1 January 1966.

Although Belgian books and periodicals began to flow in through legal deposit, although the budgets were divided and both parts increased steadily during the late fifties, and more particularly during the golden sixties, I was the sad witness of the diminishing proportion allotted to the purchase of books in the overall budget of the Library. After some initial efforts, thirty percent of the whole budget was allocated to book purchases. Fifteen years later this figure was down to fifteen percent. One day this made me say with resignation to the minister: "We are better and better paid to do less and less with books." I said this with fits and starts. It was not because the salaries and the book prices went up steadily that the staff was better paid.

As soon as I was appointed I looked for able staff members to send to the United States. I scouted for all possible fellowships and finally had more offers than candidates. From time to time I even had to slightly twist an arm. It was not long before nearly all single staff members had spent a few months or a year in the United States. The fellowships which were available did not cover the expenses of married couples, but fortunately libraries generally have a good average of single persons on their staff.

Once I had two single librarians at the same time on the other side of the Ocean, August Cockx who was spending a year at the Linda Hall Library in Kansas City, and Elly Indestege who was a fellow at the Folger Shakespeare Library in Washington, DC. It was customary at the time that at the end of their stay visiting librarians were offered a trip through the United States. Mary Ann Adams at the Library of Congress organized these trips, and when she found two Belgians on her list, she decided to put them on the same planes and to send them on to the same cities. What was due to happen, happened. They got married as soon as they were back in Belgium, although both had been working previously for quite some time at the Royal Library without looking at one another. Enriched by their American experience, they gave an enhanced service to the Library. Elly went back to her fifteenth- and sixteenth-century printed books. I remember that she was the only candidate who knew something about books before she entered the Library. She had been trained by her father who had deep interest in a wide variety of fields. He was a member of the Flemish Academy as a distinguished poet, and he had been teaching English language and literature most of his life, except for the happy years in Italy when he taught Dutch to the incoming art historians from the University of Padova and wrote the exquisite *Quaderno Fiorentino*. Finally he also was quite knowledgeable in the field of the history of the book, more particularly on Flemish blind-stamped bindings. Before I leave the father for the daughter, I want to recall the visit I paid him in Venice. At the time, the secretary of the department of the University called his students together with *"Fiamminghi avanti."* Since it was my first visit to Venice a ride on a gondola was a must. My wife and I went with him to the embarkation point and he ordered us to leave the bargaining of the price to him. A discussion, of which I understood nothing, went on for a few minutes and then he said "Let's go" and he went on in Dutch saying to us that as soon as we reached the corner, the gondolier would shout that he agreed with the price. And it went that way and I was very much impressed. In the boat he said that he had been sure it would work because he had not

spoken Italian, but Venetian. I was even more impressed. Everything was perfect, except when I realized that we were gondoliered
home half an hour before the others, notwithstanding the local
accent of my friend Luc Indestege.

Daughter Elly felt more and more at home in her beloved
sixteenth century, and her Folger experience added a lot of pleasure to her work. She was involved in all major bibliographic
enterprises related in one way or another to humanism in the Low
Countries. I remember as a particularly rewarding period the
months she spent on the catalogue of the illustrated fifteenth- and
sixteenth-century books which Lessing Rosenwald had bought
from the renowned Arenberg collection of Belgian origin. I shall
not be able to avoid coming back later to this collection, but here I
would only like to recall how pleasant it was to Elly and to us all to
work with Lessing Rosenwald. He and Edith came over for the
opening of the exhibition of these books both at the Museum
Meermanno-Westreenianum in The Hague and at the Royal Library in Brussels. I can still hear Edith saying, while we were eating
sweetbreads *demi-deuil* in one of the better Brussels restaurants,
"Lessing, we shall never travel again without an exhibition."

This exhibition was also the life's dream of Marie Kronenberg,
the dean of all bibliographers in the Low Countries, who had been
refused access year after year to the Arenberg collection because
she was a "Dutch Protestant serpent". This sad story, which ended
well thanks to Lessing Rosenwald, has been told in the wittiest way
by Marie Kronenberg herself. What a wonderful woman and, in
the Library, Elly knew her best. The Rosenwald exhibition contained a unique copy of an old Dutch cookbook and Elly fell in love
with it. This love affair ended, however, in a rather original way,
because it led to a highly scholarly publication with an impressive
critical and philological apparatus. It is indeed much more difficult to be accurate about a medieval recipe than about a scholastic
treatise. When Lessing Rosenwald showed some of his books in
Brussels and The Hague, he had already given them to the Library
of Congress, as he had offered his drawings and prints to the
National Gallery. He owed it to the nation, he told me and many
others, which had given him a chance to be happy in this world.
Since he had retained lifelong interest in his collection I had the
opportunity of visiting it several times in his elegant Alverthorpe
Gallery near Philadelphia. He and Edith were perfect hosts and

they were as generous to intruding visitors as they were to the works of art of the best minds of past centuries.

And now from the wife to the husband. August discovered a new vocation in Kansas City, where Joseph Shipman, the director of the Linda Hall Library, introduced him to the vast world of scientific and technological documentation and information. For one year he familiarized himself with this fastly evolving and expanding field. I had not the slightest idea of what was ahead of me when he came back to Belgium. I had hardly congratulated him on his wedding when he wanted me to set up a whole new department in the Library where the old stuff and the old-fashioned readers would no longer have their place. This came rather as a shock to me and although I did not exactly have the reputation of being a conservative librarian, my heart was still with books and with readers, while pre-prints, patents, information retrieval, users and computers still sounded rather barbarous to me.

During days, weeks and months I listened to August to try to understand what it was all about. When it was finally clear to me, I had difficulty in making up my mind, a feeling which I did not like at all. My first reaction to his proposal was to support him in setting up a National Documentation and Information Centre for Science and Technology outside the Library. He had some sound arguments for staying within the Library, the main one being that our collection of scholarly journals was outstanding. Finally I gave in with the restriction, however, that if he should feel, after a certain time, that the Library acted as a brake to the development of the new Centre, he would have my blessing to try his success elsewhere. My main problem was actually that I was tempted by his proposal, but did not want to lose or sacrifice anything of the Library's responsibility on the traditional side.

Once the decision was taken, the new Centre put a larger claim on my time than any other department. In fact the Centre remained a separate entity under the same roof as the Library, with August in charge, but with me to bear the ultimate responsibility. Although I fully trusted him, this responsibility was a heavy one. We had to find ways and means. Fortunately much was still possible in the sixties, which were ahead of us, and a general political decision had been taken to encourage the creation of national or inter-university centres. On a small scale I had already availed myself of this opportunity by encouraging some colleagues to set up national research centres in the Library. After a couple of years we found ourselves enriched with a National Centre for the Archeology and History of the Book, and a National Centre for the History of Science. Some centres had different names but had the same relation with the Library, such as the American Studies Center and the Museum of French-Belgian Literature. All these centres were means to expand the scope of the Library's responsibility and were financed through specific programmes approved by the government which should not last longer than three years. These centres have now been in existence for over twenty years, and there was a period when more staff was working in the centres than in the Library itself. This was indeed an awkward imbalance, but had the central administration of the ministry allowed the development of the Library in a logical way, I would not have been compelled to use the detour of the centres.

Although these centres did a good job and issued many important and useful publications, they did not represent a major change in the long tradition of the Library. They were just a new and opportunistic means of carrying out functions which a general research library could not ignore if it wanted to reach a respectable level of operation. With the National Documentation and Information Centre for Science and Technology it was completely different. We were adding a completely new institution which brought to the Library a very different mentality, within the staff as well as within the users. Physics, chemistry, agriculture, medicine and engineering entered into the Library through the front door. A staff which counted historians, philologists, art historians and lawyers began to see among its members physicians, physicists, biologists, botanists, chemists, even sociologists and economists. The range of responsibility was wide indeed. If someone asked me what the Library exactly covered, I had a ready made answer: "Everything that separates Mrs. from Mr. Cockx!"

In approaching the dedication ceremony of the new building in 1969 I began to think about preparing a memorial volume in which the old and the recent past of the Library would be described as well as a prospect for the immediate future. [1] The recurring pattern of the first part seemed to indicate that the best

---

[1] *Mémorial 1559-1969* (Bruxelles, Bibliothèque Royale Albert Ier, 1969).

periods were those when the Library was a conscious expression, in its specific field, of the lively forces of the society to which it belonged. If I understood correctly the dozen or so years which preceded the dedication I would be tempted to recognize such forces as, above all, a sign of true confidence in life after the nightmare of the war years. This regained confidence had many positive aspects, but also some drawbacks which would ultimately lead to the much decried consumer's society. After the reconstruction of the heavily mutilated country, financial means became available to institutions like libraries. I took full advantage of this trend and tried to spend as much money as possible. I had no bad conscience because resources were plenty and none of the money given to the library was taken away from other institutions. I admit, however, that I sacrificed a bit too much to the exterior aspects of the expansion.

As such I participated in the *nouveaux riches* mentality of the country. I did it quite consciously, trusting that the more fundamental issues which were at stake would benefit from it. The cost level of the building which was imposed upon me was too high, but I used it to find ways and means to expand the collections and the staff. I convinced none of the authorities but they agreed. My main argument was "You cannot force us to live in a palace like paupers." It worked to a certain point. I would have been happier if it had been understood as I meant it.

In each library the major components are the collections, the building and obviously the financial resources each of them presupposes. Here I would like to dwell somewhat on the quantitative and qualitative adaptation of the staff which I felt to be a high priority. I had known the time in the Library when there was hardly any intermediary staff between the academically-trained librarians and the office boys, between very highbrow intellectuals and poor veterans from the first world war. The first intermediaries began to show up while I was a young librarian, and when I was in charge I brought them in massively. I never had the feeling that it was a revolutionary decision but only a late recognition of an unavoidable adaption. Quite a number of routine jobs were transferred from the professional to the subprofessional level. It freed the mind of the former and it enhanced the status of the latter. The free mind did not always prove to be eager to be filled, while new assistants nearly always performed an improved job. I do not like people who live in the shadow of their degree but I do like people whose quality of work makes one forget whether they have a degree or not. When this proportionally large group of intermediaries was integrated I wanted to widen the range of the research staff. I failed nearly completely and the Royal Library of Belgium is probably the only research library in the world whose academic staff is not larger than before the war.

All I could achieve required a kind of bypassing of the governmental authorities. The legal deposit law was voted in parliament before I informed the administration. Its reaction was exactly what I expected: would the new law justify a budget reduction? My "No" must have been so convincing that they did not insist. It went the same *fait accompli*-way with the American Studies Center. An initial grant from the American Council of Learned Societies gave me some freedom of action. The same Council had been supporting an important Center in West-Berlin and I thought this was a mistake because of the isolation of the city. In Brussels a good centre would be able to serve easily a much larger public than the local one. The European avocation was a powerful argument and the Belgian authorities matched the American grant. The research collection of the Center is continuously expanding and has reached a satisfactory level. Thanks to a dedicated, though too-small staff, it has become one of liveliest places of the Library.

Just for the satisfaction of writing down the names once again I would like to make a final comment on the National Information Centre for Science and Technology, the National Centre for the Archeology of the Book, and the National Centre for the History of Science. When the ministry refused systematically an expansion of the research staff I bypassed this refusal by creating these centres with . . . money from the ministry. It gave with the left hand what it refused with the right one. Nothing was secret in my strategy and I even declared publicly that this detour was more expansive than a regular expansion. Finally I found myself running a private business with government money. I gave fringe benefits to the staff because it did not have the status of permanent affiliation with the government like civil servants. Since the allocations always came late I borrowed money from the bank and paid interest. At a certain moment I even had a financial reserve, but here I was severely punished and it was taken away from me. That happened only once because afterwards I was very careful to be always in the red figures. What about research programmes in these financial, economic and social exercises? I tried to keep the latter for myself and allow the staff members to give all their time to do exactly what they were supposed to do. I had, of course, to give them a free hand and I never had a reason to regret my unchosen trust.

Among the innovations I have not yet found an opportunity to discuss was the *Musée de la Littérature*. It will allow me to introduce some local idiosyncracies. Because the Flemish part of the population has been oppressed, it developed from the middle of the nineteenth century onwards a national consciousness in which language and literature were major contributions. This movement towards authenticity was not confined to this part of Europe and many similar trends appeared rather simultaneously. In Belgium, Flemish literary archives were soon to be an important asset of the Flemish movement and in Antwerp a literary museum and archive was officially inaugurated in 1933 and has since been continuously developed as an independent branch of the local public library, the oldest and richest public library of the country. When a new building was inaugurated in 1959 I said rather naughtily to the director that the museum was better than the literature, which was not true at all.

There was no parallel French literary archive or museum in Belgium. The explanation was simple: the political incentive did not exist and the experts on manuscripts of the Royal Library were always overwhelmed by the wealth of its medieval collections and neglected the nineteenth and twentieth century autographs and literary archives, the vast majority of which were written in French. The imbalance between the literary heritage of the two national communities began to worry me and I forgot that my mother tongue is Flemish. (Actually Dutch, but I do not feel this to be the place to explain the difference between Dutch and Flemish, let it suffice to say here that every educated Fleming speaks Dutch). A joint venture of the Belgian Royal Academy of French Language and Literature and the Royal Library led to the creation of the Archives et Musée de la Littérature with headquarters in the Library. It started slowly but developed steadily and although it has not yet reached the level of its Flemish counterpart, it is now a well-established institution. To baffle the reader I shall add, without explanation, that its strongest holdings are those of Flemish authors writing in French. It would take a long time to explain why the best French-writing authors in Belgium are Flemings (Maurice Maeterlinck, Emile Verhaeren, Marie Gevers, Suzanne Lilar).

The Royal Library serves equally the two Belgian communities and the Musée naturally only one. This created some problems. When the politicians began to worry about a fair balance between the two communities this had an unexpected influence on the Musée. One day the minister of education was supposed to give to the Musée, let us say, an allocation of 1.000.000 Belgian Francs, and I received 2.000.000,–. A reduction to 500.000,– would have been normal, but 2.000.000,– was a shock and I was ready to revise my opinion of the Minister. But before this happened I got the explanation. The Minister wanted me to give half of it to the Flemish Museum in Antwerp and sent the money to me because he did not know the name of the director and the address of the Museum. When I called my Flemish colleague, Ger Schmook, to ask him how I could transfer this subsidy, he refused: this was a municipal institution and he did not want to lose his independence by accepting money from the government. What a happy man! I faithfully reported his refusal to the Minister and asked him if I could keep the money. He said no. I insisted and promised to buy only French translations from Dutch authors. He still refused and I had to give back the money. The very idea of having to give back money to the government killed me. So, I went to Antwerp and implored my friend to accept the money which I longed to keep for myself. Finally he accepted but said I should not try a second time. In the meanwhile, heaven granted us two ministers of culture, on top of two ministers of education, and he and the Antwerp museum have regularly accepted subsidies which had been cleared politically and linguistically, if not necessarily literarily.

Dedication Day: 17 February 1969.

For the team which had worked like mad to be ready with a huge building, its interior design, its redeployed collections, its reinvigorated staff, this was the beginning of a new and brilliant era in the history of the Library. For the higher authorities it was, on the contrary, the end of a period of harassing pressure, heavy expenditure, not a new departure but a point of long awaited arrival. Of course nobody in the Library was aware of this ominous attitude, which may not even have been conscious at the time but which became plainly apparent too soon after the event.

The day itself came close to perfection. Thirty-five years after the death of King Albert, to whose memory the Library was dedicated, and fifteen years after the laying of the cornerstone, the Library was opened to the public. The whole Royal Family attended the dedication ceremony, which was opened by the ministers of education and culture, and followed by a message to the nation read by the King himself. During a tour of the new premises the Royal Family, surrounded by a thousand guests, was introduced successively to important benefactors, a group of foreign librarians, the members of the scientific board, the trustees, representatives of the "Friends of the Library" and, on their way, they had met the whole staff spread over the various services. After the Royal Family had left, the Library was turned into an open house and a two days' international symposium on "Large General Libraries in the Last Quarter of the XXth Century" started. In the evening, as is customary in Belgium, a banquet was organized which was also the dedication of the cafetaria, the quality of the food being slightly better than what was going to be served on the next and following days. There were of course a series of toasts. Mine was nothing else than a continuous expression of gratitude, although I have been told afterwards that too many nuances marred my generous feelings. Bob Vosper from the University of California, Los Angeles, spoke with his customary elegance on behalf of the foreign librarians and Pierre Vermeylen, minister of education, closed the series and ended by thanking me "for what I had done with and against the government." This was a nice formula and everybody, I included, smiled.

That beautiful dream of 17 February 1969 has been recorded in factual detail in a published report which I have had to glance through again, to read carefully its table of contents, to spell out the names of the distinguished people who were present, to look at the illustrations, in order to believe today that it really happened.

Here I should make a lengthy inventory of all my sad failures, but this would detract from the assignment which I put upon myself in writing down these professional reminiscences. I guess I can use a few anecdotes to convey the ambiance in which I have been working during the five years I spent in the Library after the dedication of the new building. What these unimportant stories will not convey is the rewarding consolation I always found inside the Library itself among staff and readers, outside the Library among colleagues, publishers, book dealers, printers, authors, artists and a few old friends.

In 1968, one of the rank and file staff members, Serge Reding, won a silver medal at the Olympic Games in Mexico as a weight lifter. All of us were very proud. Before the game all his stack companions had helped him, they did his work while he was more regularly absent than present because of the many hours of daily training. Even I contributed to his success. One day he came to see me and asked for a weekly half-day off. I asked him why. To walk in the main street, he answered, because my life is miserable. I work daily in the Library until 4 p.m. and then I start training for five hours, afterwards I go home to have dinner, and, by the way, my salary in the Library is not enough to pay for the meat in my training diet (he was as large as he was tall) and I never see anybody. I gave him his half-day off. When he came back from Mexico as a champion, the minister of education gave a party in his honour. The Minister made a long speech to underscore the importance of sport and then he turned to me to add "of course this is difficult to understand for a library director." I interrupted him and said "I apologize, Mr. Minister, but when I was the same age as Serge Reding, I played with the national basket-ball team." Somewhat later I went on, but *in aparte* with him, about the wonderful experience which a team sport had been in my youth and how useful it had proved to be later in my professional work. I also added that sport was the origin of the fact that I never smoked, but also that I had acquired a bad knee with a torn meniscus. This was, however, a small price for the immense satisfaction that the very notion of belonging to a team had always given me. Nothing can be achieved if in one way or another one does not have the feeling of belonging to a team.

Not so long after the dedication, the reading room of the Library was occupied by students from Brussels University who refused to leave at closing time. I tried to talk to them, but it took a long time before any kind of silence was reached. I first had to listen to their list of grievances. I had some difficulty in understanding them because two or three talked at the same time and did not voice the same opinions. I tried to look for familiar faces, but there were not many, which was not surprising since the leaders had distributed pamphlets at large among the student body to explain where to find the Library. I thought I understood that out of solidarity with the working class they wanted an extension of the regular hours, that in Moscow the libraries were open twenty-four hours a day, and that I, being a representative of the establishment, did not understand the needs of the new generation which preferred books to marble on the floor, etc. To give force to their arguments, they had decided to start with a sit-in strike to the finish. While they shouted and whistled, I could think my reaction over. I first answered, with a slight demagogical inclination, that I shared most of their opinions, except when it came to factual mistakes. I told them I happened to know the Soviet libraries and that it was not correct to pretend that they never closed. The hours were better indeed and I wished I could open the Library more widely. But in the Soviet libraries they would have to queue a few times: at the entrance, checking in, at the cloak-room, at the catalogue room, at the reading room and the reverse when leaving. Our new Library, as opposed to the old one, had solved this problem. I also offered to give them a list of books for which they would look in vain in Soviet libraries, and when I suggested that they might try to organize a sit-down strike in Moscow I had some trouble in continuing.

As to the choice between marble and books, I could not agree more with their preference. When I tried to explain that I needed the marble to get the money to buy books, they thought that I was kidding. It takes indeed more than the innocence of youth to understand that an overexpensive building was an argument that I could use to beg some Belgian francs to improve its contents. What I needed was more staff to increase the number of hours that the Library would be open to the public. I then made the mistake of thinking that they were serious in what they were doing and tried to explain that in all libraries of the world the real problem was to strike the right balance between the staff which is assigned to public services and those working in the wings, that it was today that we had to order the books which would be needed by their successors, and that if they were so insistent on using the library (which actually was not true) it was because my predecessors had built the collections (which was close to the truth) and that I wanted to do the same. They couldn't have cared less.

I thought that I could redirect their animosity to the proper quarter and pointed out that they had put the blame on the wrong library. The National Library was not a university library, I re-

minded them, and would never, as long as I was reponsible, turn
itself into one. If the collections in their university library were
scandalously poor, and the hours during which they had access to
them even fewer than in the National Library, that was not my
fault. I then gave a lecture on the difference between a university
library and a national library and I ended with an image which I
had invented on the spot "in a national library the reader looks for
the books, in a university library the books look for the reader."
Most of them did not listen and some began to leave the reading
room. It was about time to use my secret weapon. Were they still
decided upon a sit-down to the finish? Yes. Did they realize that
the staff also had to stay? Yes and no. So, that being that, I ordered
all the doors to be closed and said "Let's have a cosy get together."
and I casually took a reference book from the shelves pretending
to read. If I remember correctly it was the Oxford Dictionary of
Quotations which fell open at "you should have banged the youth
into dumbness" (Shakespeare). But I was worried. Would they
revert to violence when there was so much glass in the Library?
(One of my big ideas had been to put glass partitions everywhere in
order to insure acoustic isolation and keep visible simultaneously
as many books and readers as possible). At that very moment I
could see a tree in the garden through six glass partitions. What
was going to happen? There was silence and whispering in small
groups. Two girls and a boy came to me and told me that they had
been assigned to buy drinks and food for the others and asked if
they could leave. I said no, a serious action implied a minimum of
sacrifice and that after all it was forbidden to drink and to eat in the
reading room. Then up came an elderly gentleman who was
certainly not part of the odd two hundred students and asked me if
he could go home where he was expected. I said of course as far as
I was concerned but that these young people lived on the principle
of solidarity and that I was not sure that they would let him go.
They talked it over among themselves and their spokesman came
to me. "We all shall leave and come back tomorow." That was
all right with me and I was sure they wouldn't come.

    The next morning everything was normal, but a few days later
they were there, equipped with drinks, food and guitars, and they
made it quite clear to me that they were going to stay. I called the
Minister and asked what I was supposed to do. "Ask them to come
to my office and you come too." "When?" "Immediately." I went

back to the reading room and told them "The Minister wants to see a delegation at once." "But we are not ready now, we haven't prepared a statement." I told them they had better accept the proposal, which would allow me to keep the police out of the Library. Half a dozen went and, independently, I went also. We met again in the waiting room. Somewhat later we were called to a conference room adjacent to the minister's office. He waited for us behind a large table and when we came in, he made a sign to me and the students that we should sit down. I said candidly "Don't you think, Mr. Minister, that I'd better sit on your side of the table, because I do not feel that I belong to the students' side?"

This digression about the students shows nevertheless that the Royal Library acts, beyond its official assignment, as a university library. As far as I know there is no national library in the industrial world which has such a large proportion of undergraduate students among its regular readers. Indirectly this fact is recognized in its organization of the services for the public which provides for a reading room for privileged readers (actually the only type of readers who should use the facilities of a central research library). This being said, the students have always been welcome, though it was not easy to explain to them that the deficiency of the local university libraries was the real reason for this favour. "Favour" – what a horrible word to use at any time!

As if the double function of national and university library were not enough, attempts have also been made to entrust the Royal Library with the function of public library of the city. Here the resistance has been most stubborn, though it was impossible to deter some readers from coming to the Library who should have gone to a public library, where they were entitled to a better service than the one we were prepared to give. Brussels is probably the only civilized capital in the world without a public library. Until recently Paris was also on this blacklist, but since Beaubourg it no longer appears. My hope that the city authorities would follow the French example was a faint one. In my city, as in my country, we are extremely good at imitating the poorer sides of France and we do not seem to be aware of the better qualities of our southern neighbours. Once the mayor told me, after I had complained about the lack of a public library in his city, that he would give me the money to set up such a library service. Though I was undecided about accepting the proposal, I asked him how much he would give. He quoted a figure and my reaction was that I would not even consider the idea with a hundred-fold the amount. This just goes to show that the first representative of the city authorities had not the slightest idea of what a public library means.

Incomprehension, indifference to the real problems with which a library is faced in its daily routine work worried me more and more. But day after day brought also professional and other satisfactions. The true source however of what I never admitted to be discouragement was not in short-term difficulties. It was the systematic antagonism of the bureaucrats sitting in their dull offices of the central administration.

Ionesco has explained this phenomenon of the bureaucrats taking over in his own particular way, in his own style, with his own words, and with an extraordinary lucidity. It is a malaise which has marked my relations with bureaucracies. In his *Antidotes*, he has collected a series of articles he published in newspapers and magazines under the explicit title "Culture is not the Government's Business." [2] I would like to line up a few quotations in their original sequence. Paraphrasing Karl Marx, whom he hates, he cries out, "Intellectuals, scholars, artists of all countries unite for the benefit of the people." Ionesco reminds us that for Simone Weil culture was a tool manipulated by professors to produce professors who in turn will produce professors. "In our days," Ionesco adds, "culture seems to be a tool manipulated by civil servants to produce civil servants who in turn will produce other civil servants."

"The officials and the bureaucrats who think they have to decide upon cultural policies never think of asking themselves the question whether power is the authentic expression of society, whether it does not exist outside society, whether it is not above society, whether it is not society's oppressor." "A new exploitation of man by man and a new alienation seem to show up dangerously: exploitation of the artists by the bureaucrats who would be their employers, the bosses of the creators, whose ideas they would distribute, whose ideologies they would sell." "The danger of marshalling and managing culture is tempting. In the west it has the appearance of being done by our bureaucrats in a more liberal

---

[2] *La Culture n'est pas l'affaire de l'Etat*, in *Antidotes* (Paris, 1977).

fashion but just as insidiously and more hypocritically, perhaps, while in the other countries at least one hears them coming with their heavy shoes and big boots."

In 1958 Ionesco was the guest of honour of the International Theatre Institute meeting in Helsinki and after his lecture the Soviet delegation said that he was mentally ill. It was the first time he had been recommended to a psychiatric hospital. Speaking about the PEN Club, before Pierre Emmanuel took over as chairman, Ionesco used this incisive phrase "In fact, the people of the PEN Club gave the floor only to those who refused to give it to the others." Ionesco is at odds with UNESCO because it is an organized expression of the dangers besieging culture. It considers artists to be children who haven't grown up, if it dared it would do the same with scholars, instead of promoting great scientific discoveries and great works of art. Ionesco, being a writer, would give equal opportunities to Pasternak and Eluard, to Mailer and Cholokov, to Marx and the Bible, and comes to his own conclusion "literature prevents men from being indifferent to men."

I could go on along this sad line, but it is about time to breathe some fresh air. I once met Ionesco and it was in Provence, at the typographical school of Lurs, where I arrived straight from Helsinki. If I had known at the time that Helsinki had played an important role in Ionesco's inner life, I would have talked to him about it and we would probably have agreed with the leading Flemish novelist, Marnix Gijsen, who always talked about Helstinki. In Finland I had attended a librarian's meeting and when it was over I flew to Marseilles (over my native city) and with a feeling that after all western Europe was something. The meeting at Lurs had been in full sway for a couple of days when I arrived and its big boss, Maximilien Vox, put me in a Maurassian way in the chair, while Massin was explaining how he had produced his whimsical edition of *La Cantatrice chauve* and he had brought its author along as a guest. I understood nothing of the lecture, I did not very well realize where I was (my only friend among the Lursiens, Fernand Baudin, who had induced me to attend the meeting, was himself absent), and Ionesco and I remained silent all the time. Upon a sign from Maximilien Vox I said "The meeting is adjourned." At the end of the dinner, where Ionesco was sitting at quite a distance from me, a waiter came to me with a bottle of red wine and said "with the compliments of Mr. Ionesco." I asked him why and he came back with a slip of paper "because you have been a silent chairman."

From Lurs to Brussels. When Belgium became an independent country in 1830 it blended a British constitution with a French institutional framework. In the administration the influence of France was overwhelming (when it rains in Paris you open your umbrella in Brussels) and the result was an overheavy centralization and concentration. Paris being France, Brussels ought to be Belgium. In the nineteenth century this was not too bad for an institution like a national library because the government did not care about art and sciences. To set up the Royal Library in 1837, as one of the first new institutions related to the recently acquired independence, the government bought a private library and paid an amount equal to the whole science and arts budget. The private library was that of Charles van Hulthem, considered as one of the twenty-five most important encyclopedic libraries extant at the time. Even today it is a commonplace in the Library to ask, if someone has vainly tried to locate a rare book: "Did you not forget to look it up in van Hulthem?"

Everything has changed since the nineteenth century, except the mentality of the central administration. We, the people in the field, are a nuisance. Administration has become a purpose in itself, and those who think in terms of books and users are out of touch with reality. Books and users, and for that libraries, laboratories, archives, and museums are a nuisance, except when it comes to applying obsolete regulations or, even worse, new regulations which aim at eradicating the last nooks and crannies of independence. At the appropriate place I shall tell the story of the finance inspector who blamed me for buying too many medieval bibles. It was indeed at the time that the administration had invented a new regulation to thwart our normal work. For each acquisition above a certain price I had to submit a report with the arguments justifying the expenditure. As if they could evaluate our arguments, as if we had no professional conscience. These reports gradually became wonderful literary exercises where we mixed gross errors with subtle lies, or from time to time the other way round. The only accurate information was the figures: size, number of pages and illustrations, price, etc. I always suspected that they realized that we were fooling them, but when one deliberately confuses the fields of competence, one best behaves quietly.

The regulations were not only nonsensical with regard to expensive books. The Library which came under the ministry of education could not buy the ministry's own publications. There was on the one hand the sacrosanct rule that it was forbidden to pay with public money for merchandise which had not yet been delivered, and the same ministry refused to deliver it if not prepaid! We bought the publications of course, not that they were so important but because we wanted to collect exhaustively domestic publications. How we bought them would be one of the many examples of sinning against imposed rules. If I look backward I would be tempted to say that the more positive results of my work were all directly related to the fact that I ignored the administrative rules. I write this down with mixed feelings. It would have been so much easier, cheaper and more pleasant for everyone concerned to trust me in matters related to my job, to fire me if I blundered, to give me precise instructions, to pin me down on matters of general policy. Nothing so simple as that.

It took me quite a long time to realize that I had never been sent abroad as an expert by my own government. For UNESCO I went several times to Asia. The American, the French, the Iranian governments thought that they could make some use of my professional experience. In Belgium, no. That is to say with one exception and one I want to recall. In 1957 I was suddenly sent to the then still Belgian Congo. I had not the slightest idea of the country, except for a few western commonplaces learned at school, and I had no time for some background reading. I got all my shots the day before I left, which meant that most of the time I was lying flat on my stomach in the plane. My assignment was a simple one: to inspect the libraries of the country. I landed in Stanleyville, today Kisangani, and met my friend Jan Van Overloop, who had been director of the Belgian Broadcasting Corporation in the Congo immediately after the war. He knew the country very well and was a born geographer as well. We stayed together for nearly the whole trip and this was all to my advantage. In Stan, there was no library and so we proceeded to Kigali and Bujumbura. No libraries either. I began to feel rather uneasy and tried to meet some Belgians who needed books to carry out their jobs. I found them at the headquarters of IRSAC (the Institute for

Scientific Research in Central Africa), at Lwiro. What a place! A
villa half-way between a Flemish farm and an Italian palazzo built
by the director himself, Louis van den Berghe. We were welcomed
there in the grand manner and if the director's reputation had not
preceded him, I would have thought that his budget depended on
our report. I do not remember much of the library, but since there
was plenty of everything I am sure that they had all the subscrip-
tions to the journals they needed. The whole institute had an
unrivalled reputation in Africa south of the Sahara.

After a couple of more attempts I began to realize that there
were no public libraries in the Congo and that I had to wait for the
capital Leopoldville, now Kinshasa, to see one. So I forgot about
books and looked at wild life, of which there was plenty. I could tell
quite a number of pleasant stories, such as the one when our car
got stuck in a *passage à gué*, in the middle of the jungle. Nobody was
around, at least I thought so. But when our driver clapped his
hands, immediately twenty or thirty people appeared from behind
the bushes. There was a lot of argument in what must have been
Swahili in that part of the country and finally a dozen of them
lifted our car, where we had quietly remained seated all the time.
Unfortunately one of them slipped and all the others began to
laugh, dropping us again in the shallow water. After one or two
other attempts we safely reached the other bank. Laughing and
childish joy was precisely the picture I brought home of all the
black people I had met.

I also remember a conversation with a local Belgian civil servant
of some age. He was expecting a dropping of paratroopers the
next day and told us that he had long forgotton Durkheim's
theories about the primitive soul and that after a quarter of a
century in Africa he had to admit that he knew nothing about the
population with which he had been living, but that he was sure that
they would all run away when they saw those big birds falling from
the sky next morning. I ran into him a couple of days later in a
neighbouring city and asked him about the drop. "Well, I am here
to visit a dozen villagers in the hospital because they were injured
when they ran towards the paratroopers and tried to catch them in
their arms." Quite different is my reminiscence of Guy De Leyn,
whom I met as game officer in Rwanda and with whom I visited the
Kagera National Park. He was a fine man, a trained biologist in
love with Africa, its people, its animals, its nature. Looking at

animals with him as a guide was a unique experience. The day
after we left him he was supposed to move a herd of several
elephants over a long distance of a hundred kilometers towards
the game reserve. After the end of the Belgian trusteeship he was
one of the few who remained in the country and the political
change did not affect his local relations and interests. In that time
he lived in the park and was liked by the whole local population.
One day Tutsi terrorists shot him by automatic pistol and the
courage of his wife saved him from ritual mutilation. The death of
such a man is even worse for a young country than for an older one.

This sad story brings to my mind another unpleasant recollection. I participated in the dedication of the Dag Hammarskjöld
Library of the United Nations in New York in 1961. When the
formal part was over there was a cocktail and as it happens at
cocktails I began to talk to someone I did not know. He asked me if
I were the delegate from Belgium and upon my acquiescing reaction he said rather aggressively "I hope that next time there will be
Congolese librarians here." I looked around and answered "And
Italians too." There was no Italian delegate in the room and it had
been announced that very morning that the whole crew of an
Italian aircraft which had made a crash landing in the Congo had
fallen in the hands of cannibals. That was the end of our conversation and I found out that I had been talking to Andrew Cordier,
assistant secretary general of the United Nations. Later I met him
again in Brussels and in Colorado, where he had retired, and we
talked about the good old days. Among them was my first and last
Congo experience. The report I submitted about this assignment
must have been a rather original piece of writing. Later I realized
that I had been sent to the Congo to counter a critical report
written by a Chilean staff member of UNESCO, Miss Summers. I
finally met the lady in question when I began to visit the UNESCO
headquarters and we discovered that our reports were concom-
itant.

To the day one hundred years after Dr. Livingstone died in the
heart of Africa, I started on 1 May 1973 working as a consultant to
the Council on Library Resources in Washington, DC. My library
experience in Belgium had lasted for nearly thirty years, but over
the years I grew gradually more and more interested in international work. I also began to realize that my interest in my own
library and its national environment was reaching a very low level.

Parallel to this development on the home front my American friends opened the Council to me step by step. The exchange of a directorship in Brussels, for a consultantship in Washington was the most natural thing in the world which could have happened to me. The reason why I left the Council after eight months and went back to Belgium falls outside the scope of this book, but it certainly was not the result of a decision that I took.

3. American, European and International Librarianship *

MAY I START with what the French call *une précaution oratoire,* an informal warning: no extensive research went into this paper, but it is based on a lifelong experience, the better part of which was devoted to international cooperation. I have been too much of an actor, too little of a detached observer.

Shortly after I entered the profession, close to the end of World War II, a senior colleague told me a story that four young American librarians had reorganized the old Vatican library. For a long time I believed that it was a joke to oppose a dynamic American counterculture to the static wisdom embedded in a centuries-old collection of secular and religious manuscripts. When I realized that the story was true, I faced at once a problem which has never left me since – library techniques versus subject knowledge. Time and again this tension turned up when I tried to compare American and European librarianship. Over the years I have expressed it in many different ways. If I remember one of the better ones, I would say in retrospect what I said about five or six years ago on the occasion of the dedication of a new library building at UCLA: "In Europe, the libraries are better than the librarians," sternly refusing to add the expected second part of the sentence. The fact that one day I would dedicate a new American library could not have occurred to me when I entered the profession, but if it had, I

---

* After some hesitation I decided to retain the spoken version in this chapter. As explained in the Preface I delivered this paper at the centennial meeting of the American Library Association (ALA) in Chicago in 1976. Some friends think my speaking is more lively than my writing. This did not prevent me from slightly altering some parts after the paper was delivered and published by ALA.

would have considered it to be a joke, like that of the young
American librarians reorganizing the Vatican library.

You should know that I never had any formal library training, as
is the case still today with nearly all librarians from the European
continent working in research libraries. The only relationship of
these librarians with formal training is that they nearly all teach in
library schools at the sub-university level. I committed the same
sin, but only for a short time. I even had to look up my poorly kept
archives to see what course I gave. Also like these other librarians I
had an academic training. In my case it was Dutch poetry of the
nineteenth century. This subject was never of any use in my
professional work, but the training it supplied has always been an
invaluable asset. So you will easily understand that professional
training, in the sense that you use the word, has not the same
importance in my thinking as it does in yours. It is one of the
advantages of comparative librarianship that it forces one to question the automaticity of priorities.

I started this paper with the direct question of library techniques
versus subject knowledge because it has been my life's experience
that you need a few ideas – they may even be preconceived ideas –
to face the reality of the surrounding world. This reality being a
library, the complexity of the relationship between form and con-
tent, between library technique and subject knowledge, between
typography and literary quality, represents one such idea. Modern
linguistics has given a new dimension to the distinction the old
antinomy made between *le contenant et le contenu,* the signifier and
the signified. I guess that such a need for fixed ideas is what was
called in the nineteenth century a philosophy of life. For me this
has also meant a never-ending crossing of the ocean to try to
understand on both sides the roots and the flowers of the professional trees. In my contacts with American librarianship, the Library of Congress came before ALA. My love affair with the Library of Congress (LC) started more than a quarter of a century
ago. That was when the Librarian of Congress issued a notice
saying that some false rumours were spread that he was going to
accept an important international appointment. His name was
Luther H. Evans, soon to become director-general of UNESCO.

Early in 1951 I was appointed consultant at LC for a six-week
period, which allowed me to say, until two years ago, at every
reception in the Whittall Pavilion, that I was the oldest staff

member, each time, however, being corrected by Walter Ristow, who protested, rightly, that he was the oldest one. He is now retired, but I am too in a certain way. This is not just an anecdote. It indicates one of the aspects of American librarianship which frequently strikes me: the turnover of the staff and its mobility. In Europe, more particularly in the Latin part of Europe, something is wrong with you if you change from one library to another. In the United States, something is wrong with you if you do not change. I stayed for thirty years in the same library, and when I left it was not for another library. After a long period of observation, I would be tempted to conclude that both traditions have more weaknesses than advantages. These diverging traditions are, of course, not limited to the library field but belong to two different forms of society. This is one of my other *idées fixes*: a community has the library it deserves and the library has the staff it deserves. That is, of course, not completely true, but it nearly is.

The difference between the two traditions, however, is not as sharp today as it was twenty-five years ago. International cooperation has something to do with this change, but we should not exaggerate its impact. When the American Memorial Library was built in Berlin immediately after World War II, as a symbol of democratic freedom opposed to the recent Nazi nightmare, it was gradually turned into a good German public library concept. No harm in that – quite the contrary. It is better that international cooperation bends slightly in the direction of the national environment, rather than being left at the neutral level of grandiloquent speeches about peace and so on.

After my consultantship at the Library of Congress was over, my admiration for American librarianship began. During my first stay in the United States, I visited one hundred libraries in three months, and I would never do that again. This may explain why in later years I always said that I preferred librarians to libraries. Actually my order of preference early in my career was: libraries, books, librarians. In later years it changed into: librarians, books, libraries.

Though I spent a few days in Chicago in 1951, I did not visit the ALA headquarters and I did not meet the newly appointed executive director, David Clift, who became later a good friend. The reason was very simple: I did not know of the existence of ALA. I guess I have to apologize, but it's the truth. In the United States the librarians I met in 1951 hardly had time to talk about their own libraries, and when the shoptalk was over, they questioned me about Europe, not about libraries in Europe, but about that old continent with its idiosyncracies which they liked so much. In my home country I was a nonactive member of a library association which meant nothing to the profession. Still today many library associations in Europe, and once again I must stress more particularly in the Latin part of Europe, do not mean much to the profession.

Some years ago I said that the British Library Association has twenty thousand members and the French association two hundred. The two figures are wrong, but the difference is correct! In countries like France and Belgium where the government does everything or pretends to do everything, library associations look more like learned societies. The members listen to a scholarly paper about an unknown manuscript and the closest they come to matters of professional interest is in the description of bibliographical ghosts. Many of these associations bring together librarians and archivists, the latter often being the more active members. I developed a theory that in those countries where archivists and librarians were members of the same association, the libraries were in a state of underdevelopment. I was never very popular among archivists, but I am still not convinced that I might have been wrong.

In 1957, when I had not yet discovered the professional world outside the United States, the director of the USIS library in Brussels, John Brown, took an initiative which led me to my first comparison of American and European librarianship. John Brown was very popular and knew French so well that he wrote an outstanding book *Panorama de la Littérature Contemporaine aux Etats-Unis* (1954). He brought about thirty European librarians with an American experience together in Brussels. John Brown's Belgian assistant, Madame A. Anciaux, had the good idea of suggesting Douglas Bryant, librarian at Harvard, as a keynote speaker on "American Librarianship in the Mid-Fifties". The meeting was chaired by Sir Frank Francis and I wrote the report which was published in the United States under the title *European Librarianship in the Mid-Fifties*. This was a good reunion and it should have been followed by similar ones. At the time I had just ended a period of rest because I had been suffering from labyrinthitis, which is an uncommon illness that is supposed to be the outcome of all kinds of unusual constraints. When I could use my eyes again Clark Stillman sent me an issue of the *New Yorker* in which a contributor described his labyrinthitis. He was a librarian.

IFLA, the International Federation of Library Associations, introduced ALA to me, though the relationship between the two organizations existed long before I was aware of it. I would like to recall my first acquaintance with ALA because I think it is rather typical for a number of European librarians. It was at an IFLA General Council meeting in Madrid in 1958 that, during a trip to the Escurial, Douglas Bryant introduced me to John Cory and Jack Dalton. Douglas Bryant had just finished his term on IFLA's Executive Board and Jack Dalton was taking over. The latter was still sitting on the Board when I became a member in Rome in 1964. It was, however, with Foster Mohrhardt, a former ALA president, who joined the Board in 1965, that I had the longest association.

I was surprised to discover that these American Board members got their travel expenses paid by their library association. In my part of Europe we always had to rely on government funds. I gradually began to realize that library associations were important for the development of the profession, both nationally and internationally. Moreover, these colleagues from the New World were highly qualified and had an open-mindedness toward the world at large that strongly impressed me. What I also discovered with some surprise was that they were the only members of the Board who reported home about the IFLA Board meetings. They came to the meetings well prepared, with or without instructions, and their remarks were always a bit more formal but much more to the point than ours. At the time I did not know that international commitments were a point of issue within ALA, as is the case again today, unfortunately, as I understand it. I simply thought that ALA naturally owed its cooperation to IFLA because of the high degree of development of American librarianship. I would like to add a footnote to this recollection of my first encounter with American librarians outside the United States. All of them were perfect ambassadors of their native country abroad. This is a positive way to introduce a negative remark: over the years I have met many outstanding American librarians who lost all their qualities and qualifications once they were outside their home country. I am not referring at all, or hardly at all, to their pronunciation of the English language, but to their basic mistake, which was to assume that the institutional framework, within which one had to work, was American all over the world. Some of these librarians, who were to fail in their missions abroad, never realized that the simple word "library" had a different meaning along the shores of the Potomac than along the Seine, not to mention the Ganges. This would probably also be true of other–than–American peaceful conquerors of the world, but I have not met them, except for a couple of my French or British friends.

Actually, ALA was present at the very inception of IFLA. This happened half a century ago and the details of the story have been written down elsewhere. Next year, on the occasion of the fiftieth anniversary of IFLA, it will receive full treatment again. May it suffice to say here that this early cooperation between American and European professional organizations is typical of the development of international nongovernmental organizations; just as the adherence of the socialist countries in the fifties and of the developing countries in the seventies is reflecting a general trend in transnational cooperation. Notwithstanding its name, IFLA was for a long time not exactly an international organization, but much more of a European-American venture. In the early history of IFLA, ALA contributed a president, William W. Bishop, a leading librarian of his day and chairman of ALA's International Relations Committee. He had no American successor, however, just as the limited IFLA meeting in Chicago in 1933 was unique until the recent General Council meeting in Washington in 1974. Thirty-five participated in 1933, one thousand in 1974. There was a depression in 1933, an economic decline in 1974. Besides William W. Bishop and Carl H. Milam, executive secretary of ALA, one or two other American librarians appear on the lists of participants in the early meetings in Europe. The preponderance of Europeans was obvious. Each year a small group of American librarians crossed the ocean, and glancing through the IFLA proceedings of those years, one cannot avoid the feeling that they were the happy few who could afford a return to the sources, as we say in French. In those days – that means until the outbreak of World War II – IFLA was not a professional international organization, but rather a distinguished gentlemen's club, where old friends, who happened to be librarians, talked for a few days every year, at the invitation of one of them, about matters of common interest, and had a good time. This image of IFLA was revived after the war in 1947 and I would not pretend that all its features are gone today. This is a period in the history of European-American library cooperation which I have termed amateurish. We were professionals in our libraries, in our national library organizations – at least in some Anglo-Saxon countries or countries which developed under their influence – but we stepped down to the amateur level in reaching the international scene. Effective results of this form of cooperation are difficult to detect, but it undoubtedly paved the way for the multilateral stream of ideas and programmes with which we are familiar today.

From this vantage point it is strange to read again the welcoming speech with which William W. Bishop addressed the European guests in Chicago in 1933. It sounds like the incunabulum era of international cooperation. "I should like to dwell briefly," said Bishop, "on some conditions and characteristics of American library development which I find all too frequently unfamiliar to my European colleagues."

The use of the term "public" libraries allowed him to stress the fact of the historic division of the United States into quasi-independent states, and "an even more marked centrifugal divorce of our cities and counties from our State governments, as well as from national, Federal control. Local public opinion is in the end the only driving force compelling the establishment and support of such means of both culture and education as schools, libraries, museums and galleries of art." "However," he adds rightly, "It would be wholly unbecoming in this connection to fail to point out the enormous practical assistance to all American libraries of the work of the Library of Congress, an assistance, however, based on voluntary cooperation and in no way upon control or direction." And then follows a nearly prophetic remark: "To me the power of this conception – that means of individual service which the research libraries have taken over from the public libraries – of library service in the American scientific libraries holds out great promise for the future. If once we can come through this trying financial crisis, with our ideals of service unimpaired, we shall go forward to a development of mechanical apparatus, of mutual aid, of cooperative efforts in all directions which will enable us to use to the full the books we have spent so much time and money in gathering." In passing he gives tribute to the special libraries and their Association "in spite of the greatest possible diversity of interest and of subject matter in its constituent librarians and libraries."

William W. Bishop ends with a laudatory presentation of ALA to the European members of his audience. "Without ALA, librarianship in America would today have stood on a far lower plane," but I do not feel it to be my duty to quote at length from these compliments.

Within the last few years, though, the pattern of cooperation has changed drastically. ALA is no longer alone in the United States in its approach to the international library community. Other American IFLA-member associations are the Music Library Association, the American Association of Law Libraries, the Medical Library Association, the Art Libraries Association, and the Association of Research Libraries. There are also one hundred and twelve institutional members. SLA, it is worth noting, had already invited foreign librarians to a dinner party during the 1933 Chicago session.

But IFLA also is no longer alone. Actually, it never has been, because the International Federation for Documentation is a much older organization with similar interests, to which I shall come back in a few moments. But the main factor of change, for better or for worse, is the existence of UNESCO. The prewar International Institute of Intellectual Cooperation never meant for the international dimension of our profession what UNESCO now means. In other words, governmental influence has never been as powerful as nowadays, both at the national and the international levels. This induced me to say at the opening of the fortieth General Council in Washington (1974), "Let's be aware of the danger that politics and profession may appear in the wrong order of importance, let us avoid putting at the top what belongs at the bottom and vice versa." May I use the opportunity which is offered to me here, before such a large audience, to appeal to individual ALA members to participate actively in international cooperation. The strength of international nongovernmental organizations, such as IFLA, will guarantee automatically the eminence of the profession over politics and will gradually counterbalance an international community of governments with an international community of people.

In my following comments I may be biased toward ALA and

IFLA, and this may even be unfair to other national and international organizations, both governmental and nongovernmental, but the general trend of my thinking will remain close, at least I hope so, to the reality of international cooperation.

After World War II, ALA stepped boldly outside the borders of the United States through an enhanced programme of its International Relations Office. In the David Clift *Festschrift* issue of *American Libraries* (July-August 1972), Emerson Greenaway contributes an excellent paper on "Progress in International Librarianship." I would like to quote somewhat at random:

"*Education of Librarians*. Emphasis was rightly given to education for librarianship and most of this activity centered in Asian countries. The US Department of State provided funds for the projects to *provide* library school study and in service training for nine Indian university librarians. The University of Delhi received fiscal support in the expansion and development of its program of library education from the Rockefeller Foundation. This same Foundation aided also in the strengthening of the Japan library school at Keio University; assistance in the development of a graduate program of library education at the University of the Philippines; and the establishment of a library school at the National Taiwan University. In the Middle East, the Ford Foundation assisted in the establishment of a library education program at the University of Ankara."

On reading this paragraph, however, I could not avoid noting that all of the countries mentioned – not the "institutions" as such – still lack a decent library system and have hardly any interest in international cooperation. Take India, for example, still struggling with that nonsensical legacy of the British Empire, with its national library in Calcutta symbolically located between prison and zoo. There is no generally representative library association, but instead a series of competing state library associations, the whole purpose of which seems to be an occasional meeting at which invited "messages" from abroad are read. In most university libraries, three parallel classification systems exist. The ghost of Ranganathan is still floundering around. Japan is another case at hand, with an isolated Library of Congress, called the Diet Library, refusing or accepting very reluctantly to take national leadership, and a Japan Library Association behaving like a group of librarians from a developing country. If one compares the strong international impact of Japanese publishers with the lack of international interest on the part of Japanese librarians, it is almost a shame for our profession. This truth is even sadder when one realizes the intensity of the professional traffic between the United States and Japan over the years.

I could go on, but it seems to me more useful to look for an explanation. In my humble opinion – as people in the East say when they have not the slightest reservation about their opinion – the problem is not the old one of whether it is more profitable to send librarians abroad for training or to receive at home professional teachers from abroad. This seems to me to be a false problem. There is enough experience gained so that we can agree on the efficiency of undergraduate training at home and graduate training abroad, with, of course, a number of exceptions, as with all general rules. I would not press again the point that training as such may probably not be the best answer. What I want to stress is that library development relies on the quality of a limited number of persons, in developed as well as in developing countries. The only difference between the two types of countries is that in the latter these men or women are far too rare. If you have such a man, let's say, in Malaysia, he will feel the need to travel to the United States, to Europe, and to Japan, to be exposed to different library experiences, to talk to the few librarians from whom he can learn the strategy of selling the library idea at home, because the major problem is to convince local and national authorities of the genuine library solution that has to be given in particular circumstances. This requires a high degree of professional experience, intellectual power, and strong character. Not many people combine these qualities, in or outside the library profession.

Governments are not good at finding such persons or even at recognizing them when they present themselves, which happens sometimes. And here I have a first but sharp criticism to address to an intergovernmental organization like UNESCO. I think I can speak with some authority about UNESCO: for over a period of fifteen years, I have been sent by UNESCO to developing countries on short assignments, and I have been for many years a member of UNESCO's International Advisory Committee on Documentation, Libraries and Archives. Service to UNESCO is extremely frustrating. The Secretariat – these are the officials in Paris – live in a world apart. Generally they are not chosen for their competence, but by a criterion of geographical distribution that is, in fact, political distribution. This is unavoidable in the world in which we live, but people chosen in that way should at least be modest when they meet us, the professionals. The contrary is the case. In a language which is not always understandable they build up a theoretical framework, – which is just empire building of one UNESCO division against another – in which they try to encompass some of the ideas they may have picked up when they happened to be listening to us.

This is, in turn, no theoretical attack. I shall give you two examples. They may seem to lead me away from my subject, but I think that they will show rather well the reality of international cooperation: UNISIST and Universal Bibliographic Control. Let me, however, repeat once more – and very explicitly – that international cooperation is worth all the troubles. It enriches everyone, even those who never had the opportunity to participate directly in cosmopolitan forums.

UNISIST is a brilliant example of successful international manœuvring. A couple of clever people at the International Council of Scientific Unions' Abstracting Board realized that the science information division of UNESCO had a very weak programme and proposed to them to reinvent the wheel. The acronym UNISIST stands for a world science information system. Each generation has had its UNISIST but under another name. I know one of the pre-UNISISTS rather well because it was launched in my native city of Brussels under the title *Institut International de Bibliographie* in 1895. Just like UNISIST, it was a philosophy, a movement, and a programme. Although one of the founders, Henri La Fontaine, received the Nobel Prize for Peace in 1913, it failed. In Brussels you can dig today in the archeology of international scientific and technical information. The site is called Mundaneum. Some by-products of the Institute are however still with us: the International Federation for Documentation and the Universal Decimal Classification. I hope that in about ten to twenty years' time we shall have the benefit of such important by-products of UNISIST.

UNISIST is viewed in terms of an international movement toward increased voluntary cooperation among the national and the international participating systems and services, using common rules and media, but with varying degrees and modalities of interconnection. When the UNISIST idea was launched about ten years ago, some critics wrote that it was going to be successful because both the United States and Soviet Union wanted it. On the surface this was confirmed by the fact that the UNESCO Intergovernmental Conference of experts in 1971 adopted UNISIST, and the following General Conference confirmed this adoption; UNISIST became part of UNESCO's 1972-73 programme.

UNESCO is such a dream world that I was elected a vice-president of the UNISIST Intergovernmental Conference at the very moment that I was looking outside the conference hall for an Italian candidate, having been instructed by my government to do so. Later at the General Conference, I voted for UNISIST and its overgrown budget because I did not want to distinguish myself from other delegates. Cooperation with UNESCO is very often a question of conscience.

Such a generalization is never completely true and is even unfair up to a certain point. In my case, it is based upon the intensity of my relation with a division of UNESCO, called DBA, which stands for libraries, documentation, and archives. It would be easy to change my conclusion if it could be related to other divisions of UNESCO, for example, book promotion. Here I had only a sporadic but rewarding experience, centered around International Book Year 1972. But this was, of course, marginal to my main professional interest which I am trying to reflect here.

The reason why UNISIST was phony from the very beginning is simple indeed. The UNISIST scheme is a fantasy linked to a consumer's society and has nothing to do with the basic problems of developing countries for which UNESCO pretends to stand. When I first voiced this criticism at UNESCO the answer was: two of the twenty-two recommendations of the UNISIST programme are devoted to developing countries, and those countries request networks for scientific and technical documentation. Let's be serious: first, the two paragraphs are crumbs from a rich table thrown to the poor countries in order to collect their votes; second, UNESCO sends experts to some of those countries, sometimes strange experts, I would say, to draw up government requests for documentation centres or what have you. In the developing country – an expression which does not seem to sound well in the singular – it is organized confusion. Local librarians spend years to develop a public, a university, or a national library, and then suddenly, out of the blue, comes a proposal to build a centre or a system or a network – never a simple library – which is a hundred times more expensive. And then comes the confusing sacredness of science in the minds of people and governments which have still to struggle with illiteracy problems. It is a shame for UNESCO to have equated, in too many parts of the world, computers with wisdom, science with happiness.

Before leaving UNISIST I want to tell you an anecdote. One day I was sitting at one of the numerous evaluation committees – on which UNESCO spends too much of its money and of our time – and my neighbour was a French Nobel Prize-winner for Physics. He eloquently read a paper written by someone else stating that the whole science community was backing UNISIST. When he had finished and was applauded, I asked him *in aparte*, "Why does the whole science community back UNISIST?" He answered me, "Because we want to mind our own business." I said thad this was very respectable indeed and that the librarians also wanted to mind their own business. At this point, I added that cooperation between the two communities has to be worked out. He looked at me very puzzled and said, "But librarians will never be able to distinguish the good papers from the poor ones." I said that this was evident, but I asked if the poor papers were written by librarians? At that moment, someone moved that the responsibility of the research libraries should be transferred from the library division of UNESCO to the science information division!

Universal Bibliographic Control, UBC, is exactly the contrary of UNISIST, when you look at it from its appearance in the UNESCO programme. The only clever part about UBC is its acronym. For the rest it has been a shameful courting of UNESCO by IFLA to try to convince the officials that here, with a flexible programme which did not require a neologistic jargon, an attempt has been made to improve the daily routine work of libraries all over the world, actually to reduce the routine work and to free the mind for innovative and creative work at all levels in all types of libraries. The aim of UBC could be and actually was summarized in two sentences: a world-wide system for the control and exchange of bibliographical information so as to make universally and promptly available, in a form which is internationally acceptable, basic bibliographic data on all publications issued in all countries. The concept of Universal Bibliographic Control presupposes the creation of a network made up of component national parts, each of which covers a wide range of publishing and library activities, all integrated at the international level to form a total system.

Such an objective does not require the slightest distinction between industrial countries and developing ones, between capitalistic and socialist states. This is of the utmost importance for efficient international cooperation. The implementation, however, is another story. The simple aim poses quite different problems depending on whether you work with a computer-produced MARC tape of bibliographical descriptions or try to cope with cataloguing problems in a country which has not yet been able to produce any kind of a national bibliography. Here a solid and profound cooperation between international governmental and nongovernmental organizations is an absolute must. Let us hope that in the very near future it will effectively be established. In order to include Universal Bibliographic Control in the UNESCO programme my IFLA colleagues and I had to agree to become part of another monstrous framework invented by the Library Division of the secretariat to counter UNISIST: NATIS, which stands for National Information Systems.

As for UNISIST, an intergovernmental conference was organized at the headquarters in Paris and it was in so-called cooperation with nongovernmental organizations, in this case the International Federation of Library Associations, the International Federation for Documentation and the International Council of Archives. I have already explained that at the UNISIST intergovernmental conference I was elected a vice-president by mistake. At the NATIS Intergovernmental Conference the three presidents of the cooperating nongovernmental organizations were generously given three minutes at the opening session. I decided to use plain language which was, in the UNESCO context, an act of rebellion. After my three minutes were over the director-general whispered in my ear, "I thought that you were more of a diplomat." And when it came to publishing the proceedings I received a nice telephone call from one of my girl friends at the secretariat saying, "I am not sending you the abstract of your paper because you would not agree." When I read it afterwards I was shocked, not because it was cast in noncommittal diplomatic language but because it said exactly the contrary of what I had said. I am sure that it was done in good faith. There is a kind of language, which people who are accustomed to think in UNese just do not understand anymore. It was the same with the interpreters. In Paris I had to deliver my paper in French because I was an official delegate and at the homefront I would have been blamed for not using a national language which happened also to be an official language of UNESCO, although I knew that nobody would understand the English interpretation. Not for reasons of revenge, which is a feeling that is not native to me, but to prove to my English-speaking friends that what I said in 1974 at the birth of NATIS was not pure nonsense – as the hierarchy and the interpreters wanted them to believe – I am giving here my own translation, well aware that . . . *scripta manent.*

"Mr. Director General, Ladies and Gentlemen, Dear Colleagues: Part of this audience, the part that is not librarians, will probably be disappointed because I do not appear here as an old spinster, slightly nearsighted and a bit misanthropic. This caricature of a librarian, like all caricatures, has an element of truth in it for which – all things considered – the profession has no need to blush. If the elderly lady symbolizes the modest public library, located in a poor quarter of the city or in an isolated rural area, I do not hesitate for one moment to proclaim loudly that she contributes more to individual enrichment and social development than an expensive documentation centre which devotes ninety percent of its resources and energy to becoming automated.

"It is however also true that such a caricature finds its origin in the evolution of the library itself. Being older than science, libraries encountered many problems of adaptation when science began to take the predominant place which it occupies in today's society. From nonadaptation to obsolescence the distance is short, especially when science considers itself as the religion of the twentieth century. It is my weakness to believe that science is beginning to lose its halo of sanctity to become again a highly honourable human activity which it should never have ceased to be. In other words the discussions, which have centered around the 'two cultures' are gradually becoming pointless and we, the people of books, journals, microforms and computers are soon going to stop lining up phony arguments to distinguish between libraries and documentation centres.

"An analogy to illustrate the same idea comes to my mind.

Whether it be in an old dendrological album or in a modern botanical handbook, the rendering of a tree is the same, although the old woodblock may have more charm than the mechanical plate. In both cases the tree has roots, a trunk and branches. Let us say that the unity of the profession is represented by the trunk, the archives by a thick branch growing close to the ground and that documentation is thin branches up near the top. The distinction between archives and libraries developed naturally, the one between libraries and documentation centres was created artificially. Looking at the map of the world it is easy to see that where libraries and archives developed best, they became quite independent of each other. This does not, however, mean that cooperation between them is lacking; on the contrary. The written document constitutes a permanent link and various fields of cooperation develop. Quite different is the relation between libraries and documentation centres. A second look at the map shows that good results are obtained in those places where people do not waste their time, financial resources and energy setting up parallel institutions with inevitable duplication. Haphazardly I would cite the National Library of Medicine in the United States and, tomorrow, the British Library in the United Kingdom.

"To finish with this part of my speech I would like to return for one moment to my tree, adding that all distinctions cease to exist where the tree has its roots in the soil – if you prefer – at the level of the 'infrastructure.' Therefore it is most encouraging that UNESCO has organized this conference in cooperation – I would like to be able to say in close cooperation – with the three nongovernmental organizations with which we are familiar. Here I would like to pay a tribute to the International Federation for Documentation which has created the Universal Decimal Classification – by the way in my home town – and which allows thousands of libraries to fulfil their role. I shall push false modesty far enough to remain silent about the Universal Bibliographic Control notwithstanding the fact that for our generation it is the war-horse of the International Federation of Library Associations.

"I shall use the last minute allowed to me to excuse the vocabulary I chose for this speech, which had to be cut so ridiculously short. I avoided the jargon of the working documents with one exception. A minute ago I used the word 'infrastructure,' but you will have understood that I put it between quotation marks. The choice of my words has been clumsy, but I have been clumsy intentionally. Skilfulness has done too much damage to international cooperation, both in and outside UNESCO. There is an example all of us know well: UNISIST. What a brilliant example of skilfulness: with words first, with words afterwards. UNISIST always brings to my mind that admirable façade of the palace at Jaipur in India, called the Façade of the Wind. UNISIST moved mountains of words, of paper, and also of money. We have all used this instrument. We were all happy to have it, especially to cheat our governments. Let us hope that the present conference will not lead to a UNISIST II but will replace it by an instrument, just as alluring; and that, when we are back in our institutions – there where we face the reality of every day – we shall be able to use it without cheating anyone."

I dwelled for a couple of minutes on the UNESCO part in UNISIST, NATIS and Universal Bibliographic Control to show that large government resources do not necessarily lead to the best solutions. Nongovernmental organizations, whether national or international, whether in rich or poor countries, are forced by financial pressure to rely on people, on individuals who bring to their work the necessary imagination and who never think of a cumbersome machinery. The real leaders at the international level – for large countries, I could add at the national level too – are those who modify their own ideas when the implementation of their goals runs into red tape. Nothing is more damaging to the life of the mind, in or outside any specific profession, than bureaucracy.

My negative comments on UNISIST have already given me a first opportunity to speak in a positive way about the International Federation for Documentation. Over the years, I have been induced to speak often about FID, from very different angles and more particularly about its cooperation with IFLA. It has been my pleasure to witness and to contribute to closer links between the two organizations. Will there be one day a merger? In the meanwhile I have been using many different expressions to try to understand what it is all about: problem-oriented *v.* institution-oriented, male-dominated *v.* female dominated, theorists *v.* practitioners, sciences *v.* humanities or to quote a UNESCO official: "FID may pretend to be more serious, but IFLA has much more human warmth." He knew both organizations well.

Another observation may also explain why the European antagonism between IFLA and FID has hardly existed in the United States. I can add, between brackets, that it does not explain satisfactorily why Soviet librarians and Soviet documentalists – these are experts in informatics as they like to say – do not speak to one another. A few years ago I was the first link in Moscow between a distinguished senior informaticsian (sic) and a no less distinguished senior librarian. They were kind to one another, my interpreter told me, but they had not the slightest interest in one another's work.

I would like to come back for one moment to my oversimplified thesis of science and technology versus public libraries. It is beyond any doubt that this antagonism has weakened during the last generation, also in Europe following in this context the American example. The reasons are manifold and different: active participation of SLA in IFLA, the interest of public libraries in science and technology, the development of public libraries outside the Anglo-Saxon world, for example. If I would try to draw a conclusion from the recent evolution, I would be tempted to say that within FID and within IFLA a growing number of librarians, Americans and non-Americans, are interested in one another's work, but are still aware of differences which mark their daily professional life. And so I endorse the words of the American FID vice-president who said, "Let's strengthen our links with due speed."

It is time to conclude: I would like to use the coincidence between the ALA Centennial and the US Bicentennial to try to generalize from the relationship between the ALA and IFLA to the relationship between the United States and the world. Would it, for example, be appropriate to equate, for this purpose, the International Relations Office of ALA with American Studies abroad? This possibility came to my mind when I read Denis Donoghue's comments on a recent Salzburg Seminar on the "Impact of the United States of America and Europe upon Each Other." I quote from Denis Donoghue of Dublin University:

"American studies: it is clear that this entirely reputable subject has been sustained by many different motives. American foreign policy, the rhetoric of the Cold War, the self-consciousness of American society, millenarian sentiments rampant in American feeling, and the intrinsic capacity of America to present itself as an object of interest to many people, including gifted scholars. The relation between these several motives is matter for definition and argument. It is not eccentric to find the history and the literature of the United States at least interesting. It is absurd to argue that scholars should turn away from that interest lest they be corrupted by official approval, Washington, the State Department, the American Council of Learned Societies, and the United States Information Service. But there is no merit in assuming that the official relation to American Studies is absolutely pure or disinterested."

The comparison, like most comparisons, is partly true and partly false. What is undoubtedly true is – I should rather say, was – the self-consciousness of American society, the millenarian sentiment, "what is good for us is good for you," and, up to a certain point in time, the official rubber stamp. What is undoubtedly false is that American librarianship as opposed to American Studies never had that kind of "for export only" label. On the contrary, American librarianship found in the world at large an eagerness to be understood, to be adapted to local conditions, to be translated into vernacular situations. This transfer was often very successful because it could be based on an international framework – IFLA – which American librarianship had so powerfully helped to build.

If my last words would give you the impression that, for the purpose of this lecture, I have drawn a dividing line between the United States and the world, which is partly real and partly unreal, it was just to try to explain more easily the flow of ideas which crossed this line.

May I hope that the long-standing working relationship between ALA and IFLA will continue, and even increase, because today, I think it fair to say, American librarianship will be as much an importer as an exporter. It has been an invaluable asset of my professional life, of my life *tout court,* to be a privileged witness of this intellectual migration where the United States has always been a source of inspiration.

4. Belgian Art Seminar

THIS IS A RECOLLECTION of its own, quite independent from the other reminiscences encompassed between these covers. There is indeed no reason why "the line of duty", which is a loose link between the various parts of this book, should be applied to this chapter. Today I still do not know exactly how I got involved, but in 1950 I found myself directing a summer art school in Brussels. I think that Paul Coremans, director of the Royal Institute of the Artistic Patrimonium and a world authority on the preservation of works of art, mentioned my name to the two parties involved in the organization of the seminar: the ministry of education and the Belgian American Educational Foundation (BAEF). Without any request on my part I was granted a leave of absence of two months from the Library and I was in charge before I knew what it was all about.

Before World War II Paul Rolland, a distinguished Belgian art historian, had set up summer courses in art history and had attracted quite a number of students, mainly through fellowships from the Belgian American Educational Foundation. After the war he resumed the courses and he was going to organize them for the sixth time when he suddenly died. I had never met Paul Rolland and I had to familiarize myself with his profile through conversations with people who had known him well and through the files of the summer courses. Apparently we had not very much in common and I would certainly not have taken the initiative in setting up summer courses in art history. He also did not seem to have understood what the American foundation expected from these courses. In fact the Foundation had decided to cancel its fellowships the very year that I took over. This decision was based

on the report of a former Fellow, George Wickes, a staff member
of the BAEF in New York, who had been sent over the previous year
in order to evaluate the courses from an American point of view.
The Foundation had, however, decided to keep a finger in the pie
and to pay its share in the running costs of the school. I myself was
on the eve of my first trip to the United States and did not yet know
how I was going to get along with *these* Americans.

Paul Rolland had carefully prepared the session and I had only
to look after its correct execution. When the registered students
arrived I was surprised to find that the vast majority among them,
except for one Indian, one Frenchman, one Italian and three girls
from Holland, were Belgians. Why did they need summer
courses? Why did they not go to the regular university courses (no
summer semesters at the Belgian universities)? It did not take me a
long time to understand that many were girls coming from
families of good social position, some of them very pretty indeed,
who thought that art history was an elegant way to acquire a thin
layer of erudite sensitivity. From their point of view that was quite
correct. And if in the course of the process a potential husband
showed up, this would not spoil the game.

If the student body was deliciously amateurish, the teaching
staff, on the contrary, was highly professional and competent. I
hope that I shall find an opportunity to mention them individually: I retained them all for the following years. Writing a quarter
of a century later, I cannot avoid noting that many things passed
and many people passed away. The courses lasted for one month
and at the end examinations were given, which looked a bit silly to
me. My predecessor had struggled seriously with the continental
tradition of *ex cathedra* lectures, as opposed to the American way of
teaching, and his report of the previous year, which was my main
background document, showed that this dichotomy was the major
unsolved problem. I do not remember one student, while for the
following years I remember nearly all of them. What is no longer
clear in my mind is the group to which they belonged, except
where friendships among two or three of them grew during the
seminars or even led to a marriage.

A few weeks after the 1950 session was over, I left for the United
States as a Fellow of the United States Educational Foundation
with a three months programme of library visits, more particularly
the Library of Congress. This programme, which was supposed to

cover my whole stay, turned out to occupy only its first half. About the one hundred odd libraries which I visited all over the United States I have reported elsewhere. At the end of this extensive trip, I was back in New York to talk over the Brussels summer course in art history. Instead of going home I went immediately, as a Fellow of the Belgian American Educational Foundation, on a new tour, this time to look at museums, art galleries and art schools, and to meet leading art historians, more particularly at the New York University Graduate School of Art History.

Back in Brussels three months later than scheduled, I immediately had to prepare the session of what was henceforth called the Brussels Art Seminar. The experience of the previous one, my discussions in New York (more particularly with Clark Stillman as secretary of the BAEF) and my conversations with the local teaching staff (more particularly with Paul Coremans), made it quite clear what my objective should be: a focus on one glorious period of Belgian art – the choice fell on the Flemish Primitives –; a drastic reduction of the *ex cathedra* lectures, most of the time being given to a direct contact with the works of art themselves; and above all no Belgian students but only foreign ones, actually fifteen Americans and as many non-Americans. The American graduate students came over with fellowships from the BAEF, while the European students were selected through the mixed committees of countries with which Belgium had signed a cultural agreement. From time to time UNESCO added a Fellow from Asia.

The decision to stress the actual work with the original paintings implied that one month was not enough and the Seminar was extended to six weeks. It is a well- known fact that Belgian Primitives, and for that matter other major Flemish works of art also, are better represented in foreign collections than at home. Hence trips abroad were unavoidable, and in the first year we went to Holland and France, and later Germany also was added. It should be noted here that foreign students were eager to see the places where these masterpieces were created, the genuineness of the paintings explained as well as possible by local people. Not all participants would go as far as David Carter who suddenly exclaimed, while he was in the Bruges Museum of Fine Arts "I see van Eyck!" And indeed he saw van Eyck reflected in the shoulder of St. George protecting Canon van der Paele. This was about the time that attention was given by art historians to these small reflective renderings of the artist at work. Was it as a result of Panofsky's comments on the mirror in *The Marriage of Giovanni Arnolfini* by Jan van Eyck in the National Gallery in London?

The Flemish character of cities like Bruges or Ghent was very helpful, the more so that continuous foreign armies of occupation over the years had forgotten to take away some van Eycks like the *Altarpiece* in Ghent or the *Canon van der Paele* in Bruges. My deep involvement with these seminars convinced me of the fact that the Flemish Primitives and Rubens et al. have such a glorious international reputation because they are so well represented in the great museums and collections of the world. My friends among the Belgian art historians do not like me to repeat this too often in public. It sounds as if I approved of the Spanish, Austrian and French forces who took their part of the cake. In all fairness I should add that except for Napoleon, most of the masterpieces were bought with solid foreign currency.

In my memory the Brussels Art Seminar, renamed Belgian Art Seminar in 1955 when it moved from Brussels to Antwerp or rather from the Flemish Primitives to Peter Paul Rubens, is so important that I have to impose upon myself some particular discipline in writing about it. After five seminars I knew, or at least I had the feeling of knowing, in Europe as well as in the United States, most of the top museum curators and leading art historians. This resulted mainly from my repeated visits to the major training centres where I asked the distinguished and elderly directors and professors to send their best students or younger staff members to Brussels or Antwerp. The graduate school of New York University, the Courtauld Institute in London, the School at the Louvre in Paris and the Museum itself, the Metropolitan Museum in New York, the National Gallery in Washington, the British Museum in London, the Rijksmuseum in Amsterdam, the "Zentralinstitut für Kunstgeschichte" in Munich, etc., are names which I recall with gratitude. My negotiations with the Director General of Fine Arts in Rome, the tallest civil servant in Italy as he said himself, whose office hours seemed to start at 9 p.m., and with local directors of different *Soprintendenza alle Gallerie* led to excellent participation of young Italian art historians, very often students of such outstanding professors as Roberto Longhi or Lionello Venturi.

At the very beginning I was intrigued by the fact that nearly all these Italian students came to Brussels via Monaco and since they were always late, I tried to find out what mysterious links might have existed between gambling and Flemish paintings. I was ashamed to find out rather late that Monaco is Italian for Munich or München. The Seminars generally got off to a slow start and they only got into full swing after the arrival of the Italians. My good American friends were always on time or even a couple of days early, but they were quiet, serious and dedicated, and wanted to see as quickly as possible the real works of art of which they had heard so much at home and had seen only in piles of slides and photographs, while noting particular details for checking. Although I gradually discovered strong and outspoken personalities among them the first impression was mostly one of evenness, which spread equally well over all the American students, those of Italian origin as well as those who were connoisseurs of Italian art. Completely different were the Italians themselves. They were certainly more interested in meeting their American colleagues, in discovering immediately those who spoke Italian, and they had a keen eye for good feminine profiles.

I shall never forget the late arrival of Giovanni Carandente from Rome. The morning he showed up to register I asked him, among various routine questions, where he was staying. "Hotel Stella Artois," he answered. I looked rather puzzled because Stella Artois is the name of the most popular Belgian beer and apparently he had mistaken an advertising sign for the name of the hotel. Had he no other indication? It was in a rather narrow street and the lady who ran the place was about to close it for the summer, but she let him in because he had arrived late and was very tired. I took him on a rather unusual sightseeing tour trying to find his hotel. I was very much more worried than he, because he got excited over all kinds of odd corners of old Brussels. Finally we made it and I discovered that it was a hotel where actors generally stayed and it was quite normal that the lady wanted to close it for the summer. When the theatre season stopped, the seminar began. Giovanni Carandente was a gallant Italian and it did not take him too much time to convince the landlady that it would be all right to give him the key of the hotel, and he promised to take another room every week (to enjoy clean sheets) for the six weeks he was staying in Brussels. I also heard that at the end of his sojourn he bought an old bed with canopy and that he had some trouble in shipping it into Italy.

The group was dominated quantitatively by the Americans and the Italians, but I should not be unfair to individual participants from England, the Netherlands, the Scandinavian countries, Germany (Federal Republic), Austria, Spain, Yugoslavia and France, who were generally good, often enriching the whole group with their national characteristics. I became an amused observer of these local idiosyncrasies. Differences, such as between northern and southern Europe or between the United States and Europe, have since stayed with me and have gradually compelled me to look for explanations. The homogeneity of the group from the point of view of professional interests proved to be a solid base for digging into national or regional pecularities. I committed of course the classical mistake of considering the Americans as a monolithic group. I was encouraged, however, by the geographical mobility shown by their curricula vitae.

After a couple of years I found myself in the middle of a group of Belgian art historians, museum directors and curators, art critics and collectors, for whom in turn it was curious to observe their reactions to these foreign art historians basically interested in the artistic expressions of the Low Countries. The Belgians found themselves at ease as Europeans among Europeans, with practically no language problems, but reacted very differently towards the American visitors whom they could not identify with the widespread caricature of the American tourists. Some of my compatriots had an American experience of their own, some acquired it on the occasion of the seminars and, finally, some refused to go deeper into the problem of trans-oceanic relations, hiding generally behind the language barrier. Although I tried, I was not a neutral observer and I often had serious arguments with this last group of fellow countrymen, blaming them for refusing to see that the American art historians were often of Jewish origin and were as such citizens of the world.

With these general comments in the background, individual portraits emerge and the tallest one is of Erwin Panofsky, who was not exactly tall. His arrival at the seminar in 1954 was preceded by an aura of knowledge, wisdom and wit for which his students, who had participated in the seminar since 1950, were responsible. The two impressive volumes of his *Early Netherlandish Painting* had come quite recently from the press and were an incentive to all those in and outside the United States who where working on one or other aspect of the Flemish Primitives. Before he came to Brussels I visited him at the Institute for Advanced Study in Princeton, where my colleague and friend Bob Delaissé was working under him on Burgundian miniatures. During that visit probably started the endless series of wonderful stories which he told me. He was no Adonis and spoke English with an awful German accent, but after a few seconds only his charm and wit remained. I hesitate to write down some of his stories, which I still remember, because I suppose he has told them hundreds of times and that they have probably been recorded elsewhere and better. They are, however, so prominent in my picture of the Brussels Art Seminar that without them this whole chapter would be truncated.

Was it during my first visit to his home that he told me that his cook, a black woman coming straight out of a Hollywood movie, kept a diary and that every week after his neighbour, Albert Einstein, had come for dinner she wrote down the same remark: "Eats a lot, but doesn't know what"? Or was that at a reception in New York where he was introduced as Mr. Panofsky to some guest who asked him: "Oh, are you the father of Mr. Panofsky?" and he answered, "No, he is my son"? One of his sons, I do not remember whether it was Pif or Paf, was already a famous nuclear physicist and the guest's question implied all the current difference between highly fashionable nuclear physics and old-fashioned art history. Pif and Paf hated art history indeed, having had to sacrifice too much of their childhood to museum visits with Pa and Ma, or rather with Pan and Dora, who wrote together Pandora's Box.

So much wit hid, inevitably, a vast reservoir of knowledge and also of grief. Although he rather early became the leading art historian in the United States after he was forced out of the Berlin Print Room, he could never forget that he belonged to that group of scholars who had been uprooted by the dramatic events of a Europe that had lost confidence in its own civilization. He wrote about this split condition and actually he never got over it. I can bear witness to the fact that evening after evening representatives of the new generation of German art historians came to him in his hotel room in Brussels and used every possible argument, from ethical considerations to vile money matters, to convince him to go back at least once to Germany and to lecture at one or another university. He was torn between a desire to return to his home country and the memory of what it had inflicted on mankind, more particularly on the people to which he belonged. The atmosphere was heavy and tense during these conversations and in the end he could not call up the courage to go back to Germany. Each time when the emissary, who was generally a very able and sympathetic young scholar, had left and we were alone he told me a few stories to kill the sadness of the night. I regret that I do not remember the name of the sixteenth-century painter, the subject of one of whose portraits Panofsky had identified, as usual with an arsenal of iconological, literary and theological evidence. A critic, whose name I have lost too, published a long review with a photograph of the same subject and concluded that these two portraits could not represent the same person and that consequently Panofsky's identification was wrong. Panofsky replied in the same journal with one sentence which ran about as follows, "My distinguished critic only forgot that between the two portraits the man lived for twenty years in Belgium."

One year after his Brussels lectures, the Royal Museum of Fine Arts of Belgium issued a *Miscellanea Erwin Panofsky* with contributors who in one way or another had been shaping the reputation of the seminar. On this occasion I would like to recall that one day Erwin Panofsky came to my office in the Library and told me very bluntly that he knew only three good art historians in Belgium: Guy de Schoutheete de Tervarent, Roger d'Hulst and Bob Delaissé. I took it nearly as a compliment to myself as I was on close and friendly terms with the three of them. I told Erwin Panofsky that I would not be surprised if all three should be in the Library while he was talking to me and I suggested that we should take a look. And sure enough, we found all three. Guy de Schoutheete de Tervarent, who belonged to Panofsky's generation while the other two were of my age, was working in the Reading Room on one of his iconographical finds where he jumped from Roman antiquity to northern gothic or Italian renaissance. At the time Schoutheete was a retired Ambassador and his health was very poor. He had to be driven to the Library every day, but his passion for iconographical research was stronger than the pain from which he was suffering. His scholarly wisdom enlightened his last days. We found Roger d'Hulst in the Periodical Room where he was going through the latest issues of the art-history journals. At the time he did it regularly, since he had his office next door in the Royal Museum of Fine Arts. It was quite normal to find Bob Delaissé in the Manuscript Room, since he was (poorly) paid to do his (excellent) job there. I would have been terribly disappointed if Erwin Panofsky had quoted the name of someone who was not connected in one way or another with the Royal Library.

I still cannot leave Erwin Panofsky without recalling the opening of the XVIIth International Congress of Art History in Amsterdam in 1952, attended by all participants of the seminar. The first lecture was given by René Huyghe, former director of the Louvre, who had convinced everybody that actually there was no difference between the Middle Ages and the Renaissance. The second speaker was Panofsky and nothing was more remote from him than the French rhetoric of which Huyghe was such a brilliant representative. Panofsky started with showing a slide of a Roman villa, then of a Gothic cathedral, then of a Florentine palazzo and finally he said in the dark room: "Something happened in between." Poor Huyghe, and the heavy firing followed for an hour without the slightest victorious overtone.

Among the many Panofsky students who came to Brussels I am tempted to single out Lotte Brandt Philip. When I first met her she earned her living by creating costume jewelry and on that occasion I learned that each new model had to be deposited at the Library of Congress in accordance with the copyright law. I missed that when I was in the Library of Congress. After the seminar I met her several times either in New York or in Brussels and the last I heard from her was her impressive, but controversial book on *The Ghent Altarpiece and the Art of Jan van Eyck* (1971).

Meeting the students again after the seminar seems to be the determining influence on my reminiscences. During the seminar themselves I recall a series of anecdotes, not very important but often linked to linguistic mistakes such as made by a young, beautiful American girl who was enthralled by the romantic scenery of Bruges, and since she was staying a full year in Belgium as a Fulbright fellow she said that she wanted to spend the winter in Bruges, but needed a *chambre avec chauffeur*, (she meant to say *chambre avec chauffage*, the difference being that she put a driver in her room instead of heating). I began to collect linguistic jokes and the seminar proved to be a rich source. After some years I got stuck with my collection and realized that the quality of each joke is proportional to its untranslatability. If one wants to enjoy them even with a small group of friends the different languages have to be spread evenly among the different members of the group and this hardly ever happens. I have tried them on my wife and on my children, and although they were good sports it did not last long before they finished my stories in a hurried way and that was the end. I am now alone with my collection, each item of which I can link to a given name and place within the framework of the seminar: Luigina Tiengo from Rovigo before the cathedral of Beauvais, Justina Scaglia from New York with Wilhelm Mrazek and Franz Windisch-Graetz from Vienna in a restaurant near Ostend, Anika Skovran from Belgrado in front of Nefertitis in Wiesbaden, Giovanni Carandente from Rome at the exhibition of the "Flemish Portraits from van Eyck to Moro" in Bruges, etc.

There is one I would like to tell though it has nothing to do with linguistics, and I do not yet know if it will survive the proof reading. It is however rather typical of a meeting of a couple of people with different cultural backgrounds and who do not know one another well. It happened in Paris after the group had spent two hours with the Flemish paintings of the seventeenth century at the Louvre. I was leaving the museum with Herschel Chipp from San Francisco and Maud Bennel from Stockholm and we had a drink on a terrace. It was still early in the evening and we had a second aperitif. When it was about time to think of dinner Herschel did not feel well and excused himself. I stayed alone with Maud and although my French was better than hers I did not know of a good restaurant in the neighbourhood. We decided to walk in a given direction and counted on our luck and on the good French custom of having a well-lit menu outside of the restaurant in the evening. And indeed after a few minutes we looked at such a price list of a restaurant which I think was called "Les 3 Canards" and at the bottom of the menu was printed in red *tous les vendredis dîner aux chandelles*, every Friday candle-light dinner. Since it was Friday we entered. We were immediately stopped by the barman who said that we were a bit early and had better have a drink before going into the dining hall. This was our third aperitif, and half an hour later we had our fourth one because no one had yet come in. I faintly began to suspect that we were in a queer place and had it not been for the effect of the drinks I would have suggested looking for another restaurant. While I was pondering this over the barman said that we could proceed to the other room. We went down a short flight of steps and landed in a beautiful rectangular hall with tables lined along the four walls, all lit with elegant candles, and in the middle a piano. A waitress welcomed us and put us at the first table near the entrance. It was not long before two gentlemen arrived and were seated next to us, immediately followed by two other gentlemen and less than half an hour later the whole place was full, with only one woman, my guest, besides the waitresses and the pianist. I felt rather uneasy and when the flowergirl entered and men began to offer flowers to men my mood did not improve. My main problem was trying to discover if Maud understood where we were trapped. She was young, but I was young too at the time. Indirectly I tried to find out, but I was very malapropos and her answer did not give me a clue. Finally a man came in with a woman and Maud said "Another idiot." Less of one than I, because he left immediately. Once the ice was broken we decided to get the most out of it and we added our own version to the decaying ethical standards of the city of light.

Next morning I told the story to Herschel Chipp, who was some years older than I and who was a bachelor. After the seminar was over I never saw Maud Bennel again. At the time she was with the preservation workshop at the National Museum of Sweden. From time to time I met Herschel Chipp again either in Berkeley or in Brussels because he had retained interest in contemporary Belgian artists, more particulary in James Ensor and the Art Nouveau group. In each seminar, whether it was concentrated on Flemish Primitives or Rubens and the seventeenth century, I introduced modern Belgian artists either through visits to studios, collectors or critics. A sensitive art historian like Herschel Chipp found permanent Flemish accents from Hugo van der Goes, through Breughel, to Ensor. It also was interesting to listen to enthusiastic Italian art historians who spoke about Flemish influence, more particularly in Venezia, on their national artists, while I had only heard and learned about the Italian influence on Flemish artists. I was also pleasantly surprised that they pronounced the names of the Flemish artists so well. When I tried to find out why, I discovered that they were listening to the radio comments on the bicycle championships in which the Flemings were also good.

I happened to be one of the first visitors to the Uffizi in Florence after its incredible collection had been rearranged in absolute chronological order without any consideration of local schools. This was on one of my scouting tours – not for masterpieces, but for art historians. I was however not so biased as to by-pass the Uffizi while I was in Florence. And what a shock when I entered the large hall where Botticelli's *Primavera* was facing Hugo van der Goes' *Portinari Altarpiece*. I have never been accused of being nationalistic or chauvinistic but I was proud indeed that Hugo and I had lived and worked in the same city. Some years later I was even hurt by the fact that the house in which he had been born was demolished to build my office in the new Library. I promised myself to recover the commemorative plaque and to put it up again where it had been standing for such a long time. The plaque has disappeared and I forgot my promise.

During the first two or three seminars the influence of Paul Coremans was strong and welcome. His reputation in the field of preservation was at its zenith and he attracted many foreign students to his Institute. He was a key figure in the scandal of the faked Vermeers, which created in his mind, I am afraid, some confusion between art history and detective fiction. He was close to the Belgian American Educational Foundation and to Erwin Panofsky. He supplied the latter with hundreds of photographs of Flemish Primitives, and once Panofsky said to me, speaking about photographs, "the one who has the most wins" – a sad remark by an art historian who misses the authentic works. Paul Coremans was extremely cooperative with the seminar and, with him, some of his staff members. He provided elegant and efficient headquarters with a specialized library, a collection of slides and photographs and sophisticated equipment for projections. One year I suspected him, with approval, of having kept the *Ghent Altarpiece* longer than needed at the preservation laboratory in order to allow the participants to benefit from this presence. Sometimes I had the feeling that he was running the seminar through me and I had no objections. He also benefitted from the seminar because among its participants or in its orbit he found authors for his *Corpus of Flemish Primitives*, such as Charles Cuttler for the Midwest of the United States, Anika Skovran for Yugoslavi Elisa Bermejo for Spain and others too.

One day, in the middle of a session, he became mad at me. He refused to see me and even now I have no explanation, unless he was jealous of Rubens. This is a serious supposition. He had identified himself so much with van Eyck et al. that I must have hurt him when I proposed to shift from the fifteenth to the seventeenth century. Being no art historian myself I had to rely on the advice of others and my old-time friend Roger d'Hulst, who had become a leading expert on seventeenth-century drawings, certainly influenced my proposal. Coremans and d'Hulst were not exactly what one would call friends and to say that they did not like one another would still be a British understatement. Roger d'Hulst had already been participating in previous seminars before it came to a break between Coremans and myself. I have always been rather good on forcing my friends to share my interests. Now with the move from Memlinc to Jordaens, from Brussels to Antwerp, Roger d'Hulst became the key figure. Although he pretended the contrary he enjoyed it as much as I did. We reached a climax when we convinced Ludwig Burchard from London to come over as a visiting professor for the 1955 seminar. Burchard was no Panofsky, he was shy and an introvert, soft-spoken and a poor lecturer, but he knew everything about Rubens and all his life he had been collecting material on his favourite subject. For the *cognoscenti* he was an overwhelming mine. Among his students in Antwerp he had connoisseurs as Felice Staempfle of the Pierpont Morgan Library in New York, who had ably expanded the already rich collection under her custody; Ruth Magurn from the Fogg Art Museum at Harvard, who had translated into English Rubens' collected correspondence for which he used French, Spanish, Italian, Latin and Dutch; Colin Eisler from New York University, who participated for the second time in the seminar and who started from Jean Duvet to become an authority on old masters' drawings; and Pontus Grate from Stockholm who was assistant in the National Museum of Sweden for the famous collection of drawings brought together by the eighteenth-century Swedish ambassador to France, Tessin.

If Panofsky's participation ended with a Belgian Festschrift being offered to him, with Roger d'Hulst as the general editor, the passage of Ludwig Burchard through the seminar yielded a more spectacular result. I once went with Roger d'Hulst to his house in a pleasant suburb of London first to discuss the modalities of his participation in the seminar and incidentally also to try to find out about the future of his Rubens documentation. Roger went back several times with Frans Baudouin, curator of the Rubens House and official representative of the city of Antwerp, to discuss its possible acquisition by the city. They conducted and succesfully concluded these negotiations.

After Ludwig Burchard's death the city would erect a Rubenianum to house the archives and publish a *Ludwig Burchard Corpus Rubenianum* in twenty-eight volumes, once again with Roger d'Hulst as general editor. At the time of writing seven volumes have been published and the estimates are that the *Corpus* will reach about forty in total. Here also some former students of the seminar became contributing authors. Egbert Haverkamp-Begemann issued the volume on the Achilles-series and Jay R. Judson on title pages. They were both uncommon participants in the seminar. Jud was already married to Carol when they first came to Brussels. Her French was good and after the seminar was over she translated into English the catalogue of the third part of the renowned Stoclet collection. This was a difficult job because the collection had the widest variety of objects, spread geographically as well as chronologically. Jud was already well on his way to writing a thesis on Honthorst, the Dutch Caravaggio, and improving his knowledge of the language of Rembrandt. Roger and I attended his doctoral defence in Utrecht and we have remained friends since with a casual yearly meeting somewhere in Europe. I once went to his house in Whately, a small place in New England at a time when he was still teaching at Smith College. On this occasion I discovered that the township was still run by a meeting of citizens, that Carol had a grinder in her kitchen, that Leonard Baskin was a great artist and that Jud had to grow tobacco.

When he came to Brussels to attend the seminar, Egbert Haverkamp-Begemann was a young curator at the Boymans Museum in Rotterdam. He and Roger d'Hulst found one another very easily and we spent many pleasant hours together during and after the seminar, either in Europe or in the United States. In Brussels he did not however give us all his free time. At the farewell party which I usually gave at my house, I had the feeling that he and Recie Pennock, a participant from Poughkeepsie, seemed to have a lot to say to each other and apparently it was not exclusively about the genuine characteristics of Flemish art. One year later I attended their wedding in Amsterdam and Janet Cox, another art fellow, was also a witness. On this occasion I met his father who told me that he had been a witness to the great fire of

San Francisco, which impressed me nearly as much as the wedding ceremony. On the occasion of Recie and Egbert's wedding I went back to Haarlem to see once more, all for myself, the Teyler Museum. This is in many respects the most curious museum in Europe. I never missed an opportunity to take the participants of the seminar to the Teyler Museum, though I regularly had difficulty in dragging them away from the Frans Hals Museum in the same city. Once they were in the Teyler, however, they enjoyed every minute of it. It was much more than a striking *Kunstkabinett*, although it had all its features. The entry hall was muddled with early electrical machines, monsters in alcohol were not missing, fossils, ethnologica, etc., followed, and at the end, in a large room, a unique collection of old master drawings was quietly kept and shown to connoisseurs with love. The director of the place has to be born in Haarlem, must be a painter and should preferably be a Mennonite. In fact this meant that the son of the curator had a good chance of succeeding his father when all these impossible conditions were met. The director was not yet his own boss, because he had to report to the curator of the Print Room of the Rijksmuseum in Amsterdam. Mr. Teyler was by no means a usual human being.

After a few years in Rotterdam, Recie found life in Holland too conceited, which I as a citizen of the large southern neighbouring country understood very well, and they moved to Yale University where Recie raised their four children and Egbert taught northern art and was also curator of the graphic collection. During one of my visits to Yale, Egbert gave me a guided tour of the campus which impressed me as a living museum of modern architecture. All great names were represented by striking buildings or constructions. I did not like at all Paul Rudolf's school of architecture. Egbert told me that it was very photogenic. I had no objections, but was pleased to hear a couple of years later that a fire had broken out in the school. Since there were no victims this was about the best that could happen to it.

One day Egbert came to see me in my office in Brussels and he told me that he was working on the exquisite Flemish artist Joris Hoefnagel (1542-1600), of which a few sample sheets existed in the Library. He did not understand why I smiled when I heard the name of Hoefnagel. When I gave him my explanation he laughed too. I had on my desk a letter from a certain Mr. Hoefnagel from the United States, which had arrived that very morning, inquiring about his illustrious ancestor. I gave the letter to Egbert and my correspondent probably received the best answer that a letter sent to the Royal Library ever commanded. What actually came out of their correspondence I do not know and that is the only sad part of my seminar recollections. So many interesting follow-ups took shape and are still taking shape in many parts of the world of which I am not aware, or only partially or by accident. An example of such an accident was when, in the 1 October 1964 issue of *The Times Literary Supplement*, I discovered by sheer luck the reviews of three books written by former participants in the Brussels seminars: Albert Chatelet on *French Painting from Le Nain to Fragonard*, James H. Stubblebine on *Guido da Siena* and Jan Verbeeck on *Dutch and Flemish Etchings, Engravings and Woodcuts, c. 1450-1700*.

The reading of these reviews gave me a feeling of proud satisfaction. I was probably the only person on earth to realize that they all were linked to the seminar, because the authors themselves were not in Brussels during the same time. Were it not for TLS I would never have heard of them again. I can as well tell here that for more than thirty years I have been a regular and admiring reader of TLS, although each time that I happened to know the subject of a review well, it had mistakes. I twice sent a letter to the editor and twice I got the same answer – that I was the tenth in a row to protest. I still use TLS for the acquisition of English books by the Royal Library. What I particularly like about TLS is its sharpness in judging the quality of the English language used by the author, chiefly when he is American, or by the translator, and at the same time nearly always misspelling quotations from foreign languages. One I happen to remember is *Correspondence complète de Jean Jacques Rousseau*. In all fairness I must add that it sometimes improves the French language when, for instance, it calls the inhabitants of suburbia *faubourgeoisie*.

Although all these individual profiles of outstanding participants are vivid in my mind, they keep a particular significance when I can link them to an institution or an organization. Through this connection I very often met them again in later years. When Tom Messer came to Brussels he was not yet director of the Guggenheim Museum in New York, but he was with the American Federation of Arts which circulated, in the United States, an exhibition of old drawings of the Degrez collection from the Royal

Museum of Fine Arts after he had discovered it in Brussels. Similar was my experience with Jo Ann Sukel who circulated exhibitions for the Smithsonian Institution from Washington. Helen Franc, who retired recently from the Museum of Modern Art in New York, helped me to show at the Library one of its most succesful exhibitions assembled by her Museum *Architecture Without Architects*. I could say the same about the exhibition which Albert Chatelet, director of the Palais des Beaux Arts at Lille, organized at the Library with a selection of drawings from the famous collection of Wicar. Heinz Peters, now with the leading art historical publishers in Berlin, Gebrüder Mann, was curator of the Düsseldorf Museum when he came to the seminar and afterwards welcomed following groups in his own museum. Just as Lisa Oehler did in the Kassel Museum or what Gunther Thiem would have liked to do in Augsburg, but his first son was born the very day we arrived in the most Italian of all German towns.

In extending these seminar relations I could name Wolfgang Braunfels for the visits to Aachen and Hermann Schnitzler for the Schnütgen Museum in Cologne, who each year received the seminar at their places and with whom I worked afterwards on important international exhibitions. One exhibition was on Charlemagne in Aachen in 1965, where the Royal Library lent one of its most precious manuscripts, the ninth-century *Petrus Archidiaconus* from the Palace School itself, and another, the Mosan Art exhibition in Brussels and Cologne in 1972. It might be worthwhile to note here as a point of history that the Royal Library collections developed from the fifteenth century onwards around the glorious Burgundian manuscripts, while its fine collection of early Mosan manuscripts – Mosan being a neologism, I can as well add with some pedantry that it means from the Meuse valley – was bought at the end of the nineteenth century in London from the Phillips collection, missing however the most important one of all, the *Stavelot Bible*, now in the British Library. To round off these geographical and chronological expansions of the seminar I shall finally quote Halldor Soehner, who became, soon after his participation, director of the Alte Pinakothek in Munich. He organised for the Council of Europe, shortly before his untimely death, the huge Rococo exhibition to which the Royal Library, among many other institutions, contributed various pieces.

These four- to five-day trips in France, Holland and Germany, to look at Flemish art and a bit beyond too, created lifelong friendships and some unexpected situations also. Once the Kröller-Müller Museum in Otterlo was on our programme and afterwards, a few miles north, a visit to the private van Beuningen Collection at Vierhouten was planned. The group could not leave the van Gogh collection and was staying overtime at the Kröller-Müller Museum. I was annoyed and decided to leave alone to go to Vierhouten and to apologize for being late. It was the first time that I was going to meet Mr. van Beuningen. I rang the bell and a not-too-friendly maid opened the door. I told her I wanted to talk to the master of the house. She said that she did not know where he was, but that I could try to find him. I walked through room after room of the huge villa, hardly looking at the walls full of paintings and I finally discovered the owner of the incredibly rich collection behind a large whisky and in front of a small Bosch. He looked at me and said that he had been waiting for the group for more than two hours. When I tried to explain and unfortunately let the name of Kröller-Müller pass my lips he was furious: "There is nothing to see in that place. Everything that is worthwile is here." Finally he offered me a Dutch gin while waiting for the group and, though late at night, we separated on good terms. But the following years we started with Vierhouten and went to Otterlo afterwards. He bequeathed his collection to the Boymans Museum in Rotterdam which henceforth was to be called Boymans-van Beuningen and the director, my friend Coert Ebbinge Wubben, is one of the rare custodians in the world who has seen his responsibilities to preserve masterpieces for future generations doubled.

Not all unexpected situations ended so well. We were quietly visiting the pretty Doppelkirche at Bonn-Beuel when suddenly a tiny little priest came in shouting at us in a thunderous voice. He was so mad that neither I nor any one else at first understood what it was all about. Finally we discovered the origin of his anger: the bare feet of our tiny little Norwegian girl Elie Soelseth who was innocence personified. When he threateningly approached her the tall Peter Selz, I think, thought it was enough, lifted the priest by his throat from the ground and took him out of his church. The architectural originality and the delicate ornaments of the walls were gone with him. Elie cried and still did not understand why she was blamed so roughly and protected so gallantly. In any place where she went, in the classroom, in the museums, in the restaurants, she threw her shoes off and we were already so accustomed to it that we did not notice it anymore. I still remember her arrival on the disembarkation pier at Antwerp. When everybody had left I saw a youngish girl, with long blond hair with her bicycle in her hands and sure enough, she was Elie Soelseth, art student from Oslo University. The rumour spread very fast in the seminar that her father was the judge who had condemned Quisling, traitor number one to his country. Two or three days after the Bonn incident, we crossed the Danube and Elie said that she wanted to swim in the blue river. I said that it was not on the programme and that after all she probably had no bathing suit. She looked at me with her light blue eyes as if I had objected to Rodin for having drawn nudes.

During the same trip we had to hide another female participant, Anika Skovran from Belgrado, in the bus. The shortest way from Karlsruhe, where we had visited our last museum, to Brussels was through Saarland, which at the time had not yet been returned to Germany. Close to the border we discovered that a Yugoslav citizen needed a special visa to cross the Saar, which Anika, of course, did not have. The detour was rather long and we decided to roll her in a blanket and to put her under the seats with her head at my feet, which would allow me to give her a kick when she had to be silent because she talked all the time. We twice safely passed the border, but in between the tension was so great that we decided to celebrate our good luck at the Luxemburg-Belgium border, a border which is only a pretext for a nominal occupation by a few customs officers. The celebration lasted much longer than the detour around Saarland would have taken, but it also was much more fun. Some years later Anika took my wife, a couple of friends and me on an extensive tour of all the major monasteries of her country. She, being an expert on fresco paintings, not only gave us an excellent iconographical and stylistic explanation, but she also showed us proudly all the paintings and icons which she had saved after the war. In one church she had an argument with the priest because she wanted to take us behind the iconostase and the churchman would not let her because she was a woman. She said that she was a woman when she had saved all the works of art in his choir and that it would be empty without her. Nothing helped and while I was behind the iconostase she gave me all the explanatory comments from the other side, knowing every detail by heart, and interrupting her iconographical descriptions with some expressions, at quite a lower level, about the priest. She assumed that he did not understand French.

Looking through the names of the hundred or so alumni of the seminar I am tempted to associate some of these individuals with the institutions to which they belonged when I first met them or where they landed after we separated: Dick and Poe Randall at the Walters Art Gallery in Baltimore; Elisa Bermejo at the Instituto Diego Velasquez in Madrid; Claude Lauriol coming every year to Brussels to check bibliographical references for her *Répertoire d'art et d'archéologie*; Michelangelo Muraro at the Casa d'Oro in Venice; Jan Verbeek at the Rijksmuseum in Amsterdam; Fedja Anzelewsky at the Print Room in Berlin; Pontus Grate at the Swedish Institute in Paris; Kathleen Morand at various places in London, Princeton, San Marino or Kingston, Ontario; Fernando Bologna and Raphaelo Causa at the Capodimonte in Naples; David and Louise Carter at the National Museum in Montreal; Luigi Malle at the Museo Civico in Turin; Olga Raggio at the Metropolitan Museum in New York ... Not many readers will share my pleasure in writing down these personal, institutional and geographical names, but it does not require a lot of imagination to see what treasures of unmatched beauty they cover and, as far as the individuals are concerned, of dedicated knowledge.

It is clear from this report on the seminar that the Belgian American Educational Foundation played a leading part in its organization. I have already referred to other beneficial relations I had with this Foundation, either as a Fellow, as an associate secretary or as a friend of Clark Stillman, once its secretary and later its president. I would like to leave the Foundation with these happy memories, but there is unfortunately another side of the coin and since this sad episode brought nearly all American alumni once more together I shall briefly refer to it.

In 1963 a few members of the executive committee of the Foundation decided to give $ 900.000, one quarter of the capital on which the Foundation was living, to the Hoover Memorial Library to be set up in West Branch, Iowa, the birthplace of President Hoover. Quite a number of officers felt this to be an improper decision and said so. Clark Stillman was among them and he was forced to resign. One of the arguments held against him was that he had all the defects of the Belgians, which seemed to be that he was pro-Flemish and pro-socialist. I wished it were true, not for Clark Stillman but for the Belgians. In Belgium a few elderly alumni, among them former Prime-Minister Gaston Eyskens, Fernand Chenu, a leading industrialist, and I organized the resistance. In the United States two board members, George Wickes, professor at the University of Oregon, and Sheldon Judson, professor at the University of Princeton, sued their own Foundation. The action was organized by Harry Bober, professor at the Institute of Fine Arts of New York University and member of the selection committee of the BAEF, surrounded by all the alumni he had sent to Belgium, and with the legal advice of Jerry Rubin, the husband of Ida Brophy, who had attended the 1952 seminar and who was active in New York art circles. I was appalled by the American legal system, I read hundreds of pages of affidavits in legalese which I did not understand, I still do not know if I was filed as an *amicus curiae* or not, and I began to believe in our good old-fashioned Code Napoleon. We had wonderful meetings in New York and in Brussels like reunions of old friends, we raised all the money we needed or nearly, and more than ever before we felt what the Foundation meant to us. Finally we lost the suit, but we all are convinced that we saved the Foundation – the only point that really mattered. Though this Foundation was a small one according to American standards (and had been set up after World War I as a permanent body for cooperation in the field of education between the United States and Belgium) it served as a model for the Fulbright Foundation which came into existence after World War II between the United States and former allied nations.

To counter the sad resignation of Clark Stillman, I wrote sentimentally, at least for me and a large number of Belgian and American alumni, a portrait of him and published it in 1963 in the Belgian *Alumni Journal* of which I was the editor. With some slight adaptions I reprint it here to finish this chapter on the Belgian Art Seminar in the tone which it deserves:

"About a quarter of a century ago two men were sitting together in a Liverpool streetcar. They knew of one another that they belonged to a newly formed international team of linguists working on a project of a new universal language. One Belgian and one American, they had been introduced only the day before. Sud-

denly the streetcar came to an unusual stop and the American said
to the Belgian '*de flèche is af*,' and in good spirits the journey
proceeded to the linguistic centre. This anecdote proves at least
two things: (1) that dialect is a powerful means of human communication (and those who frown upon it miss something important to international understanding); and (2) that the American
who was acquainted with such a colloquial Brussels expression
(some of my Belgian readers may need a translation, but I will not
give it because I am strongly opposed to the official view on
monolinguism) that the American was not the usual type of
American. His name was E. Clark Stillman.

"A quarter of a century later – just a couple of years ago – a
correspondent in Leopoldville of an influential American weekly
cabled to his headquarters, together with a photograph of a Belgian Minister who had just arrived, the following caption 'Snul,
they say.' The whole staff of the paper searched after the meaning
of the word *snul* – even the large Dutch colony of what was once
Nieuw Amsterdam was at a loss – but finally they found somebody
in New York who knew that *snul* meant 'pumpkinhead.' This
anecdote proves at least two things: (1) that dialect is a powerful
means of human communication and international (mis)under-
standing; and (2) that the American who was acquainted with such
a colloquial expression was not the usual type of American. His
name was E. Clark Stillman. And those who have met him know
that he is exactly the contrary of a *snul*, although he has met quite a
number of them (in New York and in Brussels).

"Those who care more about important facts in the life of Clark
Stillman can look up the Foundation's Directory and find out for
instance, that he is now 55 years old, just the age to devote all his
energy and wisdom to improving the cultural, intellectual and
educational relations between Belgium and the United States of
America. The Directory will indeed have told any inquirer that
Belgium has been in various ways the subject matter of this American citizen, born in Salt Lake City, without being a Mormon, but
certainly 'quite different,' like the believers in the church of the
Latter Day Saints. Before going a bit deeper into the Stillmanesque
Belgium, the readers of this article may be interested in a technical
opinion on the Directory just quoted. This Directory is a model of
its kind and no similar reference work with biographical information about Belgians matches its high standard. It was Clark

Stillman who was responsible for its editing and it is one of these time-consuming jobs about which nobody seems to care. One uses it quietly in his study and takes the trouble to speak only about its misprints. Incidentally the Directory mentions correctly that Clark Stillman married Frances Jennings in 1932, and all Fellows know her as well as they know him because the border-line between his office and their home was slight indeed. Clark Stillman's first image of Belgium did not allow him to distinguish it from any other West European country. There were not yet any special sentimental or intellectual ties with the young American Fellow arriving here as a student in 1933 and becoming afterwards a lecturer in 1936. Unlike nearly all other Fellows he did not leave our country after a couple of years but remained five full years.

"The positive result of all these years spent here included, as we already have seen, a good knowledge of the Brussels dialect, gleaned mostly in the small, popular streets near the Porte de Namur. He still has a weak spot in his heart for this part of Brussels, where he always pays a visit to his coiffeur (though less and less necessary) each time he is in Belgium. Of course not as often as all of us always expect because more important Foundation problems kept him in New York.

"Flemish dialect, even with a large amount of French words as it is the case in Brussels, was of course not enough for a man who had been teaching German at an American university and who had published a Spanish grammar. His knowledge of the Dutch language was so thorough that some years later he published, together with his wife, English translations of Guido Gezelle and Karel Van de Woestijne. It needs of course more than an outstanding bilinguism to translate poetry, even the relatively easy (as Clark told me) rendering of Gezelle in English as compared to Van de Woestijne. The translator must himself have a poetic inclination. Clark Stillman certainly has it, and nobody would expect that all the people he meets in the prosaic way of life would go mad about it. Even worse, his own original verse is in the humorous vein (some of it has appeared in Penguin Books) and I guess – though I may be wrong – that some simple and serious minds (on both sides of the Ocean) instinctively hold it against him. No wonder that his best friends in Belgium, before the war, were poets, artists and scholars who did not fit in that awful group of bourgeois intellectuals. Among the score of names of intimate friends I must single out Frans Olbrechts, at the time director of the Congo Museum at Tervuren and professor of ethnography at Ghent University. This has been a lifelong friendship with a common interest in, nay passion for, African sculpture. A collector of African sculpture today can be a very decent chap and this bias does not necessarily make a queer fellow of him. However it was not exactly so before the war. The small group of connoisseurs who did not need Picasso or Zadkine to discover the original value of Congo plastic was not very fashionable in those days. Valuable masks, head rests, stools or amulets did not yet command high prices on the market and attracted consequently only *les purs*. Frans Olbrechts and Clark Stillman met for the last time at the airport of Cairo, the first one on his way home from his first trip to the Congo, the second one on his way to the Congo also for the first time. Frans Olbrechts was headed for a long period of a fatal illness, Clark Stillman was going to inaugurate the new Congo programme of the Foundation which was to be as short as it was successful.

"It is a mind with a wide range which can link sensitiveness for traditional Negro wood carving to interest in modern Flemish poetry. But there is more in store for us. It has however not much sense to add an uncommon knowledge of Chinese or classical philosophy, if the result were a mere rainbow of intellectual curiosity. This undoubtedly exists in Clark Stillman but only as an accident of his deep interest in the human mind with its endless variety. A young Belgian student freshly arriving in New York generally had one or two glimpses, during his first lunch at Stouffer's, of this well-informed mind, so casual (at least in appearance) in points which were raised during a conversation which the younger partner never would forget. It took Clark Stillman a short time indeed and not many words to make the Fellow believe that the Foundation existed only to solve his own personal problems he was going to meet in the U.S. and maybe even afterwards. There is no doubt that administrative ability is too poor a qualification to cover such an attitude. It is much more indeed, and Clark Stillman, in his own way, perpetuated a venerable tradition established by his predecessor, Perrin Galpin.

"My story goes however too fast and the Foundation came too early and too often into focus. This is of course quite natural when one feels that the presidency of the BAEF to which Clark Stillman was promoted on October 26, 1962, was the logical conclusion of his long association with the Foundation, as secretary from 1947, as member and director from 1945, as Fellow since 1933. It is obvious that he was – as we say in Dutch – laid in the cradle to become president of the Foundation.

"World War II saw him in North Africa whence he proceeded to Brussels to be the first Cultural Relations Attaché and Public Affairs Officer of the American Embassy in Brussels. I have never seen him in uniform and I do not feel I missed a lot. In one way or another uniforms do not fit him. There are, of course, moments in life when uniforms, as symbols of intellectual conformity, are extremely helpful and put you on the safe side. In such moments a Bena-lulua woman, a love poem, an unorthodox idea are not the required ingredients, you are much better off with a uniform, a nice necktie or even a law degree.

"When Clark Stillman was still in New York during the war he kept close relations with some of his earlier Belgian friends. Marnix Gijsen – alias Dr. J.A. Goris – became an intimate friend while he established himself as the leading Dutch writing novelist. This reminds me that I have not yet had the opportunity, or that I missed it, to mention that Clark Stillman's spoken and written French is even better than his Dutch. Being well acquainted with the intricacies of the Belgian mind, he never would have dared to translate Gezelle and Van de Woestijne without translating simultaneously Verhaeren and Maeterlinck. To do this he needed only the ability and had plenty of it. From his lips I picked up only one sin against the French language. I heard him say: 'Il n'est pas mature' speaking of one of my best friends.

"His position with the Foundation, his basic knowledge of our country, his sentimental attitude towards it – protesting that we were only taking over the poorer sides of the American way of life – placed him in a unique position in New York. All Belgian visitors of some importance – even the rarer ones who had no formal link with the Foundation – stopped at his door and if they could afford a night off they spent it in his house, meeting there regularly the young Fellows who happened to be in town. His curious and beautiful apartment on the 10th and 11th floors of one of the older skyscrapers of Manhattan, located on old-fashioned Gramercy Park, has been for years – and will remain for years – an open house to so many of us. It gave us the best of America and we could answer it with our small local values, because they were always met with such a warm response. An engineer from Zwijndrecht was happy when he met a Foundation official – what a poor word! – who knew Zwijndrecht, which is of course only important because the engineer happened to be a Fellow.

"What are the basic features of Clark Stillman's portrait? An American and Belgian experience in university teaching, a diplomatic career in Belgium, and a leading officer of a private foundation devoted to the educational relations between Belgium and the United States of America. This will do for the outside, but not for the more important inside story. Here is paramount a personal blend of scholarly and artistic mental attitudes, rooted with body and soul in his American ancestry and simultaneously enriched by a West European cultural heritage. From this core emerge enlightened openings in all directions of the human mind. The conclusion is obvious. If it were necessary, one should invent an institution devoted to cultural relations between Belgium and America in order to make the best use of the exceptional qualities and qualifications of E. Clark Stillman."

5. New Libraries in Old Places

SIR FRANK FRANCIS, former director and principal librarian of the British Museum, and I were the two librarian members of an international jury whose responsibility was to choose an architect for the Centre Beaubourg in Paris, inaugurated in 1977 under the name of Centre Pompidou. It was President Pompidou's personal decision in 1969 to build in the heart of the French capital a cultural centre, which would include among other things exhibition spaces, a museum for contemporary art and a modern library. Hence Sir Frank and I found ourselves among museum curators and, above all, architects.

Participation in this work was in many respects a unique experience. The fact that Sir Frank had been president of the International Federation of Library Associations, from 1964 until 1969, before I took over, shows clearly that the Centre Beaubourg project had from the very start an international slant and wanted to be open to the world. Since France is hardly a foreign country to me, I was pleasantly surprised by this openmindedness which contrasted with a certain image of the country with which I was all too familiar. For the library component of the project, this was new as well as obvious. Jean-Pierre Seguin, a staff member of the Bibliothèque Nationale, one of the most conservative libraries in the world, went out to foreign countries to look at good and large public libraries. He found them in the Anglo-Saxon countries, more particularly in the United States. In the sixties and even in the seventies there was no such library in France, and the one at the Centre Pompidou today, of which Jean-Pierre Seguin was the first head, comes very close to the Donnell Library Center of the New York Public Library. The main difference between the two comes down to the fact that the latter has an independent building while the former is part of the huge and controversial Centre Pompidou.

I can note here parenthetically that I was the only jury member who voted against the winning project. Now that the new Centre stands there in old Paris I regret that I did not join the majority votes. Apparently I did not understand fully the president of the jury, the excellent French architect Jean Prouvé when he said *"Messieurs, j'espère que nous sommes tous d'accord pour éviter le geste architectural,"* asking for a general consent to choose a building without architecture. Although I fully agreed with this outlook, I did not realize that the Centre was going to be an anti-Guggenheim Museum, which was the best we could hope for. I happened to be in New York when the Guggenheim Museum was dedicated. I read all the quotations from Frank Lloyd Wright in the newspapers and understood very well why the curator, James Sweeney, resigned immediately after the dedication. The architect wanted to stand between the exhibited works of art and the visitors. He was very successful in accomplishing this. The Centre Pompidou aimed at exactly the contrary and was nearly as successful in reaching its aim.

This international slant was not only applied to the library of the Centre Pompidou but also to the other parts of the Centre. The museum component was strongly influenced by the Stockholm Cultural Centre and a striking manifestation of this trend was in the field of music and acoustics. It finally brought Pierre Boulez back to France.

The international outlook of the project led naturally to the decision to appoint an international jury for the architectural competition. Out of the nine members five were foreigners. [1] The latter discovered an aspect of France with which none of them was familiar and which is certainly a major asset in the Beaubourg experience: a France with an exceptional administrative, managerial and technical efficiency. I am tempted to say that it lies in the use – not only at Beaubourg – of a few outstanding individuals belonging to one institution, the *conseillers d'état*. If one looks carefully around, one finds a number of *conseillers d'état* in key positions in and outside France. The one responsible for Beaubourg was

---

[1] Sir Frank Francis (London), Willem Sandberg (Amsterdam and Tel Aviv), Philip Johnson (New York), Oscar Niemeyer (Brazilia) and myself (Brussels).

Robert Bordaz. He came to the project with an incredibly wide-ranging record. He was responsible for the fast traffic roads along the banks of the Seine in Paris, he had been director general of the French broadcasting corporation, he had been commissioner general of the French pavilion at the World Fair in Montreal in 1967, etc. At Beaubourg it was easy to realize why he had always and everywhere been successful. At the administrative and managerial level he was assisted by a small group of younger people who matched the perfect *énarque* [2] profile and at the technical level the architects and engineers were of no lower standing. He put all these people at the disposal of the jury members, using them strictly within the limits of their competence while he himself devoted most of his time to obtaining the main policy decisions, not least from President Pompidou himself, with whom he had close and friendly relations.

On the occasion of its first meeting, the members of the jury were invited for lunch at the Elysée. This was a memorable party. At the outset President Pompidou said "I want a monument." Everybody looked at me because just before we had left for the luncheon I had been the last speaker at the morning session and my closing words had been "Let's not build a monument but an instrument." When I had explained why my colleagues looked at me, President Pompidou went on "One does not exclude the other; I want a monument because General de Gaulle did not leave one and I need not say why mine has to be ready before 1976," referring to the end of his term of office. The building was ready in time, but President Pompidou had passed away before it was finished. His widow was present at the dedication by President Giscard d'Estaing, and the Centre was officially designated as Centre Pompidou. When President Giscard d'Estaing took over, he cancelled various urban projects of President Pompidou, but Beaubourg was not among the victims.

The tone of the luncheon was set by the "monument" intermezzo and it went on for three hours. President Pompidou was very outspoken about his international outlook: if a foreign architect wins the competition he will be entrusted with the actual building. So it happened indeed: the Italian Piano and the English Rogers associates won and built the Centre. Not all French com-

---

[2] Colloquial for graduates from the "Ecole Nationale Supérieure d'Administration."

petitors and other French architects were very happy about this firm decision. I can bear witness to the fact that the jury worked and decided in complete independence.

A peak in the luncheon was reached when our French chairman of the jury said to President Pompidou that we were fortunate in having among us one of the world's greatest architects, Oscar Niemeyer, who did us the honour of building in France the Régie Renault. Oscar Niemeyer added himself "but also the headquarters of the French Communist Party." President Pompidou looked at him, who was sitting at his right, and said "Monsieur, je ne savais pas que ce parti avait si bon goût." [3] I left the Elysée with a very pleasant feeling.

A third important aspect of the Beaubourg experience is the dependence of the library component on the other major elements of the whole enterprise. The dialogue with the museum curators was not too difficult although it took them some time to understand the relative complexity of the various library operations. It was more difficult to convince the architects of the specific needs of a modern library. Among the architects Philip Johnson had some experience in library buildings and at the time of the jury meeting in Paris he was working on the Bobst Library on Washington Square, in New York, one of the most expensive library buildings I know and also one of the least functional. Simultaneously Oscar Niemeyer was conceiving a university campus in North Africa, which included a library. He asked me if I would be willing to give him a written statement that the students should be allowed to use the books of the library. He was surprised that I was not surprised at this request. I had visited several developing countries where library directors were held personally responsible for any loss or theft from the collection and they had soon discovered that the safest way to discharge this responsibility was to keep the bookcases permanently locked. Actually this situation prevailed also in the Middle Ages in Europe, where the keepers of the King's manuscripts and/or of the crown jewels had to make a detailed inventory before they handed the collections over to their successors. Here lies the accidental origin of a fair number of early catalogues, which are today invaluable historical sources.

[3] "Sir, I did not know that that party had such good taste."

Sir Frank and I have a somewhat similar, but also very different experience with library buildings. In London he was the sad witness of endless hesitations and cancelled decisions regarding a new building for the library of the British Museum. His work with the architects remained theoretical. [4] In Brussels hesitations and cancelled decisions had been common for many years, but when I was appointed director in 1956 the corner stone of the new library had been laid exactly two years earlier. In the following pages I shall attempt to tell my local story with as little parochialism as possible. Before doing so I would however like to come back a last time to the Beaubourg experience. The French organization of the competition impressed me so much that I did not hesitate to quote it as exemplary a few years later when I was asked to advise the Iranian government on the building of a new Imperial Library in Tehran. What came out of my advice will be told at the end of this paper.

The decision to build a new National Library in Belgium was taken immediately after King Albert's death in 1934. This library was going to be the nation's homage to the King, who had gained international stature during World War I and who had been a progressive ruler until his untimely death, which occurred while he was climbing a mountain. His interests in science and in reading were well known and it was easy to reach a consensus on the idea to pay tribute to his memory through a badly needed new building for the National Library, which had been housed in a palace since its foundation in 1837. [5]

When I joined the Library in 1943, I discovered to my own surprise that nobody on the staff was interested in the project of a new building. First I thought that the war, which was not yet finished in our part of the world, was responsible for this indifference, but I soon became aware of the fact that a deep gulf separated the library staff from the board of trustees who had been designated by law to erect the new library. The only librarian on the board had left the staff of the library to take up a teaching position at the University of Louvain. So I found myself to be the only one in the Library to be seriously interested in the project.

[4] At the time of writing an impressive project had just been approved after the name of the institution had been changed to the British Library.

[5] The full story of the old library, its even older collections, and the renewal has been told in a *Memorial*, published on the occasion of the dedication of the new building, in 1969, thirty-five years after the King's death.

The board of trustees had organized a national competition in 1938 and the winner, Maurice Houyoux, had been chosen by an international jury. When everything was ready a movement was organized to change the site, and after years of discussions nothing had come out of it when World War II started.

When I had become familiar with the history of this project, the war had ended. Many years of vital reconstruction of the country were needed and nobody among the trustees or among the public authorities cared about the Library. Gradually the pre-war plans were pulled from the drawers, the board of trustees began to meet again and I, as the new director, was invited to attend the meetings. In the meanwhile I had visited dozens of new libraries in the United States late in 1950 and early in 1951 and I had a fairly good idea of what was new in library architecture since the war. At the time, modular construction was in its full sway and people like Keyes Metcalf and Ralph Ellsworth had already reached their highly regarded status. To my horror I discovered that nothing new had gone into the Brussels plans, while – I may recall – the actual building had already started when I took over.

The very beginning of the new building started in a rather original way; I could also say in a typically Belgian manner. Since the Library was to be dedicated to the memory of King Albert the first part that was ready and was inaugurated was an equestrian monument of the late King. The King wears a uniform, but has no helmet, which is heresy to the military. Public opinion, if one can use this expression when it comes to library matters, was immediately divided: on the one side were those who thought that the equestrian monument was enough to honour the King, on the other side were those who believed that once the monument was erected the rest should follow. The latter won a tedious, though sometimes funny battle.

The architect Maurice Houyoux was a sick man when I met him first. He died two years later. During the short period of our cooperation I realized that he was working on a building in which he no longer believed. He was a young architect when he won the competition; he had been forced to adapt his original project to a new site; later he had to go back to the old site but in the meanwhile his ideas had changed. He was very open to new esthetic trends, but the board of trustees was rather conservative. The main reason however for his disappointment was that several times the actual building was postponed and when it really started he was taken by surprise and had to deliver immediately the plans as he had left them a few years earlier. What was supposed to become his *Magnum Opus*, was actually for him a still-born giant.

At the personal level we had good relations. He was not interested at all in libraries and each time I made a suggestion to change one or another detail he agreed, provided I added "from a librarian's point of view." At the end of his life the only colour which appealed to him was white, and that is the reason why the main exhibition hall, with its white columns, is called today "Galerie Maurice Houyoux." On the white walls of his private house hung only a few samples of what is known in modern painting as cool abstract. It all reflects the man's character very well. He was pure and honest, and left this earth with a feeling of near failure.

A few months before his death he asked the administration to appoint as his successors two young architects, Roland Delers and Jacques Bellemans, who would be willing to finish his work "in his spirit." For once the bureaucracy took a humanitarian view of the situation and agreed to entrust it to his candidates. They were practically inexperienced when they inherited such a billion-franc mastodon and the worst was still ahead of them.

This happened when a public opinion movement was launched to keep a late Gothic chapel, which had been standing on the site for centuries, *in situ*. The controversy was passionate and ridiculous. One of the changes which I had proposed to Maurice Houyoux was precisely to preserve the chapel, but to move it so as to conform to the vertical and horizontal axes of the new building. The major argument with which I convinced the architect was not a very serious one. If an American librarian, I said, had such a prestigious collection of Gothic manuscripts as we have here he would buy a Gothic chapel, if he had the opportunity, to house it. While the inside discussion centered on the techniques to be used to move the chapel, from the outside came the very pressing cry to keep the chapel *in situ*, every journalist speaking Latin for some time. In the meanwhile the new architects had taken over and they soon began to realize that architectural skill was only a small part of their job. Together we lost the battle. Our argument, a very serious one this time, that there was no site anymore since the chapel was the only part left of the old Nassau Palace, did not carry enough weight. The result was a loss of a few years, of many million Belgian francs, a hybrid building, and a main façade which "is not the worst that could have been feared" as an official statement said.

For prospective library builders it might be noted, *en passant*, that a new international commission of architects came to exactly the opposite conclusions from the first one which had met twenty years earlier. Since not all library builders will have twenty years to change plans, it might be well to choose the members of any commission carefully so as to be sure to get the right kind of consensus.

A quelque chose malheur est bon. "No cloud without a silver lining," is the closest interpretation I can think of. The interruption of the construction in order to draw up new plans allowed me to go deeper into the design of the remaining part of the Library, mainly the public areas. The plans which the new architects and I inherited were still marked by the triumphant railroad station tradition. The railroads having conquered the world, the station halls should symbolize this power. The book having conquered the mind of man, the reading halls should bear witness to its triumph. My major contribution to the Brussels library is a few mezzanine floors which were obtained by surreptitiously sliding horizontal partitions into inhumanly high halls. The only other improvement for which I would be prepared to take credit is the visual impression one has from the entrance: one sees only books and readers. I did not want prospective readers to get the library confused with a bank – the more so in that at the time of building money in plenty was available and the materials used would not be frowned upon by a banker. To keep this visual image of a library, as much glass as possible has been used on the inside of the building. It provides acoustic isolation and does not hide readers or books. On the contrary it allows readers to look through various walls and see the trees outside. I belong to that old-fashioned race of librarians who do not think that a tree, a leaf, a bird, an inch of blue sky detract from intellectual concentration.

This viewpoint got me in trouble with a reader whom I knew well. Every morning he was standing in front of the entrance before the doors were opened and every evening we had to turn off the lights of the reading room to push him out. One day he gave me a copy of his latest book and I made the mistake of starting to read it. To my horror I discovered such a lot of undigested ideas taken from other authors that I threw the book away. What should happen happened, and the reader and I ran into one another at a moment when he wanted to complain about the slow delivery of books and when I probably had other problems on my mind. I kindly suggested to him that from time to time he should take a walk in the nearby *Bois de la Cambre*. I was very serious, although I must admit that the French *envoyer promener* could be interpreted as being sent away without any consideration. He turned his back on me and a few days later my Minister passed me a letter from him in which he complained about me, saying that it was not the business of a librarian to send a reader to the woods. In the margin the Minister had written: "What should I answer?" Under his note I added that the complaint was based on a true fact and that he badly needed some fresh air. Not long before this incident my eyes had fallen upon Samuel Johnson's "Deign on the passing world to turn thine eyes/And pause awhile from letters, to be wise."

All my efforts to avoid confusion between a bank and a library did not prevent my colleague Margarita Rudomino from Moscow from criticizing the corridors of the library as being "capitalistic." One of the reasons why I was so concerned with this possible confusion was the fact that, at the local level, the decision was taken nearly simultaneously to build a new national bank and a new national library. Nobody interfered with the plans for the first, but everybody had a personal opinion on the second. The result was that the new bank was finished in five years, but it took thirty-five years to build the new library. The Nuremberg style of the main façade of the National Bank is not better than that of the Library. The director of the Library even benefits from a kind of diabolic revenge. A railroad passes under both the bank and the library. While the director of the bank hears every train which passes under him during office hours, his colleague from the library can quietly go on reading his favourite novel.

Notwithstanding a long delay, the Royal Library in Brussels was the first new post-war national library building on the European continent. Having been present, I have not forgotten that the new building of the National Library of Scotland in Edinburgh was dedicated in 1956 by Queen Elisabeth, but Scotland is not exactly a part of the European continent and furthermore the building had been started before the war. My trip to Scotland, which was actually my first professional mission abroad after my appointment, left me with memorable impressions. One I badly want to record.

At the time, Lord Crawford was chairman of the board of trustees of the National Library of Scotland and the day after the dedication he invited us to his seat at Balcarres, where he proudly showed us his library. He was the 28th Earl of Crawford and Balcarres and from the fourteenth century onwards many of his ancestors had been book collectors with the impressive results in front of us, notwithstanding some epoch-making sales. He had more fifteenth-century Brussels imprints than we have at the National Library in Brussels and for his British guests he had taken out a few dozen books from the shelves with for each of them only a small reference "not in STC" (missing in the Short Title Catalogue of books printed before 1640).

My main recollection of this wonderful visit is, however, not related to books, as surprising as this may be. I don't remember if Lord Crawford or one of his friends told me the following story. The present Earl's father was the one exception to the family tradition of book collecting and he had even sold some important books. Lord Crawford wanted to buy them back and in order to be able to do so he had to sell a painting from his collection, since there were also some rather important paintings in the castle. That is the reason why the Boymans-Van Beuningen Museum in Rotterdam now has the beautiful portrait of Rembrandt's son Titus from the Crawford collection. After the two parties had agreed on the price, the quality, the authenticity and everything else, the Museum curator asked if, by chance, a certificate by an authority on old masters was not available. Lord Crawford said "No, but I can give you Rembrandt's invoice." [6]

---

[6] I have told this story over and over again and when I wrote it down I began to have doubts about its authenticity. At the time of the dedication William Beattie was director of the Library and I knew that after his retirement he had been appointed director of the University of Edinburgh's Institute for Advanced Studies in the Humanities. I could locate him easily and after long years of silence I wrote him a letter asking him to check my recollection. He talked to Lady Crawford, her husband having died in 1975, and he sent me her version of the facts: "There is rather a lot of inaccuracy in Herman Liebaers' draft. My father-in-law was very interested in the books and though he had to sell he also bought, but not on a comparable scale as his father and grandfather. It was he who sold the Rembrandt picture of Titus now at the Rotterdam museum, I think to a dealer with a name like Katz? I have never heard the story of Rembrandt's invoice but it is rather a nice one if genuine. I think it would have been the last picture that David would have sold, as he loved it. Isn't it

My main disappointment with regard to the Brussels library building was the fact that I was not involved with the project from the very beginning. I guess this happens often and for various reasons, and probably more often in Europe than in the United States, because decision-making and actual building go much more slowly. In Brussels, two adjacent institutions – the National Library and the National Archives – suffered from the same cause. In both institutions the directors knew that the process of erecting a new building would take so much time that they would have retired long before it was finished. So they didn't care and left all decisions to outside bodies, cutting themselves off from inside knowledge and participation. Finally, the situation of the Library evolved more favourably than that of the Archives because I was appointed at a moment when I could still interfere, while my colleague inherited a new building which was old-fashioned from the outset. Actually, my sharpest criticism of the building with which I was going to be involved for more than fifteen years and with which I had to live and to work afterwards, is one of common sense and not one at the technical level of librarianship.

Brussels must have been an extremely beautiful city from the fifteenth century onwards. Descriptions by early travellers and remnants from the past bear witness to it. The main charm of the city undoubtedly lay in its location on a slope with a real downtown and uptown, and original lines of communications between the two components. In the second half of the eighteenth century, a first basic mistake was made when a large, flat Place Royale was built in the middle of the slope. It had been decided to copy the royal plaza at Reims in France and the result was indeed a provincial interpretation of this classical example.

---

awful how one's memory misleads one?" With such a correction I decided to pursue my quest for the truth and I wrote to another friend, J.C. Ebbinge Wubben, retired director of the Museum Boymans-Van Beuningen in Rotterdam. He told me that the painting had indeed been bought by the dealer N. Katz in 1939, which meant that no curator could have asked the question about the authenticity. Besides, a good curator should know the pedigree of this famous painting and not ask such a stupid question. My friend's conclusion was *se non è vero, è ben trovato*. In the meantime Nicolas Barker published his excellent book *Bibliotheca Lindesiana* (1977), but the Rembrandt painting falls outside the scope of his subject, though he mentions its existence. Shall I never enjoy the invoice-story again? I was keen on writing this footnote because it might help the reader to understand how my memory may have twisted reality elsewhere in these pages. For a long time, however, I have been living with the idea that reality is not always on the side of the realists.

Just below the Place Royale in Brussels an early twentieth century climbing garden was still part of the urban picture, when it was decided to destroy it and to make a huge artificial flat foundation on which the new library would be built. Once again the same mistake was made: to create a complex of vast buildings with an urbanistic conception of flat land instead of matching with subtle architectural imagination the natural slope of the city. The romantic garden of the Mont-des-Arts was destroyed unnecessarily, because any competent architect could have designed as good and as functional a library as the one which is now half hidden in the slope. It was that all-pervading sense of monumentality which was responsible for the original mistake. As soon as a public building of some size was to be created the first requirement was monumental status even to the detriment of function. This of course is not a problem which is specifically linked to library buildings. When one decides to build huge blocks of offices on flat land, there is no other way to solve the light problem than to create inner courtyards, while it is so easy to use daylight when one respects the natural solution offered by a slope.

This unhappy starting point in my own experience may explain why I have been so keen on avoiding sacrificing the instrument in favour of the monument. It is possible, as President Pompidou said, to combine both, but it is extremely difficult. From that point of view I would not say that the Centre which bears his name is a success. The difficulty lies in the fact that both the public authorities and the architects are not interested in the instrument, but only in the monument. Only the librarian, if it is a library which is to be built, only the doctor if it is a hospital which is to be built, is basically interested in functionalism.

This comparison of a library with a hospital was forced upon me back in 1954 when I was the first, but temporary, librarian of the European Council of Nuclear Research (CERN) at Geneva. I was supposed to do only two things: to find a permanent librarian and to draw up a project for the library. The excellent librarian who joined the staff was Dr. H. Coblans. He was a South-African who had left his country for political reasons and who ultimately became, in the words of Arthur Koestler, a call girl of international forums. For the library it had been decided before I arrived that the work would be entrusted to a Swiss architect, Rudolf Steiger, who had just completed an outstanding hospital in, I think, Zürich.

We had very pleasant sessions with a lot of arguments, he being the senior architect and I the young inexperienced librarian having only some theoretical knowledge of what the building of a library was all about. I discovered, however, rather rapidly that the only way to convince him was just simply to say, "Well, it is exactly as in a hospital, if you accept that. . . ." We agreed most of the time.

Let me say in passing that the functionalism of a library and of a hospital have a lot in common. If readers are patients, books drugs, and librarians doctors, lines of communication between the various components, controlled traffic patterns with distinct circuits, specified areas, all offer many common features. The purpose of this paragraph, however, is to stress the importance of functionalism. It is not easy to convey this concept to an architect, because its specific library meaning is mostly new to him and, as in all fields, it is not a static notion. The function of any library is much more diversified today than it was one or two generations ago. The differences between different types of libraries have grown over the years. Various trends have to be reflected through a responsive architecture.

It is quite obvious that among the different types of libraries the national library will always have more monumentality than a branch of a public library. The real problem is that monumentality should not interfere with function. And if the library is designed from the inside, as it always should be, it is not difficult to achieve the required monumentality through adequate façades. This does not mean that a sense of grandeur should be completely eliminated from the interior design. Since most of the large libraries have rooms for rare books and special collections, it is relatively easy to give some visual distinction to these parts of the building. It is exactly as with good food: it requires a nice table and pleasant surroundings. Actually it is general experience that not only rare books require adequate furniture, but the design of the whole library governs the attitude of the public towards the collections. Those of us who have worked both in old shabby buildings and in clean new ones know the difference very well. For this reason also the ease of the upkeep of the building is of such enormous importance. Most architects have a tendency to be casual about it. For the user of the building it is as important as the care with which the collections are kept or the love with which the architect cuts his name in the foundation stone.

A last remark about my Brussels experience with library building. A few years before I took over I had been exposed, as said above, to the successful introduction of flexibility in new American library building. In Brussels the plans were of an incredible rigidity and even where I managed to replace walls by partitions, they were so well sealed to the ground and to the ceiling that no one could think of moving them. After many years I would be tempted to say that the best solution is in the middle. A building with a one hundred percent flexibility is unnecessarily expensive, while a building without any is pure nonsense. Wisdom lies in a carefully worked out compromise where stacks, public areas and offices can easily be interchanged, but within reasonable limits. Finally I should mention another pre-war inheritance: the use of the available site to the last square inch. Since the shape of the site at Brussels has a couple of queer boundaries, the inside of the library reflects carefully this queerness.

Gerhard Liebers, [7] director of the Münster University Library, coined the phrase that "It is not difficult to see whether one is looking at an architect's library or a librarian's library." It has been my experience that too many architect's libraries are spread around the world. I offer as an explanation that librarians are very often introverts, and that in front of aggressive authorities and ambitious architects they normally prefer books to bricks. This would be all right if the bricks would not end by killing the books, to everybody's loss, the architect and the university president or minister of education included.

As stated earlier my Brussels building past brought me to the Centre Pompidou in Paris and the latter brought me to Tehran, where I became the adviser to the Iranian government for the construction of a new imperial library, the National Pahlavi Library.

It all started in an unusual way. As president of the International Federation of Library Associations, I had given a series of lectures in South East Asia and on my way home I was to give a last one at

---

[7] Liebers is of course the same name as Liebaers, and I would not bother to note it if there had not been a third Liebert in the trade. His first name was Herman like mine but everybody called him Fritz. When the latter was still at the Beinecke Library at Yale, the three of us met in Brussels on the occasion of a visit of the Grolier Club from New York of which he was to become president a few years later.

the University of Jerusalem. Coming from the East the nearest airport from where one could proceed to Tel Aviv was Tehran. Having a scheduled stopover of twenty-four hours there, I had written to the only Iranian I knew in the library field, Mrs. Farideh Tehrani, asking her if I could see some libraries.

Although Mrs. Tehrani was not a librarian she was connected in some Persian way with the national library and I had met her some months earlier as Iranian expert at a seminar in Moscow and Tashkent. I guess it was during this trip that the local radio station at Tashkent wanted to interview me. This was not the first time that I was interviewed in the Soviet Union. The first time it happened was in 1970. I chaired the General Council meeting of the International Federation of Library Associations, and the TV set-up, the girls and men were all like the ones we are accustomed to see in the West. The questions were as trite and so were the answers. Journalists jump from one interview to another, from one subject to another and when I was ready to prove that libraries are the most important institutions in the world, they asked me if it were true that Lenin got upset about the poor library service in France. I answered that although he had never been to the United States, he was a great admirer of the New York Public Library. When I wanted to add that I was one too, they asked me what I thought of public library service by helicopter in the remote north of the Soviet Union. I reacted by saying that UNESCO had once made a film where one saw book delivery by helicopter, boat, donkey, etc., but not one regular counter, over which thousands of books were passing every day all over the world. This interview reminded me of one in Sweden where I could not get away from questions about book thefts in libraries. I finally had to say that libraries did not exist solely to have their books stolen.

The interview in Tashkent was funny in another way. The fellow began by being rather aggressive. He said that I could see that the mosques were open, that books were published in Uzbek, and that our capitalistic propaganda blundered when it spread the news that mosques were closed and that only the Russian language was used to spread publications among the local population. I did not like his tone at all and told him that I did not need to come to Tashkent to know that the mosques were open, that I knew exactly the figure of the number of books published in the previous year in Uzbek, and that he had better look for somebody else for the interview. The next day he came back and we met in one of the *chaykhanas*, those pleasant tea houses on the water, and he asked me kindly if I would be willing to give my impressions on the local libraries, on the restoration of the monuments of Samarkand and, if possible, on my contacts with the population. In a *chaykhana* one is always in an acquiescent mood and I asked whether I should speak English or French. "No importance," was the answer, "since it will be retransmitted in Hindi and Urdu!" I still wonder what I have been saying to my Pakistani and Indian friends.

Great was my surprise when the Belgian ambassador called on me at the hotel as soon as I had arrived in Tehran to tell me that "the Iranians wanted to talk seriously" to me. I had to attend at once a luncheon which was chaired by His Excellency Shojaeddin Shafa, Vice-Minister of the Imperial Court and, if I remember correctly, by Mrs. Lili Amir-Arjomand, Director of the Institute for Intellectual Development of Children and Young Adults and President of the Iranian Library Association. The food was excellent and the local wines also, but the luncheon was over before anything was said to me, except that I was invited to a small dinner party. The dinner party was over before anything was said to me, except that I was asked, by Minister Shafa, if I would be in Brussels one week later. Since this was the case, we made an appointment in my home town. There, an over-ambitious project was explained to me and I found the answer to two other questions which worried me. First, why did he not talk to me in Tehran? Because Western straightforwardness has no place in the Persian mind. After some years of work with my Iranian friends, I am not yet sure that I understand the twist of their minds. Secondly, why did Minister Shafa come to Belgium? Because he had another project with Professor Duchesne-Guillemin of Liège university who was publishing for him the *Acta Iranica* series.

Iran had suddenly become a rich country through the high prices paid for its oil and among the numerous grandiose building projects was an imperial library which should reflect both the centuries-old Persian civilization and the new power of the country in a vast area of the world. Minister Shafa had been told that I was the only man in the world who could help him and rather innocently I accepted the challenge. I was clever enough, however, to add two conditions: firstly that it should not be an expensive window dressing, but a real library, and secondly, that it should not be imported, *clé sur porte*, from abroad but that the Iranians themselves should be involved in all phases of the project. My experience in developing countries had taught me that they were often not cognizant of conditions which were taken for granted by me. I could mention a number of huge buildings, sometimes called national libraries, which are as useless as they were expensive. Just as it would not be difficult to give examples of libraries which were conceived by Western minds and which do not fit into the cultural landscape of a given developing country.

A first meeting was held in Tehran in August 1973. I had suggested a list of foreign experts from whom Minister Shafa could choose. [8] He took them all, which forced me to insist that as many Iranians should participate. The result was interesting and unexpected: a couple of Iranian architects showed up and also a few beautiful young women who seemed to have stepped straight out of a Persian miniature.

During that meeting, which was chaired jointly by Minister Shafa and by me, we listened to a highly intellectual lecture by the former who explained the kind of institution he had in mind. To translate his vision into a scheme which would take into account the realities of the country was not an easy task, if one realizes that all basic components were either non-existent or extremely weak: books, readers and librarians. After a week of discussion the group provided, however, an outline which struck a satisfying balance between an unrealistic monument and an ambitious but workable library.

In view of the local situation and above all of the expected development of the capital city, it was proposed to include in the new institution a national library (in the narrow sense, that is a library solely responsible for national literature), an encyclopaedic library, a national documentation centre for science and technology, and a world centre of Iranian studies, which comprised even a guest house.

Further study and deeper analysis of this preliminary sketch has been going on now for a number of years. The role I played during this phase has been a minor one because I had left the profession less than a year after I had accepted the Iranian proposal. It was,

---

[8] Ralph E. Ellsworth (Colorado), Gerhard Liebers (Münster), Jean-Pierre Seguin (Paris) and Colin St. John Wilson (London).

however, decided that I would not drop out of the project completely and would be associated with the major decisions. One of
them was to follow the example of the procedure adopted by the
Centre Pompidou regarding the organization of an international
architectural competition. A French architect, François Lombard,
closely associated with the Parisian Centre, implemented this part
of the programme, while a Swiss librarian, Jean-Pierre Clavel,
director of the canton and university library at Lausanne, advised
on all professional matters regarding collection building, staff
training, budget allowances, automation and administrative
structure. [9]

I would not like to close this paper without making two general
remarks. To have said above that there were no, or hardly any,
librarians in Iran was less than fair to a few outstanding colleagues.
The problem was that it was difficult to discover them. They were
not picked out by the local authorities for reasons which a
foreigner can try to guess but which he would never fully understand. This is typical for a developing country. I have often been
talking to or working with the wrong people. In the case of Iran it
was outside the country, at an international forum, that a few
Iranian librarians revealed themselves as extremely able and competent. They are now completely integrated in the project to
everybody's benefit. They would be the first ones to stress the
necessity to develop an ambitious training plan, because of the lack
of qualified librarians in the country.

My next remark is related to the difficulties of working outside
one's own area of culture. A European is not an Iranian. Although
Shojaeddin Shafa and I became good friends over the years, we
tend to react differently towards given situations. I am afraid that
such basic differences will explain quite a lot of frustrations in
international cooperation. It convinced me once again that the
only guiding line when dealing with people from countries which
honour a different way of life – and more and more of us meet
such situations – is to abide as closely as possible to one's own
professional standards and dignity.

---

[9] At the time of writing a major milestone has been reached. The international
architectural competition has been organized and a winning project has been selected. The
jury was received by the Shabanou in her private library and the prizes were handed out by
the Shah in his *Grand Salon*. Since I was representing the jury at this last ceremony I
attended both.

6. Small Talk about Great Books

THERE IS NOT MUCH inside information available on the present-day collection-building in public institutions, except, of course, on the much publicized bulk transfers of famous private collections. I have been actively involved for nearly twenty years in that process at the Royal Library in Brussels and now that I begin to look back at my active and responsible years in the library world, I thought that it might be worthwhile to write down the *petite histoire* of my own experience in this field.

I first thought of taking the various items in their chronological sequence of acquisition, but this proved to be impossible, with one type of a book or document bringing a similar one to my mind. I had, however, no second thoughts about it, because a chronological listing had in itself no logic, and since logic has not much to do with the subject under consideration, I forgot about it. Nearly all the books or documents are described in detail, bibliographically and historically, in the two following exhibition catalogues: *Quinze années d'acquisitions, 1954-1969*, and *Cinq années d'acquisitions, 1969-1973*, quoted respectively in the footnotes here as *Quinze Années* and *Cinq Années* followed by the number under which a given book or document is described. Some major books auctioned during the period under consideration are not listed in these two catalogues because we missed them, but some stories can be linked to them too. I would call them negative acquisitions, because the empty space on the shelves is still visible to those who were involved. If an accession brings happiness, a failure to acquire leaves you with sadness. In both cases, however, time brings the right balance.

Early in my acquisitions activity an unknown Flemish manuscript appeared on the market, the *Llangattock Hours*. Bob Delaissé, a librarian of the Manuscript Room, came to see me with great excitement: this is a manuscript which could be related to the van Eyck brothers, it is of the highest artistic quality and never would the opportunity to acquire such a masterpiece present itself again. I was easily convinced of the quality, but the price? The dealer, H.P. Kraus from New York, asked $ 200.000 for it. At the time, this was a price never heard of and I was scared to death. After a sleepless night I decided to ask the advice of André Molitor, Principal Private Secretary to the King, because a normal call on the responsible cabinet member would not yield the special grant which was needed to be able to buy the book. André Molitor was so positive in his reaction that I decided to ask for the book on approval. Great was the excitement when it arrived. In the meanwhile we had gathered more information. The book had been found in a silver chest from the estate of the second Baron Llangattock, it was offered for sale in London at a Christie's auction in 1958 and Marlborough, dealer in modern paintings, had bought it for $ 32.000. A couple of years later H.P. Kraus acquired it from Marlborough for twenty percent more. Christie's catalogue described it as Ghent ± 1450. It appeared in Kraus' catalogue 100, where thirteen of the fourteen miniatures were reproduced. In the meanwhile Rosy Schilling had published an extensive study in the Wallraf Richartz Jahrbuch.

Besides the esthetic quality of the illumination, it had other unusual features: larger than normal size for a book of hours, extremely fine handwriting on pristine vellum, and a signed contemporary binding by Lievin Stuvaert. The book was carefully examined in the Manuscript Room and shown to a few connoisseurs. Then came the moment to decide. We were three: Bob Delaissé, a young librarian, François Masai, the experienced curator of the Manuscript Room, and I. It was a most dramatic discussion which lasted for hours: Bob Delaissé pleading, François Masai resisting, and I trying to be as neutral as possible, but actually wanting to support Bob Delaissé. Finally we came to the conclusion that I would inform the dealer that we were interested in the book, but that we were not convinced by his arguments supporting such a high price. As a result he decided to ask a well-known American art historian, Harry Bober, to come over to Brussels and to have with us a scholarly session on the merits of the recently discovered manuscript. Bob Delaissé and I knew Harry

Bober well personally, and he also knew the Royal Library well, because he had spent several months here, before World War II, working on its collection of Flemish manuscripts, and he had remained in contact with my predecessor, the late Frederic Lyna, an authority on Flemish miniatures.

The session with Harry Bober was no less dramatic than the first one. Going over the same pro's and con's again, emphasizing them according to the various points of view. After Harry Bober had gone back to New York, where he was teaching at the Graduate School in Art History of New York University, the three of us sat together again, each one of us sticking to his previous attitude. I suspected at the time that François Masai, whose background was completely imbued by Latin civilization, was unconsciously cool to arguments which were either written or presented in English and which were bearing on matters outside the scope of his personal interest. Finally we decided not to buy the manuscript and this was certainly a mistake. I paid a second visit to André Molitor to thank him for his support and to explain to him why we came to a negative conclusion. I was not very proud, but he understood our reasons. I had established as a rule in the Library that for major acquisitions the decisions should be taken unanimously. Unlike the national museums of our country, we had no outside acquisitions committee and we were (and still are) convinced that this was an enormous advantage. The price we were willing to pay for this privilege, was unanimity in the decision in order to avoid dissenting views being voiced outside the house. Even with the *Llangattock Hours* gone, nobody saw any reason to change this self-imposed rule which allowed us to mind our own business. After many years I heard vaguely that the German collector who had bought the book after we had returned it, sold it back to H.P. Kraus who put it again on the market. Since I still felt like a cheated lover, I decided to stay out of the way. Late information tells me that the same German collector bought it again and included it in the collection which he presented to the city of Cologne.

Actually the first important book the Library bought after I was in charge was four years before the episode of the *Llangattock Hours*. It was sold to us by the same H.P. Kraus and was another book of hours, the *Cleves Hours*. The story is, however, again not simple. Bob Delaissé located in a Kraus catalogue a Flemish book of hours, which came from the Arenberg collection. I need to make another digression before I come back to the *Cleves Hours* and mention once again the Arenberg collection. It so happened that this world-famous collection, centered on Belgian books, began to be dispersed a couple of years before I entered the book business, (because a librarian who buys enters the book business whether he likes it or not). This dispersal marked repeatedly and fundamentally my professional interest. The major curse, not to me but to my Library, was the fact of dispersal. As a young librarian in Brussels, I had heard that the Arenberg family, of German origin but settled for many generations in Belgium, had decided shortly before World War I to present their library to the Nation. Unfortunately the war came and through one or another bureaucratic decision the Arenberg possessions were considered as alien property. After the war the family did not want to have any relations with the Belgian government and the collection was shipped out of the country and began wandering through Europe. I never had the courage to check whether this story is true or apocryphal. Anyhow an American dealer bought from an heir, who had settled in Monte Carlo, a number of outstanding manuscripts which he offered in a priced catalogue in 1952. The rumour went that the mark-up staggered the owner who sold the books and that he decided afterwards to sell to other dealers, H.P. Kraus being one of them.

The catalogue with the *Cleves Hours* had various other Arenberg books in it. Fortunately, I would say, because the dealer had offered us the *Arenberg Hours* first and not the *Cleves Hours*. Bob Delaissé had become our expert on Flemish manuscripts after he had applied a new approach to manuscript documents, known as codicology or archeology of the book, a technique of analyzing sometimes also called the Brussels method, to one of the Royal Library's most prestigious manuscripts, the autograph manuscript of Thomas a Kempis' *Imitatio*, as his doctoral dissertation. After several years of hard work he organized in 1959, on the occasion of the 400th anniversary of the founding of the first Royal Library in Brussels, one of the Library's most successful exhibitions *Flemish Miniatures*, which was also shown at the Bibliothèque Nationale in Paris and at the Rijksmuseum in Amsterdam. He also published several books on the subject, among others *Medieval Illuminations*, in which he wrote brilliant comments on fifty of the most glorious miniatures from the collections of the Royal Library. He studied for two years with Erwin Panofsky at the Institute of Advanced Study at Princeton, went several times as visiting professor to American universities and finally left us to become a Fellow at All Souls College, Oxford. I was very sad to be without him, though we remained in contact. While a soldier during the war in England, he married a British girl, was severely injured during the landing in Normandy and felt uneasy about the world in which he was living. He had not been very happy in the Library and unfortunately was not going to be happier at Oxford. All his dedication could not prevent him from being a *déraciné*.

I had not much experience in buying expensive books with public money, and before placing the order for the *Arenberg Hours*, I wanted to go in detail over the matter once more. Finally I sent a cable and the answer came the same day: sold! H.P. Kraus had, however, in his catalogue another Flemish manuscript, the *Cleves Hours*, also coming from the same collection and he had sent it immediately on approval. It enchanted everyone concerned in the Library and we decided to buy it. The funny thing about this, my [1] first major acquisition for the Library, is that long after Bob Delaissé had given a public lecture announcing the acquisition of these *Cleves Hours*, Parliament approved a special grant to buy the *Arenberg Hours*. The manuscript is beautiful as a pure example of its style and has many specific features which allowed our experts to date and to localize it with a high degree of precision. [2]

Manuscripts are important in my whole acquisitions activity, a fact which can be explained in different ways. One is the uniqueness of the document, though I gladly admit that early printed books also have, very often, unique features. Another explanation would be the aggressive acquisitions policy of the manuscript people in the Royal Library, which I was happy to honour because I did not come from "special collections" and I wanted to show that a librarian who had been working with common books was not of necessity narrow minded. Actually I was the first director to ex-

---

[1] In the following pages there will be many "my's" and "I's" which actually mean the Royal Library. This confusion is by no means the result of a lack of modesty. In fact it expresses a too easily accepted identification of the institution with the person who serves it. I can as well add at once that I never bought an expensive book for myself. I avoided on purpose being faced with a conflict of interests. To satisfy a mild collector's passion I bought from time to time an African sculpture, as remote as possible from books.

[2] *Quinze Années*, 493.

pand systematically the museum collections of the Library after an interruption of more than half a century, although my predecessors had come from "special collections."

H.P. Kraus again sold us, in 1958, a manuscript of the *Armorial of the Order of the Golden Fleece.* [3] Several copies of this book are preserved, since a manuscript was generally written and decorated on the occasion of the installation of a new member of the Order. Ours is a rather late one, but one of the most beautiful of the recorded ones. It has splendid full length portraits of Philip the Good, Charles the Bold, Maximilian I, Philip the Fair and Emperor Charles V, all grand masters of the Order. This gallery of portraits induced the Belgian Post Office to issue a series of stamps based on the miniatures. It was so successful that I was able to pay H.P. Kraus with the profit from the stamp sales.

It so happened that when this book entered our collection, a Maximilian exhibition was being prepared by the National Library of Vienna. They wanted to borrow from us a number of pieces, including the *Armorial of the Order of the Golden Fleece.* We sent everything, but I told them that the latter could only be delivered the day before the opening of the exhibition because it was still at the printshop of the Post Office. I took it personally to Vienna, so I could also attend the opening. I brought the book by diplomatic pouch to be sure I would have no trouble with the customs. I went to the Belgian Embassy in Vienna to have the seal removed before taking the manuscript to the exhibition. A young diplomat was taking care of this matter and apologized that the ambassador was not present in person. I did not care about the ambassador and to shorten the time I told the story of the postage stamps to explain why this manuscript was late. When I mentioned postage stamps, the young man said, "Excuse me, I am going to call the ambassador." I asked why and he said, "The ambassador is a keen stamp collector!" When H.P. Kraus heard about the stamps, he bought several series and mounted them as a keepsake for one or another occasion.

A manuscript of *Statutes of the Order of the Golden Fleece* was bought a couple of years later, actually in 1961, from Lathrop C. Harper's, also in New York. [4] I did not buy many manuscripts

[3] *Quinze Années,* 118.
[4] *Quinze Années,* 101.

from this house, which is the oldest rare book dealer in the United States. I bought, however, quite a number of exceptionally fine or rare printed books. The first one which I think I should mention here is a unique copy of the *Tabulae Sex* of Vesalius. This is a rather romantic story. Otto Ranschburg, who was on a buying trip in Europe for L.C. Harper's came to see me in my office and told me that he was probably going to buy, in Eastern Europe, a book which would be of the utmost interest for the collection of the Royal Library, but he did not tell me which one. Three weeks later, he came back and told me that he had bought a copy of the *Tabulae Sex* with the enigmatic seventh plate. I wanted to see the book immediately, but this was impossible because it had already been mailed to New York. During the anxious weeks of waiting, I read the literature about this seventh plate, and discovered that Vesalius had complained about the circulation of an unauthorized plate which had been cut after a sketch made by a student. A nineteenth-century bibliographer, Ludwig Choulant, medical advisor to the court of Saxony, claimed to have seen the plate but no one had heard about it since. One can imagine my excitement when the book finally arrived in a contemporary binding which was a last proof of authenticity. For once I did not discuss the price. The Library issued a full-scale reprint of the seven plates, with a scholarly introduction.

I sent a copy to Yale where Cushing had based his final bibliography of Vesalius on the library's collection, and the answer expressed great interest in the find: "Your book would be Cushing 11-8." I also sent a copy to O'Malley at UCLA who had just published his excellent biography of Vesalius. It was a first contact between us. The next one was the Eugène Baie Prize of the Province of Antwerp which he received for the same book. This prize was to be given, as a decision of the Founder, to a non-Belgian who would have written the best book on a Belgian personality. Since I was a member of the jury, I was present when O'Malley received the prize and he was eager to listen to my story of the *Tabulae Septem*. Unfortunately he was to die soon afterwards, leaving an important work in the field of the history of medicine unfinished. Soon after his death I saw all his material, which was still kept together in the new library of UCLA.

The separate purchase of two important manuscripts is linked in my mind. The widow of a well-known Belgian collector came to see me with the suggestion that the Library might buy one of her husband's most prestigious manuscripts, *L'Horloge de sapience*, by Henric Suso. [5] Many handwritten versions of this text, originally written in German, survive in different languages, but this one is certainly the most beautiful, with its thirty-seven large-size miniatures of the French school of the middle of the fifteenth century. I had several rather unusual meetings with the lady in her bank's safe, and the box where she hid the book was barely large enough to contain it. At a certain moment, a Brussels dealer, Paul van der Perre (through whom her husband had acquired it some years earlier from one of the oldest Belgian noble families who had decided to sell it in order to pay for the upkeep of the castle) was in the picture. Paul van der Perre was an outstanding connoisseur not only of books but also of prints. He had a strong character, and he was as strong in his honesty as in the other features of his personality. He was no social mixer at all and this did not make him very popular in the trade, although he was very much appreciated by the book collectors. With the Royal Library his relations had always been good. Each time he offered a book for sale we bought it. He never came to the Library with a book where there might be a chance that we would not take it. There also was never a discussion about the price he asked.

When I first met Paul van der Perre the peak of his career had already passed. This has happened to me rather often with outstanding people. For a long time he was the only dealer to organize book auctions of international standing in Brussels. In the case of the *Horloge de Sapience*, however, he dropped out of the deal, for a reason which I do not remember. I bought directly from the owner. Actually she asked if I could pay the agreed price directly to her son, for tax purposes I imagine. When I met the son, he confessed to me that he also was a collector and that with the money from the manuscript he was going to add substantially to his collection of leaden soldiers. The day after I concluded the purchase of the *Horloge de Sapience* I went to London with a colleague from the Manuscript Room to try to buy a French manuscript written at Tournai in about 1351, by Gilles Li Muisis *Œuvres Poétiques*. [6]

[5] *Quinze Années*, 68.
[6] *Quinze Années*, 29.

The auction sale was to be held next morning at Sotheby's and since H.P. Kraus had shown interest in this manuscript we had agreed that he would bid for us. Upon our arrival in London, the evening before the sale, H.P. Kraus invited us to his Ritz suite, while we were staying in a hotel which was a little shabby. While we were waiting for our double whiskies, H.P. Kraus received telephone calls from all over the world, but I am not sure they were all orders. My young colleague was even less at ease than I was and warned me that our host was trying to get us drunk. I did not see why he would try to do this because we were partners, and I offered myself another drink to kill my excitement over the forthcoming sale. Next morning we were one hour in advance at the sales room, while H.P. Kraus made his grand entry just a few minutes before 11 AM. Our manuscript was 112 and we were anxiously sitting behind our dealer. It was the first time (and, for that, the last time) that I attended an auction sale. Everything went so fast and when 112 was knocked down I did not know whether we had it or not. H.P. Kraus whispered to us that we had it.

After the sale, which covered the third part of the Dyson Perrins Collection, Anthony Hobson of Sotheby's offered a luncheon, which gave me ample time to show H.P. Kraus photographs of the *Horloge de Sapience* which I had just bought. His comment was rather unexpected: "I do not know how much you paid for it, but I offer you twice as much."

I must admit that I had described the photographs in his own style. Something like:

"This is French art of the highest quality ever to be seen. French artists are well known for their altar pieces, panel paintings or even monumental fresco's, but these miniatures surpass everything French that has been given to the world. Imagine these thirty-seven large-size miniatures put together! French art would be poorer without them. And their condition of preservation: mint. Who could not be moved by their bright rich colours and powerful figures, not to mention the iconographical originality of an incredible number of details. Pure wonder. Nothing else but one of the most famous of the French cathedrals could be compared with this book. Those familiar with this type of masterpiece will find it breathtaking."

H.P. Kraus never understood, or pretended that he never understood, that I was not buying with my own money but with public money. Many public institutions in the United States are in fact privately owned, which gives their directors a freedom of action which government ruled institutions do not have. Since H.P. Kraus had a European background he should have known better. Actually I am convinced that he knew it, but it was all to his advantage to ignore my financial problems. My years of active purchasing coincided with H.P. Kraus' domination of the rare book trade. Over all these years I saw him acting as the unchallenged leader in the field, which he actually was. These were also the years that institutional budgets in Europe as well as in the United States, and apparently private budgets also, were steadily growing and H.P. Kraus took advantage of this favourable situation. Books which had remained relatively cheap as compared to other works of art became expensive and soon very expensive. H.P. Kraus had a major influence on this trend. That he was thinking in another *ordre de grandeur*, in another dimension, than we did can be exemplified by the following story. He had bought from the Heverlée Castle of the Arenbergs near Louvain three large paintings by Jean-Baptiste Bonnecroy giving bird's-eye views of Antwerp, Brussels and Amsterdam in the middle of the seventeenth century. He showed them to a group of Belgian VIP's visiting his elegant book-shop at 16 East Fourty-Sixth Street. One of the visitors was interested in purchasing the view of Brussels and they agreed on the price. When my good countryman was back home he found out that while he was taking the figure quoted to be in Belgian francs, H.P. Kraus was quoting the price in U.S. dollars! At the time, the American dollar was still at fifty Belgian francs.

I had to live with H.P. Kraus. I visited him many times in New York, looking always at tempting books, but most of the time stopped by their price. When I wanted a particular book which I found one year later still in his safe, he had raised the price. After so many years I still do not know if he is a connoisseur in the sense that Paul van der Perre was or Otto Ranschburg is. These people knew the commercial value of the books they offered for sale and they never gave them away at low prices, but with H.P. Kraus I always had the feeling that big business came first and that he wanted his customers to understand it that way. Since through him quite a number of outstanding books enriched the national patrimonium of Belgium I guess I have to be grateful. If I could leave it at that, I certainly would. But he bought two manuscripts, bidding against me, which are still heavy on my stomach, as we say in Flemish. For the first one I am sure he knew he was bidding against the Royal Library, for the second one I am not so sure. The story of the second one will be told at the end of this chapter.

The first one was a manuscript which came originally from the library of the Dukes of Burgundy. It is public knowledge that this library is the core of the Manuscript Room in Brussels with two hundred manuscripts still preserved out of the nine hundred mentioned in a fifteenth century catalogue. About one hundred are scattered over various libraries in Europe and in the United States. The rest have mostly been destroyed by five centuries of war in this part of Europe. So when a manuscript from this famed library comes up for sale, it is quite an event. I was lucky enough to buy, in 1960, at the Hôtel Drouot in Paris a *Life of Christ* [7] coming from this library. This book is one of the purest examples of a Burgundian princely book as regards size, bastarda handwriting and miniatures from the best Flemish school, attributed to Loyset Liedet.

In 1968 another manuscript from the same library turned up in a Sotheby catalogue, a *Speculum Historiale* by Vincent de Beauvais which had belonged to Charles V, the Duke of Berry and the Dukes of Burgundy and had finally landed in the well-known Chester Beatty Library in Dublin. This sale coincided with the preparation of the inauguration of the new library building in Brussels, scheduled for 17 February 1969, exactly thirty-five years after the death of King Albert to whose memory the library was dedicated. I went to see the Prime Minister and asked him if he would not be willing to allow us to buy that manuscript as a present of the government on the occasion of the dedication of the new library. The cabinet agreed and I was allowed to go somewhat beyond the estimated price. This grant was accepted very gratefully. At the sale the book went much higher than the estimate. We could not afford it and it was bought by an unknown bidder. A couple of years later it turned up in a Kraus catalogue. It is now in Paris at the Bibliothèque Nationale.

The Library did, however, not lose the whole amount of the special government grant. It so happened that Lathrop C. Harper's had just acquired a pristine copy of *Maximilian's Prayer*

---

[7] *Quinze Années*, 74.

Book, [8] one of ten copies printed on vellum. They sold it to the Royal Library and the importance of the book was fitting to the special occasion. When this gift of the government was announced, quite a number of foreign and domestic institutions and individuals followed the good example. [9]

Since I have already mentioned two or three times Lathrop C. Harper's, I must add a rather unusual footnote on this name. The current president of the corporation which runs the firm is E. Clark Stillman, my oldest American friend. As already told in a preceding chapter, I knew him through the Belgian American Educational Foundation. Early in the sixties, a basic mistake by some of the trustees of the Foundation plunged the institution into a deep crisis and forced Clark Stillman out of his job. Over the years he had developed an outstanding collection of African art and of early Belgian books. He was well known to Lathrop C. Harper's. When Harper's was to be liquidated, he was instrumental in keeping the business going. So he stepped into the book business while I stepped out of it.

This Clark Stillman intermezzo allows me to focus some major acquisitions on persons who were involved in them. It allows me further to state explicitly that books are much closer to people than most of us believe, even when day after day brings proof of it.

In 1962, Mrs. Louis Solvay decided to give her outstanding collection to the Royal Library retaining, however, lifelong interest in it. The name Solvay stands for an industrial empire of Belgian origin founded by the grandfather of Louis Solvay. Gifts to public institutions are rather exceptional in Belgium. As compared to the situation in the United States, there is hardly any fiscal incentive, although some legal improvement was started in 1966. Mrs. Solvay's library is undoubtedly the most important single gift which was bestowed upon the Royal Library. I remember vividly my visit to the notary who had to read aloud the name of the author and the title of the nearly thirteen hundred books in order to make the gift legal. After a few minutes he had reached the stage where he

---

[8] *Quinze Années*, 139.

[9] Listed in the booklet *Inauguration de la Bibliothèque Royale Albert Ier par S.M. le Roi*, on pp. 31-62. Among these gifts I would like to single out a bilingual (French and Dutch) edition of *Reynard the Fox* printed by Plantin in Antwerp in 1566 and given by Count Guillaume de Hemricourt de Grunne. (The latter was undeservedly blamed in Belgium for having sold to the Cloisters in New York the Van der Weyden triptych.)

paused after the author's name, which led to rather hilarious combinations of titles and authors as, for instance, Paul Leclère/ *Venise, seuil des eaux*, Francis Jammes/*Ma fille Bernadette*, James Joyce/*Ulysse*, Valéry/*Eupalinos ou l'Architecte* . . . or Proust/*Du côté de chez Swann*, Musset/*Les nuits*, Pierre Louys/*Chansons de Bilitis*, Ambroise Vollard/*Cézanne* . . . or Paul Morand/*Rien que la terre*, Dostoievsky/*Les Frères Karamazoff*, Poe/*Histoires extraordinaires*, René Boylesve/ . . . When all documents were signed I had the honour and the privilege, to present Mrs. Solvay with a Belgian decoration, the first time I had ever performed such a function. I was completely unable to pin it gracefully on her breast and she finally said to me that I was better with books than with women.

Franz Schauwers, curator of Rare Books, was present and this was the most rewarding moment of his long career at the Royal Library. Actually he was solely responsible for this gift because Mrs. Solvay appreciated him very much and trusted him completely. He was a modest and shy man and had never mentioned his relations with Mrs. Solvay before the gift. The friendship which had developed between them was full of books. Franz Schauwers died after he had completed the volume of the catalogue of the Solvay Collection on old books. The Collection is now covered in three volumes: old books, literary documents, and modern books. [10]

The Collection is kept in specially designed rooms, the decoration of which matches the contents of the books. They are adjacent to another specially designed room for the Max Elskamp and Henry van de Velde collections. This brings another pleasant recollection back to my mind.

In 1932, long before I had any responsibility in the Library, a part of the Max Elskamp estate came to this institution: his printshop and some memorabilia. Max Elskamp (1862-1931) was an outstanding poet, a folklorist, a designer, a printer, and foremost a lifelong friend of Henry van de Velde. More than thirty years after Max Elskamp's gift, the Library was happy to add the extensive Henry van de Velde archives. This happened through the generosity of his son Thyl and it also represented for me one of my dearest professional satisfactions. Immediately after Henry van de Velde's death in 1957 in Oberägeri, Switzerland, I paid a

---

[10] *Bibliothèque de Madame Louis Solvay*, Bruxelles, 1966-1968, 3 vol.

visit to the director of the Library of the Federal Polytechnicum at Zürich where van de Velde's papers had been on deposit for some years. The purpose of my visit was to ask permission to make a microfilm of these papers which were of the utmost importance from a national point of view, Belgium having been central to the European *Art Nouveau* movement and Henry van de Velde himself having been a key figure in it. Though I knew the director, Dr. P. Scherrer, personally, he felt that he could not grant permission to microfilm the documents. I was very much disappointed. A couple of years later I received the visit of Thyl van de Velde, who informed me of the death of his sister Nele (Thyl and Nele are the given names of the Flemish legendary figure Uylenspiegel and his wife). He told me that he was not happy with the archives of his father in Zürich and wondered if I would not like to accept them on behalf of the Royal Library. What a proposal: the originals instead of a poor microfilm! The five thousand items of the lot were promptly shipped to Brussels and then began the long and difficult work of identification and classification. After many months Claudine Lemaire brought this to a good end. Henry van de Velde appears from this vast amount of documentary evidence as a leading European intellectual who considered himself first an architect and then in decreasing order of importance, a designer, a painter and an author. Based on these archives and on Claudine's assistance, A.M. Hammacher published a new book on Henry van de Velde, the basic feature of which is a very positive reevaluation of the pictorial part of his work.

Joining these two gifts in an *Art Nouveau* setting in the new library was a real feast. Thyl van de Velde added a small but important gift when the room was dedicated: a sketch by his father of Max Elskamp. I can also add a footnote which is unknown to Henry van de Velde's son: among the papers of his father were three hundred letters from Frans Masereel. The latter added the three hundred letters from van de Velde. Other letters in the collection are by Cobden Sanderson, Edward Gordon Graig, Maurice Denis, James Ensor, Elisabeth Förster-Nietzsche, André Gide, Walther Gropius, Jean Jaurès, Harry Kessler, Annette Kolb, Jules Laforgue, Aristide Maillol, Stéphane Mallarmé, Julius Meier-Graefe, William Morris, Edward Munch, Paul Signac, Stefan Zweig, etc.

I may as well here enumerate the other special rooms which

were dedicated on the occasion of the opening of the new library building. All these rooms correspond to important gifts. The first one houses, in an eighteenth-century decor, an important *Voltaire Collection*. [11] It was presented by Count de Launoit on the occasion of the laying of the corner stone of the new building on 17 February 1954. At the time, the president of the Board of Trustees was a Jesuit, Father Willaert, and it was rather pleasant to listen to his address of acceptance of the Voltaire collection. This collection has been much used for Theodore Besterman's correspondence and works of Voltaire. The next room is a faithful reproduction of Michel de Ghelderode's workshop. Many words have been used to describe the world in which Michel de Ghelderode lived and which is reflected in his books. When one looks at his workshop, with its paintings, art objects and artifacts, one considers the qualification *"réalisme fantastique"* as much less than satisfactory. The reproduction of his workshop, with the actual contents, was actually a repetition of what happened in 1930 when Marthe Verhaeren offered to the Library her husband's workshop in St. Cloud exactly as it had been at his death, with all the manuscripts which were still in her possession and a small but unique collection of works of art by Sisley, Kees van Dongen, James Ensor and Van Rysselberghe.

Emile Verhaeren, Max Elskamp, Henry van de Velde and Michel de Ghelderode are of course all Belgian artists, but their international stature is generally recognized. This is the reason why it is pleasant to report that other gifts will be housed in rooms which still have to be designed, among them Georges Rodenbach, with the autograph manuscript of *Bruges la Morte*. After I had left the Library, it recovered Paul Delvaux' literary map of Belgium which he had painted for the Brussels World Fair in 1958. These names are a kind of symbol of the whole policy of a national library of a small country. It has to be devoted first and foremost to those artists and scholars who broaden the national horizons through their talents and achievements.

Though I have mentioned already that gifts to official institutions are rather rare in Belgium, I still would like to record some of them because they allow me to make some general comments. The main point in this connection is the quality of the relations with

---

[11] *Collection Voltairienne du Comte de Launoit*, par Madeleine Renier, Bruxelles, 1955.

private collectors. When one is ruled by bureaucrats, the protection of the quality of these relations is of daily concern. I was very unfortunate with the bureaucrats of the government, but I was extremely fortunate with the private collectors of the Société des Bibliophiles et Iconophiles de Belgique.

It started in a rather unusual way. Auguste Lambiotte revived the Société in 1954, and he invited me to a dinner party on the occasion of my appointment as director of the Library. Bibliophily and gastronomy have always been good friends. The other guest of honour was General Willems, the former president, who had ruined himself by publishing for its members outstanding facsimiles at a time when such reproductions were not yet fashionable and who had retired from the Société long before. He was an elderly general, rather deaf, and we were sitting opposite one another. It was the first time that we had met. At the soup he shouted rather loudly to me – and I am going to quote it in French in the hope that it will sound nicer: *"Votre prédécesseur était un imbécile."* I think my face turned as red as my tomato soup and before I could answer anything he himself gave the explanation: *"Parce que c'était un numismate."* I felt a bit relieved and Auguste Lambiotte, who proved to be an excellent president said, "That's an original way to start talking about books instead of speaking about coins."

In their wills both presidents, General Willems and Auguste Lambiotte, were not very generous to the Library, but indirectly the collections have benefitted from their interest. The collection of General Willems was centered on mediaeval and renaissance civilization in our part of Western Europe, while Auguste Lambiotte's was purely French, mainly from the seventeenth century onwards. Several years after the general's death, actually on the occasion of the dedication of the new buildings, some of his heirs presented their part of the original collection and this meant a substantial number of Flemish manuscripts and incunabula. During his lifetime, Auguste Lambiotte had given to the Library his outstanding collection of documents which related to the Commune of Paris, because it did not fit into his main collection of French literature. He himself had inherited this collection from his father-in-law, Victor De Meulemeester, the first socialist senator for his constituency at Bruges. I have always thought, however without the slightest proof, that Victor De Meulemeester,

who was a wealthy brewer, bought himself a good socialist conscience with a collection about the Parisian revolution of 1871.
When Auguste Lambiotte gave us the collection, he even added an
amount of money to complete it. Till his death he renewed this
amount regularly and the result is the best collection outside
France about this particular event. This was proven by the centenary exhibition which was shown in the Library and which went
afterwards to the Library of Foreign Literature in Moscow. One
word about the latter. At the end of the morning of the opening
day, the exhibition was ready and we all went out for lunch, the
formal opening being scheduled for 3 P.M. When we came back, I
saw some empty spaces. Portraits of freemasons and opponents of
the Commune had been taken away during the *zakuski*. It should
be a tribute to objectivity to add that the Bibliothèque Nationale in
Paris did not feel the need to commemorate the centenary of the
Commune, which led a number of leading French journalists to
write that if the inhabitants of Paris wanted to know what happened in their city a hundred years ago, they should go to Brussels.

Before I took over, a member of the Société des Bibliophiles et
Iconophiles de Belgique, Jules Jadot, had given the Library in
1953 a first choice of twenty books from his collection. Among
them was a copy of Baudelaire's *Fleurs du Mal*, first edition, with
important autograph letters. This formula of a limited choice has
many advantages, both from the point of view of the donor and of
the recipient. It was repeated in 1965 by Fernand Nyssen and it
allowed the Library to acquire, among other treasures, a pristine
copy of the 1481 Dante with pasted-in engravings by Botticelli. [12]
They were both good friends of Franz Schauwers.

For me the name of Franz Schauwers will not only remain linked
to that of Fernand Nyssen, Mrs. Louis Solvay and other famous
Belgian book collectors, but also to an unknown person who happened to be the owner of an unpretentious booklet, called
L'Ouverture de cuisine. It was written by Lancelot de Casteau
"Maistre Cuisinier de trois princes-évêques de Liège" in the sixteenth century and was printed in the same city by Leonard Streel
in 1604. In the nineteenth century this book was considered by the
bibliographers as lost for ever. And then in 1958 there came into
Franz Schauwers' office a tiny little man with a copy, which, I

[12] *Quinze Années*, 325.

think, he found in his attic or in an inheritance. I knew nothing about it until Franz Schauwers came to see me a few weeks later with the invoice and the following story. The man, whose name is lost forever unless he reads this page, wanted indeed to sell his *Ouverture de cuisine* and Franz Schauwers told him, "I have been following rather closely the book market of Belgian items for a quarter of a century and I have never encountered this small book. So it must be rather rare. In consequence I offer you three thousand Belgian francs instead of three hundred which would be the normal price." The owner agreed, but did not leave the room. When Franz Schauwers asked why he was still standing there, he said that he wanted his money immediately. Franz knowing that it would take the government at least six months to pay the poor fellow, wrote a personal check to him, thinking that he would easily recover the amount from me. The man had hardly left his office when a book collector from Liège came in. They looked at this unambitious *livre de cuisine* and the collector said, "But this is exactly the book that my journalist friend has been looking for for many years." To make a long story short, a paper about the book was published in a leading daily, *Le Soir*, and two days later the owner of the book came back to Franz Schauwers with a clipping from the paper. He was furious and said to my friend Franz: "Look at this article, you cheated me, it is not three thousand francs which you should have offered, but thirty thousand and I want my book back." Franz answered timidly: "But the property of the State cannot be disposed of." "Words," said the other fellow, "you bought it with your own money and here is your check. I refuse this charity," and indeed he threw the check on the desk and since Franz stubbornly refused to return the book he slammed the door cursing the Library and the Belgian government. In the meanwhile Franz had sent in the papers to recover his expenses and decided to tell me the whole story. We had a good laugh and of course the Library still has this unique copy of a book for which we finally did not pay. Our price was probably too low, and it is not fair to buy under the market price from a person who is not a dealer. But we did it in all innocence. The whole story ended with an impressive banquet offered by the mayor of Liège at the hotel school of the town, where the booklet was sitting at the head of the table and where the menu was based on the recipes from *L'Ouverture de cuisine*.

Gifts are not always the result of old friendships between a collector and a staff member, although the more important ones always are. I have constantly encouraged staff members to go out in the world to meet people and to put their expertise at the disposal of private collectors. I think I have been influenced as a young director by Wilhelm von Bode, who wrote somewhere in his memoirs that while he was building the collection for his famous Museum Insel in Berlin, he never knew who were his best curators, "those who were never in the Museum or those who were always there." I was lucky to have the two types of curators.

Furthermore gifts came really out of the blue. I shall always remember a modest Dutch collector from Bilthoven, W. Arntz, who sent me a good book from time to time, because his wife was of Belgian origin. One day Robert Hankart, the author of a biography of the Belgian novelist André Baillon came to see me and offered the Library all his André Baillon manuscripts which he himself had received from the heirs. There was however one condition, that I should accept the responsibility of the copyright. From time to time I transferred small amounts of money to a grand-niece of André Baillon who was living in Paris. Doctor Baron Ludo van Bogaert began his numerous gifts to the Library with other manuscripts of André Baillon, who had been his patient at the Salpêtrière in Paris. Later he added important documents on the Flemish painter Rik Wouters, whose wife had been treated by him for a nervous breakdown caused by her husband's untimely death at the age of thirty-three in Holland during the First World War. It should not be my purpose to praise the qualities of Belgian artists, but in the case of Rik Wouters, I cannot but regret that outside his home country, he did not achieve the reputation which he richly deserves. Ludo van Bogaert has just given his unique Rik Wouters collection of paintings to the Antwerp Museum of Fine Arts and his rich collection of manuscripts and printed books to the Royal Library. I am sorry that I am no longer in charge to accept it.

The most unexpected gift that fell on my desk was a series of Korans. A Prince of Polignac, living in the south of France, gave it to the Library in order to convert the staff and the readers to the Muslim religion. With some hesitation I pointed out that he could not expect too much proselytism from us, but he was fully aware of our position. Though the collection did not have kufic manuscripts, some items were a real enrichment of our rather poor Near Eastern holdings. Another unexpected and extremely moving gift recently came to the Library and so I was hardly involved in it. One day Mr. Massuda, director of Datsun-Belgium, was introduced to me by representative Dupré and he made it quite clear that he was so happy in his adopted country that he wanted to make three substantial gifts: one at the local level where the plant was operating, one at the provincial level and one at the national level. We easily agreed that the recipient at the national level should be the Royal Library and he made it possible for us to buy a splendid copy of the famous *Yoshiwara keisei shin bijin awase jihitsin kagami*, Edo, 1784.

Sometimes also a gift is requested, hopefully in a diplomatic way. A few years ago a dealer offered an early broadside with a woodcut of a northern Italian landscape with an oil well and the title was *S'ensuyvent les vertus de la vertueuse pétrole*. . . . [13] I could easily convince Petrofina, the only Belgian owned oil company, to buy this unique copy of an Antwerp imprint for the Library. In the sixteenth century oil was only useful as a medecine, but we have of course good reasons to forget this modest origin.

It also can happen that an acquisition stands half-way between a gift and a purchase. One day I was introduced to a member of one of the oldest Belgian families who had just inherited part of his father's estate. He wanted to sell some incunabula which apparently had been in his family for nearly five centuries. I quoted a price and he said "Oh, no, half of it is more than enough, that's what I need to restore my furniture." In the preceding paragraph I have used for the first time the word purchase. I have tried to avoid it as long as possible, because when it came to purchases, the smile which accompanies all gifts tends to disappear and is replaced by a face expressing mixed feelings. Let me start with the worst of all my recollections. One day a finance inspector – this is the super-powerful type of a Belgian bureaucrat – refused to approve the purchase of a late fifteenth century *Book of Hours* because I "bought too many Bibles!" I was so mad at him that I made a most stupid reply: "If you can provide me with a medieval copy of James Anderson's *Old Charges*, I shall be prepared to pay any price for it!" In the meanwhile he approved the purchase of

[13] *Quinze Années*, 353.

the *Book of Hours*. I still was unhappy because it was my feeling that a finance inspector is not qualified to have the power to force an opinion of his own on the contents of our acquisitions.

Once I consciously cheated a finance inspector. We had asked for a manuscript on approval from a London bookdealer, probably Maggs with whom we used to work, and brought it into the country with a form used for temporary entries. We looked carefully at the book, decided to buy it and forgot about the form. A couple of years later the inspector enquired whether we had returned the book or still had it. If we still had it we had to pay X percent of custom duties. I always resented paying such duties on works of art with which we enriched the national patrimonium. A staff member and I read carefully the form in which our fine, illuminated fifteenth-century manuscript was described as "an old book in paper weighing one kilo and a half." We looked at one another and thought of the same thing. After a few minutes he came back with a worthless old book weighing three pounds, which he would take next morning to London. Since he did not like London he decided not to stay overnight and he had arranged to take the first plane in the morning in order to be able to come back the same day. Early in the morning he was at the airport and at the customs he refused to pass without a stamp on his form proving that he had exported the described item. There was no customs officer available at the departure hall and he was advised to look for one at the arrival hall. There he found a sleepy one, who did not understand what it was all about but who stamped the form. When my distinguished staff member wanted to proceed to the aircraft the customs official did not let him pass but said that this was the exit and that he had to go back to the entrance hall. So he did, and just before he was going to pass the gate it suddenly occurred to him that there was no longer any reason to visit London. He took a bus back to the centre of town and he went immediately to the Library anxious to tell his story to me and the others.

The real weakness of my position was that I generally did not have the money to buy the books which tempted my curators or sometimes myself. I have made several public statements and I have written often about the difference between private and public buying. I have always been very keen on this point and all responsible staff members shared my opinion. To trace a valid border line is not an easy task. On both sides confusing issues may blur the ultimate outcome. Above I have already referred to the Solvay collection. One of my outstanding curators, Georges Colin, an authority on Renaissance bookbindings, insisted continually that we should buy modern French *"livres de peintres,"* those books which have been dubbed "non-books" by a British critic. I resisted stubbornly using the argument that these are the type of books which should be given to us. Thanks to Mrs. Solvay, I was right and we have them all now: Picasso, Braque, Dunoyer de Segonzac, Matisse, Dali, etc., even among them Poe's *Raven* illustated by Manet and Renard's *Histoires naturelles* with the Toulouse-Lautrec lithographs.

Some time ago I mentioned to Georges Colin that I was collecting notes on my major acquisitions and with a smile he told me "Don't forget the one which was bought without your knowledge, although you have every reason to be proud of it." I looked at him rather puzzled and wondered if his paradoxical statement was not one of his mild attacks on me when we were in disagreement. But what he added was so complimentary that I cannot resist the pleasure to tell the whole story. In 1970, when I was travelling abroad, Georges Colin received a telephone call from the Dutch book dealer, Menno Hertzberger, who is called by his colleagues the father of the International League of Antiquarian Booksellers, a real connoisseur of rare books and a shrewd businessman. He offered for sale a bound volume in which were gathered five manuscripts and eleven printed opuscula, among which a nine-page pamphlet printed at Liège by a certain Cornelius de Delft around 1500. If seven Flemish cities could claim a typographical workshop in the fifteenth century, the oldest printing house in the Walloon part of the country which could be quoted before the discovery of Menno Hertzberger, corroborated by Professor W. Hellinga, was that of Henri Rochefort who printed a tiny booklet at Liège no earlier than 1556. Consequently, Hertzberger's offer was a capital one. Capital for sure, but expensive too. He wanted one million Belgian francs. Georges Colin did not hesitate for one second and answered, "Send me the book at once and if it is all right the Library will buy it at the quoted price." And it did, while I was still away. Georges Colin had, however, a very clever explanation. "Actually," he told me sometime later, "we owe this major acquisition to you because I would never have engaged the Library in such an important commitment if I hadn't been convinced from the outset that I acted in full accordance with your own views in such matters." How right he was! Time having passed, I am even tempted to say that it was a bargain. Besides the opusculum which enabled us to gain half a century in the introduction of typography at Liège (for those familiar with local politics an achievement far beyond bibliographical niceties), the volume contained nine incunabula, one of which, printed at Cologne by the Augustinus Printer, was completely unknown.

Another aspect of the borderline between private and public collecting is a balanced cooperation between the two parties. I have been lucky in this way. Among different outstanding private book collectors I would cite Robert de Belder from Kalmthout-Antwerp who had brought together an exceptionally good botanical library over a rather limited number of years. When he went to London for book auctions we often agreed on specific lots where I gave my upper limit and which he or his dealer would try to buy for the Library, but which he would buy for himself if the bid had to be higher. It sometimes happened that he even left the book with us when it was knocked down at a higher price than the one upon which we had agreed. It was of course easy to come to a basic agreement, a connivence as the French would say, because botanical literature is a congenial field. The Royal Library in Brussels had been fortunate at the time of its official founding in 1837 to acquire the library of Charles van Hulthem (1764-1832), the owner being as fond of books as of plants. The botanical items in this library were numerous and of high quality and his interest in botany matched his appetite for books. A rose had been named after him and Robert de Belder went to Uzbekistan to find a rare specimen. With such leanings it is easy to respect any borderline or to ignore it when it is more convenient.

Belgium is the cradle of the first book printed in the English language and the first one in French too, both by Caxton at Bruges, probably in 1474 and 1475. About the first one, everyone agrees on the priority; about the second one, discordant points of view exist. This is quite normal since it is difficult to admit, at least for a large number of people, that the first book in the language of Villon could have been printed outside of France. This is however an unimportant detail in my story. Since I would never be in a position to buy a Gutenberg Bible which is still conspicuously missing in the national book collections, although my old friend

Kraus had one for sale, [14] I decided to try to buy a Bruges Caxton of which none were on the shelves of the Library. Once again, H.P. Kraus had a copy of the *Recuyell of the historyes of Troye*, Caxton's first book printed at Bruges. Since we could not afford it, I finally was able to buy a copy of Caxton's second Bruges book, *The Game and Play of the Chess*, [15] which actually was a duplicate from the Pierpont Morgan Library in New York and which had been put up for sale at Sotheby's. The price was incredibly high and I did not have the slightest idea how I would bring the required amount of money together. Finally a friend, Marcel Van Audenhove, who was the director of a public bank, granted me a loan without interest and the book was ours. It was my firm belief at the time and it still is today, that the national library of the country which introduced typography in English to the wide world, needed to own a good old Caxton. And one is not enough.

Since the Bruges Caxton was the most expensive book which the Library had bought up till then I could stop my purchasing story here. I can, however, not resist the temptation to recall the story of the acquisition of a complete set of the Kelmscott Press publications. [16] At the time I was envious of the Royal Library in the Hague, which had not only a complete set, but even a specially designed cupboard to keep it in. When R.C.H. Briggs, secretary of the William Morris Society in London, asked me if the Library would be willing to house a commemorative William Morris exhibition, I did not hesitate for one minute to accept this proposal. At the time, I did not yet have the slightest idea that one day the Library would acquire the Henry van de Velde Archives, but I had already published my first article, "*William Morris in Flanders*," to which Henry van de Velde was central. Thanks to R.C.H. Briggs, the Library was able to buy from Quaritch in 1958, with whom we were not accustomed to deal, a complete Kelmscott Press set at a most reasonable price. For many years R.C.H. Briggs and I kept our correspondence alive and William Morris generated in the Library an interest in private presses which is shared by a number of staff members.

[14] While correcting the proofs I learned that he sold it to the city where it was printed more than five hundred years ago.

[15] *Cinq Années*, 131.

[16] *Quinze Années*, 407.

As a rule the Library would only afford to buy "Belgian" books, either in Belgium, or, mostly, abroad. When we published *Quinze Années d'Acquisitions* in 1969, I decided to mention for each entry the name of the dealer from whom we bought it. This was a rather revolutionary decision in my opinion because the vast majority of our acquisitions were purchased abroad and I expected that the local book dealers would protest. There was not the slightest reaction and I was disappointed.

As an exception to the rule of "Belgian" books, I would mention the acquisition of foreign books which were owned by Belgian collectors and which turned up for sale. One such example was the *Horloge de Sapience* to which I referred earlier. Another one is the purchase of a collection of one thousand Japanese books of the seventeenth, eighteenth and nineteenth centuries. A physician, Professor at the University of Liège, Hans de Winiwarter, had spent a lifetime assembling this collection, which showed his real connoisseurship of Japanese literature. His heirs and I knew nothing about the subject, except that we shared an equal delight in the many woodcuts of the collection. Marcel Florkin, a distinguished biologist of Liège University, had brought us together, not because of his biological interest but he was also an outstanding art critic and was very much interested in Japanese prints. We agreed that each of us would look for an expert to estimate the value of the collection. Since at the time I went rather regularly to the British Museum, I asked the director, Sir Frank Francis, if he had a staff member who was an expert on Japanese books. Of course he had an outstanding one, Kenneth Gardner, and through his good offices we were easily able to come to an agreement with the owner and to buy the collection. This smooth transaction left me with three unrelated recollections: Marcel Florkin getting a few prints out of the deal; Chantal Kozyreff-Rouffart, a staff member of the Royal Museum of Art and History at Brussels, being the only person in Belgium able to catalogue the collection and still working on it after many years; Kenneth Gardner, a delightful man, being for a short time Francis' successor in the British Museum, but apparently old Japanese books befitting him better than modern British bureaucracy, resigned his post and went back to his beloved books.

This is no way to end the pages on purchases. Fortunately there is no way to end adequately this ongoing process. So, rather arbitrarily I shall pick a last acquisition which will allow me to illustrate one more unexpected aspect of public book buying. Since the Library acquired (immediately after the French Revolution as a result of the secularization of religious properties) the autograph manuscript of Thomas a Kempis' *Imitatio* – the most read book after the Bible, which came from the Museum Bollandium in Antwerp – it had been collecting systematically the different editions of this classic of religious literature. This was of course an ambitious programme, since more than three thousand editions and over seven hundred manuscripts have been recorded. A unique opportunity to expand its holdings presented itself in 1961 when a Liège bookdealer, Halbart, offered in the catalogue of an auction the well-known Ancion collection of 762 Kempisiana. The curator of manuscripts, François Masai, told the dealer that we were interested in the whole collection and the latter decided to apply a rather unusual technique to his auction. At the opening he announced that at the end of the sale, he would aggregate all the lots, *faire la masse*, as he said. All the dealers in the room left as one man and we bought shamefully the whole set for a ridiculously low price. It brought our Thomas a Kempis' collection to about fifty manuscripts, twenty-five incunabula and short of a thousand later editions. A nice way to end this story would be to note that to compensate for the rather forced transfer of the religious collections to the national public collection after the French Revolution, the board of trustees of the Royal Library always had, from the very beginning, a Bollandist as a member. He was always an internationally esteemed expert on medieval manuscripts. The one I knew best was Father M. Coens who was familiar with all dead languages and who wrote simple poetry in his mother tongue, Dutch. He was the sweetest man one could imagine and I, who liked him very much, was not exactly sweet when I asked him from time to time, "Which volume of the *Acta Sanctorum* was put on the Index?" His soft answer was each time, "You know very well which one."

Auguste Lambiotte, president of the Société des Bibliophiles et Iconophiles de Belgique was instrumental in setting up a Society of Friends of the Royal Library. He wanted to start immediately with the organization after we met for the first time but I favoured temporizing in order to wait for the dedication of the new building before starting a drive for members. Before the new society was on

its way, Auguste Lambiotte had died and its first president was one
of his oldest friends, Achilles van Acker from Bruges, a distinguished but unconventional Belgian statesman. Before he entered
politics he was a modest bookdealer in his home town. After half a
century of public life – he was to become prime minister after
World War II and he ended his career as Speaker of the House –
his interest in books was still great. He not only collected them but
he read them. He was not in the French sense of the word a
bibliophile, because most of his books were not expensive. He
confined his interest to local folklore and popular literature.
Popular is the best word to characterize his strange personality. He
spoke a language of his own and he had difficulty in pronouncing
the sound "ch" which led to an unending number of jokes. I always
suspected him of having invented some himself. To the American
officers who liberated the country at the end of World War II and
who had to deal with him on basic issues such as food supply, he
was   an   impenetrable   sphinx   notwithstanding   his   open-
mindedness. He used this technique as a stronghold to the benefit
of the population as a whole. How often did he tell me the story of
the American general who wanted to organize the coal supply of
the country. Achilles van Acker answered all his arguments with
the simple words, "It is impossible." When at the end the general
insisted to know why everything was impossible, he showed the full
measure of his impregnability in his reply, "It is impossible because it is impossible." He rose, looked the general in the eye,
shook hands warmly with him and said, "We understand each
other, don't we?" He had it his way and it was the right way because
our houses were heated again.

Under his presidency, the Friends of the Library developed well
and year after year they added important documents to the collections of the Library. Most of them have been drawings, by Jacob
Jordaens among others. But also an extremely rare and important
Plantin binding, and even a Japanese *dahrani*. The Society often
distributed among its members reproductions of the original
which had been given to the Library. One of the most pleasant was
a fifteenth-century drawing, preparatory to a tapestry, of the
Chemin de paradis by Jean Germain. [17] Friends are undoubtedly an

---

[17] *Cinq Années*, 40.

important link for a public institution with the society at large which it tries to serve. These links are successful when they are considered by both sides as a privilege.

A last gift which I want to mention is the coin collection discovered at Liberchies, [18] a small Roman settlement about twenty-five miles south of Brussels. It allows me to recall that the national coin collection belongs to the National Library, which is rather unusual and to tell a beautiful story. The treasure was discovered by an amateur, P. Claes, who had been digging at the place for nearly twenty years. All the usual details followed: immense excitement, lack of confidence in other people, dedication to numismatics, etc. Finally through the good offices of a friend, the National Bank decided to buy the find and to present it to the Royal Library. A gift from one public institution to another public institution can only happen in a broad-minded country or, to put it less modestly, in the broad-minded representatives of public institutions. In the meanwhile the Coin Room of the Library is proud to have the largest single find, but for one in Naples, of 368 gold items of uninterrupted Roman emperors of the first and second centuries, (63-166 A.D.). Among them is an elsewhere unrecorded Vespasian-De Ludaeis coin.

Although I have already announced a couple of times "the last gift" I cannot omit John Slocum's copy of Justus Lipsius' *De Constantia* [19] which he gave to the Library upon my departure as a symbol of our long-standing friendship. John and I met first in Brussels where he was responsible for the public relations of the American pavilion at the World's Fair in 1958. I always wondered how he took care of his job, because he was at the Royal Library all the time. His own book collection, mainly Flemish sixteenth-century books, was packed in the cellar of the Folger Shakespeare Library in Washington, where some years later he was going to become president of the Society of Friends. I stayed with John and Eileen in Cairo in 1962, where he was with USIS and I had a UNESCO assignment. I brought many Egyptian visitors to his house, about which he was extremely happy because they were often reluctant to accept American invitations. My international

[18] *Cinq Années*, 94.

[19] The book is described in detail in the first pages of *Cinq Années d'Acquisition 1969-1973*.

status apparently helped a lot. In Cairo his interest in coins began to outweigh the one he had in books and there, also, started his passion for Armenian culture, on which he is an authority now. Most of the time we met in Washington or Newport and we visited many private libraries. Although a Harvard alumnus, he has given his James Joyce collection to Yale, because the latter was willing not to restrict its use to scholars belonging to its own community. This is a type of decision for which I always had a weak spot in my heart.

I started these recollections with the story of the *Llangattock Hours* for which I went to see the Principal Private Secretary of the King in order to obtain a special grant to buy this outstanding manuscript. For the reason which I explained earlier, the Library did not acquire the book. Now I am going to close the circle, as we say in French. Another completely unknown Flemish manuscript, *The Spinola Hours*, was offered for sale at Sotheby's in June 1976. It was much later than the *Llangattock Hours*, 1510, and a product of the Ghent-Bruges school. Bob Delaissé's successor, Georges Dogaer, was the one to be excited now, more so since his doctoral dissertation had been devoted to the last Flemish school of manuscript illustration. If Bob Delaissé looked towards the van Eyck brothers, Georges Dogaer compared the new discovery to the renowned *Grimani Hours*. When the *Spinola Hours* came up for sale I was no longer at the Library and my successor came to see me at the Royal Palace. The whole story of the *Llangattock Hours* came back to my mind and I promised to help. It really did not take too much time and effort to find ways and means to be able to bid up to $ 500.000, a staggering figure for such a late *Book of Hours*. It was knocked down at $ 750.000. The Library missed it and it was bought by H.P. Kraus, who has been both my benediction and my curse during the years I was able to buy books for the national collections. At the time I vaguely remembered what H.P. Kraus had said when he presented his book collection on horses to Yale University: one of my ideals is to bring the right book to the right place... In all fairness I should add that we were not even the underbidders.

Postscript 1: This chapter was written and I had already left the book trade for some time, when H.P. and I met again indirectly and professionally. He and I were interested in the same book which came up at an auction in London. Through a Belgian book dealer, who was on friendly terms with both of us, I asked him not to bid and leave the book to my agent. Though he was shocked at my proposal he accepted and I remain grateful to him for his withdrawal.

Postscript 2: Postscript 1 was written when H.P. published his autobiography *A Rare Book Saga*. It contains his version of the purchase of the *Llangattock Hours*. It is curious to discover how differently we remember the same events.

7. *More Small Talk about Great Books* [1]

OVER A PERIOD of about twenty years, Jan Deschamps had bought so many Middle Dutch manuscripts that I kiddingly told him that he should get ready for a large exhibition. A good occasion presented itself sooner than expected when a local Flemish literary and historical society wanted to celebrate its one hundredth anniversary. Over the years this society had done a tremendous job in re-evaluating Flemish literature of the Middle Ages, which from the thirteenth to the sixteenth century had an importance equal to French, German or English literature. All over Europe similar societies, which based their interest on a romantic view of the national past (which was always glorious) were active in reviving popular, vernacular literature of a given region. Never was I so much aware of the international impact of this movement as during my visit to the *Matica Slovenská* at Martin, a small city between Bratislava and the Tatra mountains. This national library started modestly in 1863 as a local society interested in Slovak language, literature, history and culture.

---

[1] In the preceding chapter I did not refer to acquisitions by the Royal Library of medieval manuscripts in the Dutch language, because I was saving them for a paper I had promised to write for the Kurt Köster Festschrift. Since the Library honoured the good old maxim to "build on strength", it was very active in the field of Dutch literature of the Middle Ages. Another explanation of the priority which this field received was the zeal of one staff member, Jan Deschamps. When I was ready with a first draft of my paper for the Festschrift I gave it to him for translation. When it came back to me it was twice as long as the original version, many times as accurate, and I would naughtily say, half as readable. For the purpose of this chapter I have retranslated it again into English and I have resisted the temptation to cut down the *apparatus criticus* except for footnotes and call numbers. My relations with Kurt Köster have been transferred to a more appropriate part of this book.

My colleague Jan Deschamps organized the exhibition of 125 items for which he borrowed from fifty libraries in Europe and in the United States, notwithstanding the wealth of our own collection. He also wrote the catalogue, which was out of print three weeks after its publication. The well-known firm of E. J. Brill at Leiden, Holland, brought a second edition on the market. It had never happened before that a catalogue of the Library was taken over by a commercial firm. Unique also about this catalogue was the fact that it was issued only in Dutch, while the Belgian law on publications by national institutions required that the two national languages should be treated on equal terms. At the Library we always abided strictly by this law and why we sinned in this case is explained in the following chapter.

When I started to work with Jan Deschamps I did not have the slightest idea of what was in store for me. He is the most happy man I ever met in my professional life. For him the only topic of importance existing on earth is Flemish literature of the Middle Ages. It protected him marvellously against the hardships of daily life, which he was not spared. Unfortunately it forced me, over many years, to give more attention to his favourite subject than I was prepared to do. At a certain moment he made me act as if any good library collection had to fall into two parts: on the one hand Flemish medieval manuscripts and on the other hand all the rest. He was irresistible and I made many mistakes which I do not regret. One day his boss, who was to become my successor, said to me about him: "If he could exchange me, in a north African *souk*, for a fragment of a Flemish manuscript, he would not hesitate for one moment." They were and remain on good terms.

Jan Deschamps added to the collection about 180 manuscripts, either fully or partially written in Dutch, which brought the Library's holdings to a total of 800, by far the largest in the world. I am going to tell the story of only 5 among them: the mystic play *Die eerste bliscap van Maria;* a volume with nine tracts by the mystic author Jan van Leeuwen; the unique manuscript copy of the moral play *Elckerlyc;* six fragments of the animal epic *Van den vos Reynaerde;* and the only known complete copy of Jacob van Maerlant's novel, *Die hystorie van Troyen.*

The Dominican monk St. G. Axters, the author of an authoritative book on mystic and ascetic literature from the Low Countries and a faithful visitor to our Manuscript Room, told me some time early in the sixties, that he had heard in Zürich about a manuscript with seven Middle Dutch mysteries offered for sale by a local bookdealer and that I could collect more information from L. Caflisch, vice-director of the city's central library. I talked it over with Jan Deschamps who guessed immediately that it could not be a manuscript with seven mystery plays, but probably the unique copy of the hidden mystery of *Die eerste bliscap van Maria,* which was indeed known as the first in a row of seven. Of course he proved to be right. In the middle of the fifteenth century the city authorities of Brussels announced that a mystic play with one of the seven joys of Our Lady would be performed each year after the procession. The seven mysteries were performed for the first time in 1448-1454 and for the last time in 1560-1566. Only the first and the last of the plays have been preserved in a manuscript written by the same hand. The seventh one, called *Die sevenste bliscap van onser vrouwen,* had already been acquired by the Library in 1882, while the first play had been put on auction in Brussels in 1866 by the collector P. C. Serrure and bought, together with other precious items, by the Duke of Arenberg. As stated in the preceding chapter the latter's library was taken out of the country at the end of World War I and was kept secretly in different places, where the books were inaccessible to scholars. Parts of the library came on the market in the early fifties and the Royal Library looked in vain for *Die eerste bliscap* while it bought other books from the Arenberg collection from two New York dealers.

Following Father Axters' advice, Jan Deschamps wrote to L. Caflisch, who confirmed that it was indeed the manuscript of the Bliscap, and very prudently took an option with the dealer to prevent his selling it to another customer. He quoted the price, adding that it was rather high because two New York dealers had shown interest in the book. Jan Deschamps and I agreed easily on the wording of our answer. First the two dealers, as Caflisch had already suggested, were acting on our behalf and secondly no other library, in Belgium or even in Holland, would care to pay an exaggerated price for thirty-eight small parchment leaves. Consequently we offered a price three or four times lower than the quoted one. In view of such a difference L. Caflisch backed out, but gave us the name of the dealer. After a calculated silence Jan Deschamps wrote to the dealer and asked him to quote a price. After a calculated silence the bookseller sent us the manuscript on approval and quoted a price which was higher than the one that L. Caflisch had given to us.

I was furious and ordered Jan Deschamps to send the manuscript back immediately. He however was clever enough to ask permission to keep it for a few days in order to study it carefully after it had been hidden for such a long time. Apparently he was counting on a change of mind on my part and in agreement with the senior librarian in the manuscript room, but without my knowledge, he put it in the safe for as long as I or the dealer would not inquire about it. For many days I was uncertain and changed my mind all the time about whether to send it back or not, whether to keep the literary value in mind and forget about the price or to ignore the intellectual temptation and to decide that the price was impossible. It happened that at the time I ran into my friend Garmt Stuiveling, professor of Dutch literature at the University of Amsterdam, and I put my whole problem on his shoulders without giving the quoted price, but asking him how much he would be prepared to pay for it. His price was quite a bit higher and with a feeling of relief I decided on the spot to buy the book. I asked the dealer for the invoice and told him that I would appreciate a generous discount. He gave us ten percent off and the first Bliscap joined the seventh one on our shelves. When the accession was made public I received a lot of congratulations. Today, after so many years, I am not yet sure that I met Garmt Stuiveling by accident and that his price was a spontaneous answer to my question. When I pressed Jan Deschamps on this point he denied everything with saintly innocence.

The purchase of the *Jan van Leeuwen codex* was somewhat simpler than that of the Bliscap. It was again Father Axters who put us on the right track. Early in the war he saw in the Dominican monastery of Lier, a small town south-east of Antwerp, an imposing parchment volume with nine tracts by Jan van Leeuwen, who is known in Dutch literature as the "good cook" – goede coc – because he cooked for thirty-four years for the monks of the Groenendael priory near Brussels, where he was a disciple of Jan van Ruusbroec. I may as well add here that the French Revolution brought the important manuscripts of Jan van Ruusbroec to the Royal Library where they are one of the treasures of medieval Dutch writing, with a stunning devotional power as well as an exceptional literary style. The Belgian Nobel prize winner,

Maurice Maeterlinck, has translated some parts of Jan van Ruusbroec into French under the title of *Ornements des noces spirituelles* (Dutch: *Die Cierheyt der Gheestelicker Brulocht*). *The Adornment of the Spiritual Marriage*, was the title of an English translation published in 1916 and reprinted later.

Jan van Leeuwen collected his writings in 1400, but the manuscript has been lost, except for six leaves. Fortunately half a century after the original manuscript had been written a copy in two volumes was made, of which only one – the Lier codex – has been preserved. Near the end of the war Father Axters published a study on Jan van Leeuwen and included large extracts from his writings. In interested circles the significance of the author had taken shape and when Jan Deschamps was entrusted with microfilming all relevant medieval Dutch manuscripts preserved in Belgian libraries, Jan van Leeuwen was naturally included. It is worthwhile recording that the initiative of microfilming the literary inheritance of the Low Countries was taken by the library division of the General Conference of Dutch Letters. This conference had been held yearly since 1951, in turn in Holland and in Belgium. Through meetings of writers, playwrights and journalists it recognized the living unity and diversity of Dutch language and literature in the two countries, while it recorded the same facts through its publishers and librarians. From the very beginning the decision was taken that every six years the Queen of Holland would give the Grand Prize of Dutch Letters to a Flemish author, while every other sixth year the King of the Belgians would honour a Dutch writer. Up till now Herman Teirlinck (1956), Adriaan Roland Holst (1959), Stijn Streuvels (1962), Jacques Bloem (1965), Gerard Walschap (1968), Simon Vestdijk (1971), Marnix Gijsen (1974), Willem Frederik Hermans (1977) have been the prize winners.

For most of them English translations are available. One of them, Marnix Gijsen, was for twenty-three years director of the Belgian information service in New York, where he was caught by the outbreak of World War II, and has written a lot in English – no fiction however. Actually his Dutch fiction hardly deserves this name since the contents are always autobiographical. Through its style it reaches the realm of fiction. The most recent Dutch laureate, Willem Frederik Hermans, is a curious phenomenon. After a lectureship at the Dutch University of Groningen he turned his back on his native country, except in the use of his mother tongue. He studied the geological formation of a Belgian region and afterwards went south to live in France. When he accepted the prize from the hands of the King he surprised all those present by imploring the Belgians to protect the integrity of the Dutch language against the contempt with which it was treated by the Dutch authorities. This way of speaking is not often heard either north or south of the political border between the two countries. The Flemish novelist Maurice Roelants who started these Conferences must have turned over in his grave for pure joy when he heard it.

W. F. Hermans who worries about the preservation of the Dutch language, and who collects typewriters, would certainly be interested in Jan Deschamps' microfilming gadgetry, if not in Jan van Leeuwen himself. The Lier codex was brought to the Royal Library for microfilming and its value was assessed for insurance reasons. Before it came to the Library Jan Deschamps had gone to Lier to have a careful look at the book. Meditation must have raised his eyes now and then, from the page to the ceiling, and to his horror – or to his satisfaction? – he discovered that the venerable manuscript was constantly exposed to the dangers of fire. He inspected the attics and his conclusion was abundantly clear. Back in Brussels he talked to Father Axters, who in turn talked to his colleagues in religion. The agreement on the price was easy and the codex joined the other three volumes of Jan van Leeuwen on the shelves of the Library. Nearly all extant writings of the author are now available for scholars in Brussels. Jan Deschamps was still intrigued by the history of the Lier codex, which had an erased ex libris. He finally could identify the original owner as Johan IV, count of Nassau Dillenburg (1410-1475), who is not unknown to Dutch historians.

Elckerlyc, "Everyman," is a title which belongs to the literature of the world. The Royal Library owes to Jan Deschamps the acquisition of the unique Dutch manuscript version of the moralizing text by Petrus Diesthemius. Way back in the thirties an expert on Dutch medieval literature, L. Willems, gave a lecture on the attribution of the text to a new author and based his argument on a critical analysis of the text. The archivist of the city of Antwerp, F. Prims, was in the audience and told L. Willems that he recently had become the owner of a sixteenth-century manuscript with the text of *Elckerlyc*. Upon Willems' question as to whether it was a copy of the printed editions of 1495, ± 1501 or ± 1525 he could give no answer but promised to send him the manuscript. Its careful examination led L. Willems to two conclusions: first that the text had so many variations from the printed versions that it must have been a copy of a lost printed edition, and secondly that the manuscript was written at the end of the sixteenth century and contained other texts most of which had disappeared because 85 folios had been lost and only 109 were still present. Librarians have always been intrigued by manuscript copies of printed books. Curt Buhler of the Pierpont Morgan Library in New York has written very well about this unnatural relation in his *The Fifteenth-Century Book*. I for myself will never forget that late-sixteenth-century miniature which represents a . . . printing press, in the *Chants royaux sur la conception*.

F. Prims had been generous to L. Willems, but afterwards he and his brother who inherited the manuscript became very reluctant to show it to interested scholars or to have it photographed. The enhanced commercial value of an unpublished document may have influenced their attitude. Anyhow Jan Deschamps ran into the son of the owner at the University of Louvain, and there is no reason to tell once more the story of the arguments used which resulted in the sale of the book to the Library. In this case, however, the paper of the eight loose quires was in bad shape and a serious job of repairing had to be done in order to prevent further decay. As regards the last two books I was hardly aware of Jan Deschamps' dealings with the owners, but the same is not true for the two following ones.

What all connoisseurs of medieval Dutch literature wholeheartedly hope for, but nearly fail to achieve, is the discovery of an unknown version of a literary masterpiece. This happened to Jan Deschamps in 1971 or, as he would have it, to the book dealer A. van Loock who was a neighbour and a friend of the Library. In the binding of a small Bible, fragments of a fifth reading of the epical animal tale *Van den vos Reynaerde* (Reynard the Fox) were found. Van Loock had bought from a dealer in Monte Carlo a beautifully bound volume with the sixth and the fifth parts – in this order – of an edition of the Old Testament printed in six parts by Johannes Knobloch in Strassburg in 1552. Jan Deschamps looked at the binding and saw on the innerside of the back cover a pasted parchment with a Dutch poem unknown to him. He asked Van Loock if he would be willing to detach the parchment folio from the binding and sell it to the Library – to which the dealer agreed immediately. A few days later both met again with the loose leaf and the bound volume. Jan Deschamps identified the fragment of the poem (a prologue of twenty-six lines and the first twenty-eight verses of the poem proper) as belonging to the life of a saint, who turned out later to be Alexius.

Once the parchment had been taken away it was easy to realize that the binding consisted of different layers of paper pasted together and Jan Deschamps suggested again to detach them and see if they did not yield one or another interesting text. From the front and back cover twenty-two pieces of paper were taken out which belonged to five different manuscripts and one printed book. Five pieces from the front cover and one from the back had a Reynaert text of which other fragments have not yet been found. Though the Library had an option on the first parchment, I wanted to buy the whole lot as quickly as possible. A. van Loock had been so happy with the discovery that it was loudly announced in the press and I began to worry about the price. I also had to leave the country for a rather long period and I did not want to take the risk that my Flemish friends would blame me for missing this new version of their beloved Reynaert, which had shown up in the shadow of the Library. Before the dealer entered my office to conclude the sale I took one of the most risky decisions of my life. As soon as he sat down I said "Whatever your price may be, I buy the fragments. Quote a price and I accept." He looked a bit puzzled at me and quoted his price. Somewhat later he told me that his price was twenty-five percent lower than the one he had in his mind when he entered my office and which was based on consultation with colleagues in Belgium and in Holland. Much later, after having paid a stupendous amount of taxes on the sale, he told me that it would have been better for all concerned, if he had made us a present of the fragments. (I said to myself that I had to fight to the bitter end with the government to add five percent to my budget, while it was making a profit of at least fifty percent on the books which I bought). I imagine he had acquired that volume, the first two missing, for next to nothing. And what about those two missing volumes? What are they hiding in their bindings? Incomplete sets are a curse to any collection, private as well as public, but in this case Jan Deschamps is already smelling his prey.

As Jan Deschamps always studied thoroughly the contents of his new acquisitions, he came to the conclusion that the manuscript, which must have counted 55 folios and 369 lines, was written around 1425 and showed original textual variations from the other known versions. At an international seminar on medieval tales held at Louvain he gave a lecture based on the new fragments, which he published somewhat later.

The last medieval Dutch manuscript to be mentioned here is the most precious one; the story of its acquisition is a long one, but deserves to be told in full. The complete version of Jacob van Maerlant's *Hystorie van Troyen,* written in two columns on paper folios, entered Jan Deschamps' life in the middle of 1969 and entered the collection of the Library in the middle of 1973. Jacob van Maerlant, the prince of Dutch literature in the Middle Ages, had written his history of Troy around 1264, as a free adaptation of Benoît de Sainte-More's novel, adding extracts from Virgil's Aeneid and Statius' Achilleid and reaching 41.000 lines, where Benoît de Sainte-More had only 30.000.

Jan Deschamps' attention was drawn to the manuscript by F. Dressler, curator of the Manuscript Room of the Bayerische Staatsbibliothek in Munich, where the former was working to prepare the exhibition mentioned above. The manuscript had been offered for sale to the Bavarian library, which felt that it could not afford such an expensive purchase for a document belonging to a foreign culture. Munich was not *der richtige Ort.* F. Dressler advised Jan Deschamps to see the owner, Count Friedrich von Loë at castle Wissen near Kevelaer, located between the Dutch border and the Rhine, in order to borrow the manuscript for the exhibition and possibly to buy it for the Royal Library where it belonged. At this stage Jan Deschamps decided to inform me adding immediately that this would be our last chance to acquire a chivalric romance by Jacob van Maerlant and to fill at the same time a distressing gap in our otherwise outstanding collections. The manuscript was written in 1470-80 in an eastern variant of Dutch that was common at the time between Cleves and Guelder. Most probably it was commissioned by Wessel IV van den Loe who had lived in Wissen since 1461 and whose name appears on the inside of the front cover. It had remained ever since in the family, whose name was Germanized to von Loë. Jan Deschamps knew the contents of the manuscript because it had already been referred to in 1861 by J. D. Wolff. Two years later J. Verdam had published large extracts, and finally, in 1889-1892, N. De Paux and E. Gaillard had edited the whole text in four volumes.

Direct relations with the owner started with Jan Deschamps asking permission to borrow the manuscript for the exhibition and requesting a price if it were for sale. Count von Loë agreed to the loan and quoted a price which I could not justify with the government because it was too high. We suggested that he should personally bring the manuscript to the exhibition, so that we could examine it carefully on this occasion and talk face to face about the price with the purpose of coming to an agreement. Although he accepted our proposal, he himself could not come for one reason or another to the exhibition and the book was brought from Wissen to Brussels by a messenger. A few months later Jan Deschamps took it back but the owner was absent. Again some months passed and finally we agreed on a date to go together, Jan Deschamps and I, to Wissen.

On our way to the Rhineland we staged a rehearsal where I would quote all the arguments to bring the price down and Jan Deschamps would counter them with the Count's view on the matter. My first point was that the manuscript was written on paper and not on parchment. Jan looked at me with commiseration because I did not know that all such manuscripts were written on paper. When he began to quote examples I stopped him, anxious to use my second and more powerful argument. The manuscript had not the slightest illumination, not one miniature. This time he held me in sovereign contempt. This was a highly literary text which no one in the middle ages would have thought of adorning with pictures. I faintly remembered that in Brussels we had a beautiful Jacob van Maerlant manuscript of the thirteenth century on vellum and illustrated with small but outstanding miniatures, but I was afraid to mention it in the present context, knowing it would prove again my ignorance of the real cultural tradition. And after all I relied on my last and third argument: the text was written two centuries after the author's death. This blow he did not expect since he remained silent for a while. His silence had however another purpose, because it allowed him to collect his courage to answer such a stupid remark. Did I know that it was the first full text of the long novel by Jacob van Maerlant? Did I know that full texts of this type are practically non-existent? Did I know that we had none in the Library? Whether I knew it or not I do not remember, as I do not remember that we actually had this discussion in the car to Wissen. It is Jan Deschamps who remembers it all.

Where we fully agree in our recollections is that we had lunch in the house of the manager, the castle being under repair. When entering the grounds I saw the roof partly removed and I said to myself (not to Jan Deschamps) this manuscript is going to be ours, because I knew of some precious books that had to be sold to repair roofs of castles and cloisters. Everything which we ate and drank was home-made and we talked for a long time about the charms of rural life before the siege of Troy began. It was then, I think, that our discussion about the weaknesses and strengths of the manuscript began, with the silent countess on my side, and the not always sufficiently silent Jan Deschamps on the other side of the fence. Anyhow we parted on good terms with a bridgeable distance between the two prices. On our way home Jan Deschamps acted as if we had already bought the book and, I think, he even congratulated me.

Another trimester passed before the Count and the Countess came to Brussels to conclude the deal. My luncheon was in an urban setting and I chose a faculty club in a last attempt to impress the owner with our purely intellectual interest in the manuscript and to agree on a price which the scholarly community could afford. The final agreement is not yet the end of the story. The count shared the ownership with his sister who had to be convinced to sell. Afterwards the University Library of Bonn had to state that it had no objections and finally the fiat of the Kultus-ministerium of the Land of Nordrhein-Westfalen had to be secured. When the book was officially registered in the inventory I had just left the Library but Jan Deschamps sent me a nice note.

Middle Dutch, medieval Dutch, Flemish, Netherlandish, Low Countries, all this double Dutch used in the preceding pages is rather confusing. If one asks a businessman in Rotterdam or a tourist guide in Bruges for an explanation the answers will be quite different, both rather remote from reality and both given in good faith. Many social, historical, geographical and even linguistical nuances are involved in the most superficial comments. Not that I have so many original observations to make about this rather complex state of affairs, but circumstances have forced me into it and I neither closed my eyes nor my ears. In the Middle Ages the Flemings, the southerners for the Dutch, established the common language through a number of literary texts such as those of which I have been talking above. In the seventeenth century the *spraeckmakende gemeent* – the "community which shaped the language" as the great Dutch poet Hooft said – shifted to the north, to what is today The Netherlands, and has remained there since. To avoid protests from the south I have to add immediately that the Flemish movement, to which I have referred already, has also, and to a certain point successfully, defended the idea that the same literary language was spoken or had to be spoken north and south of the political border which separates the two countries. For the present generation this is obvious, a bit more in the south than in the north where some conservative circles cannot imagine that Flemings would be able to speak Dutch.

It would of course not have much sense to pretend that there are no longer any linguistic differences between the two Dutch-speaking communities. The distinction is much smaller however than between English English and American English. The spelling is the same or the different spellings do not follow the borderline between the two countries. I am tempted to add here that some are using a Catholic spelling in the south – like one has Calvinist department stores in the north – but this would only confuse the issue. Spelling is anyhow no major component of a language, and languages which have a limited geographical distribution – for instance Dutch as compared with English or French – have a tendency to change their spelling rules more rapidly. The major differences, however are in pronunciation and vocabulary. Each country has its series of dialects and with some effort two common denominators in Holland and in Flanders may be identified. It is easy to hear if someone comes from the Hague or Antwerp. Brussels is more difficult because in this city being the southern-most outpost of the Dutch language a larger number of the small Dutch-speaking population makes a conscientious effort to avoid dialectal influences.

The difference in vocabulary results mainly from an unevenly distributed French and English influence, the Flemings knowing French better, the Dutch English better. Since in language matters nothing is ever simple a very typical Flemish reaction is a puritanical attitude towards French words. A Dutch newspaper will use more French words than a Flemish one, which will make an effort to adapt these words, often rather clumsily. Afrikaans goes even farther in this direction, actually for the same reason but in this case the big brother is English. And to complicate the analysis even a bit more, it would be correct to admit that the philologist easily detects more gallicisms in southern than in northern Dutch.

My able colleague and good friend, Kees Reedijk, director of the Royal Library in the Hague, and I have been observing for many years our common language phenomenon, he from the north and I from the south, both rather familiar with one another's vantage points. Since our basic agreement is quite large we have an un-avowed preference for differences. It so happens that neither of us is a devout church goer, but he has said more than once to me, "When I am talking to you I suffer from Calvinistic whiffs," whereupon my redundant answer is, "It is strange because you make me feel like a *pilaarbijter* (a pilaarbijter is a Flemish col-loquialism to designate someone who spends all his time in a Catholic church, literally someone who bites the pillar). It is quite natural to land immediately in the sphere of religion. In modern times religion no longer has the importance it used to command, but over the centuries it penetrated men's attitudes which now express themselves more in collective than in individual reactions. A Fleming will celebrate his sixtieth birthday, a Dutchman hopes to celebrate it. There is nothing anecdotical about this difference, it only shows how today the use of language denotes a split which occurred in the sixteenth century when Spanish forces kept the southern part of the Low Countries in the Roman church, while one can still argue whether the independence of the north is due to the Reformation or *vice versa*.

This difference has far-reaching consequences and brings me immediately back to my *idée fixe* about the horizontal borderline which separates Latin Europe from Germanic Europe, starting from Brussels and going as far as Munich with some meddling in the Helvetian cantons. There is no reason here to evoke the infalli-bility of the Pope as opposed to the democratic interpretations of the Bible to explain that Kees Reedijk and I have been giving the best parts of our life to two libraries which have not much more in common than their names, both being called royal, which stands in both cases for national.

The Royal Library in The Hague being part of a widely decentralized institutional framework has a clear-cut responsibility; whereas the French example of over-centralization having been copied with gusto in Belgium, the Royal Library in Brussels has a claim to wide competence. To say that both institutions are similar as regards the narrow field of the national book collection is not even true. As far as medieval and Renaissance manuscripts are concerned there is some similarity indeed. With modern literary autographs the difference is already apparent: in The Hague, the literary museum and archives is independent from the Royal Library, except that the director of the latter is *ex officio* director of the former; in Brussels the museum and archives of modern literary manuscripts is part of the Royal Library, although it has an independent budget and, as I have explained earlier, covers only French documents.

When it comes to printed books the gap widens. Traditionally the Hague library did not collect systematically the whole national book production and merely included those books published in Holland which fitted into its outspoken humanistic collection building. In Brussels the library has always considered it to be its prime responsibility to collect the national book production, in Dutch as well as in French, while its general collection building has customarily been encyclopedic. Behind this difference lures the long-standing and high-level tradition of Dutch publishing with its impressive roots in the cosmopolitan seventeenth century, while Belgian book production, in either language, had a very slow start in the second half of the nineteenth century only and is still struggling to establish its identity, towards the Dutch as well as the French predominance. Leading Flemish authors prefer as a rule a Dutch publisher, while a French-writing Belgian never frowns upon a Parisian publisher. These different backgrounds explain easily why the two national libraries, when they recently began to be involved in legal deposit legislation, did it from quite different angles.

Once we come to non-book material The Hague and Brussels belong to two worlds apart. The Royal Library of Belgium being a faithful copy of the Bibliothèque Nationale of France, it has a series of national collections under its roof which are spread over various institutions in Holland. The most extreme example is the national coins collection, *le médaillier national*. In The Hague a separate institution discharges this responsibility, while Paris and

Brussels are the only national libraries in the world which have numismatic departments. The national print collections are another instance at hand. In Belgium it is an important part of the national library, while in Holland the largest collection is to be found at the Rijksmuseum in Amsterdam. If one were to look in Holland for the equivalent of the map department of the Belgian national library, one would almost certainly end up in the national archives in The Hague. This allows me to boast of the *'s Grooten Atlas* in Brussels which has the best and oldest map of the port of Rotterdam.

As if the profiles of the two national libraries were not yet different enough, the last decade has added the vast area of national scientific and technical documentation, on the different handling of which a whole psychological treatise of national characteristics could be written. I am not going to do it, but it allows me to dwell for a few moments upon an incongruity, *the système D*, which not one Dutchman understands. Discussion is still open as to the origin of the expression – D has certainly something to do with *débrouillard* – its meaning however is clear to any Belgian regardless of sex and age. Some think that it appeared for the first time among the troops in the First World War, where circumstances were indeed favourable to describe an attitude of life where one had to try to make the best out of the worst, where small means justified small ends, where logical reasoning would lead nowhere, where one who is in an awkward situation gets out of it in a tricky way, where shortage of everything added a dimension to trifles. Well *système D* means all that and something more too. There is nothing grand, nothing noble, nothing brilliant about it, but in adversity it helps. The expression which comes closest to it in Belgian French is probably *tirer son plan*.

I came to use it in connection with the Belgian solution to the problem of scientific and technical documentation. In Holland the matter was handled in a considerate way, a high level-committee was set up representing all public and private authorities interested in the matter, reports on foreign solutions were evaluated in view of the specific national situation, a long-term programme was established and a carefully estimated budget was attached to it. All this took time, but progress was steady. In Belgium nothing of all that. Supported or pushed from the back by a few colleagues I tried to have immediately a service in operation, *vaille que vaille*, starting from an existing situation, which meant shifting around some persons and small parts of the budget, and finding out after two or three years of operation that we had managed to scrape along, that something comparable to a documentation centre began to take shape and deciding that it was about time to draw up a plan, to establish a programme and to look for adequate financial support. A kind of centre was operational while the Dutch were still busy with their feasibility study. But, once the Dutch got started the whole outfit was much better structured, the programme better balanced, the financial means more appropriate. The different handling of scientific and technical information and documentation is only one example among many, but it certainly is typical.

Instead of adding other instances I am going to come back a last time to the two Royal Libraries. When I compare the range of responsibilities of The Hague with Brussels it would be tempting to conclude that the latter is much more important than the former. From a short-sighted point of view this seems to be true, but looking at the services rendered and the available means of all the quoted Dutch institutions combined, there is not the slightest reason to be proud of the local Belgian achievements and more particularly the services to the users. I have once been induced to compare the National Library of Bavaria in Munich with the Royal Library in Brussels. Although I am much less familiar with the situation in Germany than in Holland, I discovered quite a number of similarities between the two libraries, also regarding their visibility in the society they were serving. Through this short investigation it became rapidly clear to me that Bavaria was the most centralized land of the German Federal Republic, that the size of the population was comparable to that of Belgium and that the Bavarians were as Catholic as the Belgians. Instinctively I had found my dividing line between Reformed and Roman Europe again.

8. *Of Men and Books*

IF SOMEONE SHOULD ASK me what was the purpose of my life, I would simply answer: to make books. To make books in all the senses of the phrase. When I was a young librarian I discovered by accident Frank Gardner's book entitled *Letters to a Younger Librarian*. I read it eagerly because I agreed completely with the opinions of the elderly librarian, mainly when it came to warnings about too much interest in book production problems. Although I basically understood his sound advice, I found myself fully imbued with the exaggeration of a special feeling for the physical sensuousness of paper, of the unmatchable smell of deep black ink, of the delicate linking of the right paper with the right ink, of the incredibly difficult scanning of printing plates, of the even more difficult matching of the right screening with the right printing. I could go on endlessly with all these delicacies and if this brings a pastry shop to mind I have no objections, provided one can keep his own inclinations for different kinds of flavours when it comes to books. Indeed, I could go on with the ingredients of bindings and all the other visible and invisible features of what is so easily called a book.

Before coming to the contents of books, which after all have some importance, or rather before talking discursively about the contents of some books, I should mention that if most people's biographies read like a series of chapters of a book, mine is simply a jump from one book to another. Let me make it clear from the very outset that not one of these books was written by me. I did everything for these books, except write them. If some of them have an introduction signed by me, it is not even certain that I wrote it myself. To correct this overmodest statement I should add immediately that quite a number of prefaces and speeches by Belgian ministers of education were only signed or read by them, and, when related to library matters, written by me.

"*Tout au monde existe pour aboutir à un livre,*" said Mallarmé, meaning that all life's experience had to end in writing. I fully agree with the symbolist author, although I give a completely different meaning to this beautiful quotation, which I have used over and over again for many years. My other favourite quotation about books was by Montaigne, "*La meilleure munition que j'aye trouvée à cet humain voyage,*" which to my own surprise I have not yet used. When I try to remember how I came to be interested in the physical world of books, I think it all started with typography. Like most librarians I knew nothing about types, their design, their use, their qualities, their weaknesses, their esthetic or utilitarian properties, etc. Immediately after the war I was secretary of the Flemish Club in Brussels and I had to send out invitations to lectures and exhibitions. I discovered rather easily, all by myself I would say, that an invitation card could be elegant or ugly and if you gave it to the printer without specific instructions it always turned out to be hideous. So without any expertise I began to choose the types myself. I think the most revolutionary decision I took was to use only one type throughout the whole text of the invitation card. Names like De Roos and van Krimpen began to gain some meaning. Like most of the beginners in the late forties and early fifties I used too many De Roos types. Some of these job-printing ephemera of which I was very proud at the time, look awful to me now when they happen to meet my eyes, which fortunately seldom occurs.

I never met Sjoerd De Roos, but I quite often saw Jan van Krimpen. It actually started with an exhibition at the Royal Library in 1953 organized on the occasion of the 250th anniversary of the Dutch printing firm Joh. Enschedé & Zonen in Haarlem. Why this exhibition was held in Brussels after it was held in Haarlem I don't remember. Anyhow it was responsible for the fact that Sem Hartz, Jan van Krimpen's assistant at the time, and I became friends. He and the late Netty Hoeflake were the people from Enschedé who had to mount the exhibition in Brussels, and the director of the Royal Library had instructed me to be available for any assistance. It would be closer to reality to say that I had instructed myself to do so. It was an extremely pleasant cooperation during which I discovered, through the persons of Jan van Krimpen and Sem Hartz, the wonderful world of postage stamp and banknote printing, with adjacent fields like type design, calligraphy, layout and all other printing wonders. After the exhibition was closed I received as a present John Dreyfus' study of *The Works of Jan van Krimpen* (1952), with a foreword by Stanley Morison, specially bound in Morocco with an HL monogram by Sem Hartz. Jan van Krimpen's frontispiece portrait was also a woodcut by Sem Hartz. It is one of the most cherished items of my small collection of memorabilia.

I hope to meet John Dreyfus again in these pages, but since this may not occur I would like to write down immediately that Fernand Baudin, who helped me to get acquainted with the best typographers of our times and to understand their work, remained a lively link between John Dreyfus and me. The Royal Library organized, over the years, exhibitions of a series of typographers, the quality of which was always inversely proportional to their success. What a pleiad of names: at the outset the master of us all, Stanley Morison (the catalogue was written by Fernand Baudin and used for the first time Chris Brand's Albertina of which I was a kind of spiritual father), Hermann Zapf (Frankfurt), Giovanni Mardersteig (Verona), the Spiral Press of Joseph Blumenthal (New York), Sem Hartz (Haarlem) – but let's first go back to 1953.

Jan van Krimpen and Sem Hartz were names which would grow in importance along with my deeper involvement in typography and book production. Jan van Krimpen was chairman at the time of the Nonpareil Society in Amsterdam. I was to become its first non-Dutch member. Nonpareil is the name of a very small, six-point, typeface, and the membership of the club was strictly limited to a few bookmen: two authors, two publishers, two bookdealers, two printers, two bookbinders, etc. and also two librarians (the other one being Herman de la Fontaine Verwey, more Francophile than I, if that could be possible). I have not been a faithful member, but each time I attended a meeting – a "borrel" dinner at Hotel Schiller, in Amsterdam – I promised myself to go more regularly to the Club, but this seldom went beyond good intentions.

Here I have to open a non-book parenthesis. My good intentions were always stronger than my best friendships. Even in this respect I neglected the fundamental issues. From 1 January until 31 December my existence was filled with trifles or, to put it more elegantly, with urgent decisions. I could give many examples but I shall limit myself to my truncated relations with Yassu Gauclère. We met in Vienna in 1958 at a UNESCO conference, which was actually my first experience in multilateral cooperation. She was chief translator and explained all the differences to me between the work of a translator and an interpreter. Since that time I have not the slightest hesitation: everything for the first one and not very much for the second: *verba volant.* . . . We talked a lot. She told me about her life with Etiemble and since we were in a German speaking country I gave her my concentration camp story. We met again a couple of times in Paris. She gave me her books – I remember more particularly *L'Orange bleue* – and, that is my point, invited me to spend a few days with her and Etiemble in their summer house in the Jura mountains. I postponed this visit from season to season and suddenly she died. Etiemble wrote moving pages on this unjust death and I have a lively recollection of this visit which never took place. All my fault and end of the parenthesis.

A few paragraphs ago I said that the other librarian member of Nonpareil was Herman de la Fontaine Verwey. We shared a basic interest in the history of the printed book, but he proved, through an impressive series of publications, that his interest was serious, while I could only claim it by repeated statements. When the idea of offering him a Festschrift in 1966 was suggested, I had the privilege of being invited to write the foreword. Actually the Festschrift was presented to him with only my foreword printed, and the rest of the volume was blank leaves. [1] A few months later the real book was ready. I do not write much, but I always meet my deadlines.

With the Nonpareil Society I went to Oxford as guest of the Double Crown Club. [2] Another Belgian member of the party was Leon Voet, curator of the Plantin Moretus Museum at Antwerp, of whom I have always been jealous because his Museum was not a part of the Royal Library. This being said, he and his former

[1] No relation whatsoever to the society *La feuille blanche* in Auvergne of which I was a member.

[2] The non-typically interested reader in typography should know that all traditional paper sizes have beautiful names: double crown, double foolscap, superroyal, demi elephant and, at least in French, *petit jésus, grand raisin,* etc.

assistant, Dis Vervliet, have done an excellent job at the Museum. A number of American and British experts on type history, like John Carter, Ray Nash, Mike Parker, would certainly agree with me. This trip to Oxford left me with all kinds of recollections, mostly unrelated to books, however. The dinner was at All Souls College. The setting was superb, but at the table an old saying came back to my mind, "God invented food, but the English invented the table manners." The strawberries with old port wine were the only civilized part of the dinner. When some foreigner wanted to smoke at the end of the dinner, the chairman knocked on the table and said "No smoking because this room was built before tobacco was introduced into these Isles."

It was only my second contact with England. The first one was a few years after the war. I accompanied a well-known French physicist, Lou Kowarski, who had spent a part of the war in England, and we were going to visit the nuclear Harwell Laboratory. That was in 1954 when I was, for a short period, librarian of the European Nuclear Research Centre (CERN) at Geneva. Here again my recollections are unrelated to physics. When we set foot on British soil, L. Kowarski said to me, "If you want to eat decently in England, avoid the meals." How right he was, at the time. He should however have added, "and don't sit next to me." When we finally reached our destination, after numerous checkings and recheckings of our security papers, we saw the backs of a bunch of people with white blouses. Some turned their heads to us and asked us to remain silent. Had we entered the room at the historical conclusion of a new experiment? Not exactly. They were all religiously listening to a new record, "Voices and Noises," by Peter Ustinov.

Parallel with my typographical initiation, I began to feel the need to print short texts. A pleasant occasion offered itself when I began to work for the Belgian American Educational Foundation in 1954. Its secretary in New York, Clark Stillman, was open to any suggestion and actually knew more about typography than I did, as he knew and knows more about any subject than I do. At a time when I did not yet see the difference between a manuscript and a printed book, he was on friendly relations with Eric Gill in England. But that is not my story. In the Royal Library in Brussels we had a unique copy of Christopher Columbus' famous letter on the discovery of America printed at Antwerp in ± 1493. My friend

Louis Baekelants had translated the Latin text into French and Dutch, and we wanted to make a trilingual edition, plagiarizing a fifteenth- or sixteenth-century legal typographical layout: the original Latin text in the middle, with the other languages in glossary form left and right in smaller type. I thought of using this booklet as season's greetings of the Belgian American Educational Foundation. These were going to be rather expensive greeting cards for a philanthropic foundation which should spend its income on fellowships. So I looked for a financial sponsor outside of the Foundation and I found one, Maurits Naessens, and it became the beginning of a most exciting adventure. Who could guess that a Christopher Columbus letter, used as Christmas greetings by both a foundation and a bank (Maurits Naessens being director of the Banque de Paris et des Pays-Bas in Brussels) would be the starting point of a most ambitious publications programme?

Maurits Naessens was ten years older than I. He had known my father rather well in a pacifist league before the war. Like many other people who had met my father, he had admired him for a short time and then they separated on angry terms. When I was a candidate to be appointed director of the Royal Library, he supported me "though nobody had ever offended him as deeply as my father." His support was a strong one, because he was very clever in using his unique position as a powerful socialist banker. In my case he convinced his old friend, and mine to be, Achilles van Acker, Prime Minister at the time, to appoint me to the Library. When I first met the Prime Minister he welcomed me with nearly the same words as Maurits Naessens' about my father. The latter must have had a hidden charm which I never discovered. This may be true of Maurits Naessens also. During the many years that we had close contacts, the situations of conflict into which we regularly fell, were, in my opinion, always the result of his too extreme egocentrism. He never tried to understand the point of view of the other side. In many angry moments I have always tried to keep in mind that I was morally in his debt.

The Christopher Columbus booklet and some ephemera were printed by my lifelong friend Jan van Hoorick in Brussels. We had been to high school together; we spent our vacations together in the Ardennes where I helped him with his mathematics. We were roommates in Ghent where we were both students at the University. After one year he joined the print shop which had been founded by his father and I stayed at Ghent for another three years. In the early fifties he even followed a course I gave on the layout of periodicals at the Plantin Moretus Museum in Antwerp. I should have mentioned earlier that Bert Pelckmans, a leading publisher in Antwerp, had convinced the city authorities to set up a typographical school at the Museum in order to improve the quality of Belgian printing. He had wisely decided that a large proportion of the staff should come from Holland because the average quality of Dutch printing was strikingly higher than in our country. Since I was among the very few people interested in typography, he wanted me on his staff. Actually he had not much choice. Because I was an amateur and not an expert, he had to invent a course for which no real expert was available. The result was layout of periodicals. The students were nearly all, like my friend Jan van Hoorick, sons of owners of printing shops. For a number of years it was fun on both sides and the average quality of Belgian printing improved. In this connection the Plantin school appears, in retrospect, to be the third component of my vocation as a maker of books.

The first book, or rather volume which Maurits Naessens and I produced was *Mon Pays*, one hundred woodcuts by Frans Masereel. Naessens had had friendly relations for many years with the famous left-wing artist and had convinced him to tell the story of his own country, Belgium, in a series of woodcuts as he had done in earlier days with his social *Geschichte ohne Worte (Ein Roman in Bildern)*, which had made him famous as a privileged witness of the social revolution of his time. When the cuts were ready and when I had lost my fight with Maurits to reduce the number of blocks – half of them would produce a book twice as good – I took them all to Jan van Hoorick. It happened in 1956 and it is pleasant to remember now the old-fashioned craftsmanship with which these blocks were printed. When one or another did not came out well on the paper, the printer took it out, spit on it and pressed it firmly against the glowing pot of the stove. The result was wonderful: it could not be blacker. The book was so successful that it needed a second edition for wich I wrote the introduction, already well on my way to writing forewords to books written by others.

The first real book with a text was *Le Miroir de la Belgique* by Carlo Bronne (1957). The author was a well-known Belgian historian who had collected a number of quotations from famous foreign writers about Belgium. Carlo Bronne was also chairman of the board of trustees of the Royal Library and it was quite normal that I was a link between him and Maurits Naessens. At the time I did not know that he and Maurits Naessens had met several years before at the foot of the Ruwenzori, in the heart of black Africa, and had envisaged such a collection of opinions of foreigners about our own country. Through this book which was printed by Enschedé in Haarlem, we had many pleasant meetings in the city, which once claimed to be the cradle of printing. Laurens Janszoon Coster still has his monument there, but the real monument to typography in the city is the firm of Enschedé. Carlo Bronne's text was illustrated with views of Belgian cities by foreign artists. I remember more particularly the album which George Hunt published in London in 1825 and which had three views of Ostend, two of Ghent, three of Brussels, two of Antwerp, one of Laeken (the present Royal Castle) and six of Waterloo, without counting thirty tombstones. We used it heavily. The house style of the books which were going to follow was set by Sem Hartz, mainly through the square vellum back of the binding. The queer thing about this book is that the author's background, way of life and writing is purely French, while the physical appearance of his book is Dutch *à outrance*. And with that everybody was happy.

Here somewhere – or is it already late? – I have to include Mardersteig's *Pacioli*. Unfortunately I do not remember who drew my attention to this wonderfully beautiful book, but the circumstances in which I showed it to Maurits Naessens are still vivid in my mind. I did not stress too much the quality of the binding, the elegance of the title page, the perfect typesetting and printing at the Officina Bodoni, the texture of the paper, . . . but I insisted on the fact that a fifteenth-century manuscript codex from the Ambrosian library in Milan had been used to make an outstanding modern book at the initiative of a bank, the Mediobanca di Milano. The title of Luca Pacioli's treatise, *De Divina Proportione*, sounded in my ears like a well-balanced programme for future cooperation.

Not surprisingly, the next one in the row was *Medieval Illuminations* by Bob Delaissé. Another step in Maurits Naessens' direction: larger size, more colour plates, and publication in four languages. Well on our way to produce coffee-table books. Fortunately Bob Delaissé's text, like the plates, was of first quality. It consists of fifty-two pages of comments on fifty miniatures from the collections of the Royal Library. Starting with the ninth-century "Author at his writing Desk" and ending with "Jesus Crowned with Thorns" from the Hennessy Hours (Bruges, approx. 1540). If Carlo Bronne's *Miroir de la Belgique* was produced completely outside Belgium, *Medieval Illuminations* introduced the first Belgian component into our book production programme: photogravure De Schutter, an Antwerp firm with which I had already worked on a series of small projects. Now, however, we were striving towards an ambitious set of colour reproductions. To use miniatures as a point of departure was not exactly the right choice, since everybody knows that the reproduction of the original gold creates an incredible number of technical problems. Carl De Schutter, who shares the ownership of the firm with his brother and some of their children, solved all these problems and the result was the highest quality anybody could hope for. I always have thought that De Schutter could achieve an international reputation because he has on his payroll on the one hand a group of experienced craftsmen and on the other hand a number of young artists, whom paradoxically he is able to bring together to work harmoniously to the advantage of all, his customers included.

Since the publication of *Medieval Illuminations* was as much a matter of physical production as of publishing promotion, Maurits Naessens contracted with the well-known German art publishers DuMont Schauberg. This does not necessarily mean that Belgian printers were not able to produce the same book, or that Belgian publishers would not be capable of putting it on the market. It remains however a fact that the book we had in mind and which finally came out did not yet exist in Belgium. When DuMont Schauberg agreed to work with De Schutter, the latter warned the former "I am expensive" and the answer was wonderful "Cheap plates have cost us too much money!"

Since the Naessens books were originally conceived as Christmas gifts to the Bank's clientèle, we were always struggling with impossible deadlines. To be ready three weeks before Christmas with four volumes, each one in a different language (French, Dutch, English and German) was no mean objective. In the case of the *Medieval Illuminations* this led to the curious situation that three or four staff members of the Royal Library spent a large part of the month of November 1958 in Cologne, where the printing plant of DuMont Schauberg was located, to correct proofs either in their hotel rooms near the railroad station or on the premises of the print shop. The book was ready on time and was to become a great success, also from a commercial point of view, which was not exactly my contribution to the enterprise. Maurits Naessens used to say that I lightly spent the money which he so painfully earned in his bank. As a facetious remark I would gladly have accepted this definition of our relations, but he meant it seriously and that is where he was wrong.

Another misunderstanding arose between us while *Medieval Illuminations* was in the process of being completed. A few months before it came out, the Library celebrated the four hundredth anniversary of the founding in Brussels in 1559 of the first royal library by Philip II. [3] Inevitably the celebration took the form of an exhibition of Burgundian manuscripts which gave the best picture of the original library. Bob Delaissé mounted the exhibition and wrote the catalogue. Since the occasion was such a solemn one I wanted to issue a good and beautiful catalogue. Its size was a small in-quarto, the type was Bembo, it had eight colour plates and sixty-four black-and-white illustrations. When I proudly showed the catalogue to Maurits Naessens he was suddenly mad at me. The catalogue was going to be a competitor of the forthcoming book! I could not believe my ears and he of course did not listen to my arguments. It disturbed me only for a short time, because I knew better and I awaited with full assurance the publication of the book. Naessens' wrong reaction had, however, a positive result. Henceforth I would ask my people in the Library, and a growing number of experts outside the Library, to aim at the highest possible standards, scholarly and physically, in our exhibition catalogues. We have been successful. Over the years an impressive row of such catalogues have been published and are still being published. The Royal Library was the first Belgian public institution to spend so much time, effort and money on its catalogues. Other institutions in Belgium and abroad are now currently doing the same or are issuing even more impressive catalogues. Our

---

[3] I cannot resist the temptation to add a footnote. When we celebrated in 1959 this historical event we discovered by sheer luck the original act which mentions that King Philip II appointed as his first librarian Viglius ab Aytta, president of the privy council. From the court to the library, I said to myself, not realizing of course that some fifteen years later it was going to be exactly the other way round for me.

exhibition catalogues have proved to be the Library's most efficient public relations tool.

This had happened already with the first one, the *Flemish
Miniatures*. It was quite unusual for the Royal Library to export an
exhibition to places like Amsterdam and Paris, and within these
cities to prestigious institutions like the Rijksmuseum and the
Bibliothèque Nationale. The whole staff went to Amsterdam, in
two shifts in order to leave the Library normally open to the public.
The minister of education went to Paris. Two days before the
opening he called and suggested that we might go one day early,
that meant the next day, to Paris and attend a performance at the
Comédie française the night before the opening of the exhibition.
That was a bit complicated for me because I was supposed to catch
the boat-train immediately after the opening and to leave for New
York. It was however easy to be ready twenty-four hours earlier
than planned and a couple of hours before leaving for Paris I
found out that it was going to be a gala performance of Molière
with General de Gaulle present. I tried to see if my minister knew
about it, but he had already left for Paris. Having enough luggage
to carry to the United States I decided to take no evening clothes.

Half an hour before the beginning of the performance I was
waiting in the theatre hall for my minister, where seeing all the
men in white tie with decorations, and all the ladies in long dresses
passing, I began to feel rather naked. How was the minister going
to show up? Finally he arrived dressed like me. I felt relieved and
he felt worried. "Apparently we made a mistake," he said to me,
while we proceeded to the ticket window. The minister said to the
clerk who was wearing an impressive dark uniform: "I am the
minister of education of Belgium and this is my guest." The man
looked down at us twice from top to toe and said "The minister? . . .
quatrième balcon." So he sent us up to the cheapest places where
hardly anybody could see us, but where we could see all the heads
of the men and the bosoms of the women of the area. From our
angle General de Gaulle was no taller than the other spectators.
The performance started, appropriately for my unhappy minister, with the one-act play *Les précieuses ridicules* and he left immediately afterwards. I enjoyed Molière and the situation, and
stayed until the end.

Next morning the opening of the exhibition at the Bibliothèque
Nationale was going to be performed by Minister André Malraux

and he arrived a few minutes early. He immediately got hold of me and told me that he had read the catalogue (I said to myself: Oh, Oh, a minister who has read the catalogue!) and congratulated me that it was in three parts, but that he himself was only interested in the first one, the pre-Burgundian book illumination. He wanted to look immediately at these manuscripts, but I suggested timidly that my own minister was in town and that we had better wait a few minutes. No problem for André Malraux. He began to ask me all kinds of questions about book production in the Low Countries before the dukes of Burgundy. I could not answer these questions and looked for my manuscript curator, but he also had not yet arrived. Fortunately André Malraux suggested answers himself to all the questions he raised. In the meanwhile the Belgian minister arrived, there was hardly any exchange of greetings before André Malraux took me by the arm and eagerly wanted me to show him the pre-Burgundian manuscripts. I caught with my free hand the arm of my other minister and dragged him with us heading towards the first books at a pace which was not normal at all for the formal opening of an exhibition. With the solid grip of Malraux on my left arm, and a no less solid one of my right hand on my minister's left arm, we proceeded very slowly from one book to another, André Malraux having much to say or to ask not only about each miniature, but about the handwriting, the decoration, the vellum, etc. I began to worry about my boat-train and was trying to find out how I could slip away discreetly from between two ministers. Time was getting short and André Malraux' brilliant art historical comments did not interest me any longer. The solution came unexpectedly when a horde of photographers rushed into the exhibition. With a certain aggressiveness in my voice I suggested that the two ministers pose together before a French translation of St. Augustin's *Civitas Dei*, and I escaped while everybody's attention was caught by the flashlights. I did not miss the train, nor hence the boat to New York.

Everyone who has had responsibility for an exhibition knows how difficult it is to be ready at the opening with the catalogue. But to be ready with two catalogues in different languages was a real challenge. In the Royal Library we failed only twice. The first time it was due to the fact that technical reasons compelled us to use a new printer. This implies a well-deserved compliment to our usual printer, Erasmus Inc. at Ghent, who always delivered the catalogues on time. Very often the ink and the binding were still wet, but thanks to overtime and nightwork they were there and that was the only thing that mattered.

Before I quote the second example of delay, I may as well add a second compliment to our printer. The Boymans-Van Beuningen Museum in Rotterdam, the Institut Néerlandais in Paris and the Royal Library in Brussels had organized together, in 1972-1973, an exhibition of Dutch and Flemish seventeenth-century drawings to be shown in the Pushkin Museum in Moscow, the Hermitage in Leningrad and the Museum in Kiev. (The Soviet authorities sent from their own collections a similar exhibition to Brussels, Paris and Rotterdam). The catalogue was printed by Erasmus Inc. and the plates were engraved by De Schutter. Since that time the Institut Néerlandais in Paris has used the services of Erasmus and De Schutter for the catalogue of its own collections which will amount to twenty-eight volumes! The story is a pleasant one although it does not match the epic story of the catalogue of the Frick Collection in New York, the twelve folio volumes of which were completed on hand presses of the University of Pittsburgh, while the text was composed in a special modification by Bruce Rogers of Jan van Krimpen's "Lutetia" type.

The second delay was a rather voluntary one, and in fact was no delay at all. As already mentioned earlier Jan Deschamps organized in the Library, on the occasion of the centenary of a local Flemish literary society, an exhibition of Dutch manuscripts of the Middle Ages and published an extremely successful catalogue on the subject. Considering that it needed more of a philologist's knowledge of Dutch than a common one to read the catalogue, I decided rather arbitrarily to replace a French translation with an anthology of French adaptations of Dutch medieval poetry. It may be noted in passing that in the Middle Ages Dutch, French, English and German languages were closer to each other than in our times. At the university I had a professor who each year gave a lecture under the title "Do you want to hear Shakespeare speaking Dutch?" It included a series of striking examples, stressing some words which retained their Shakespearian sense in modern Dutch and had lost it in English.

That anthology idea was a pleasant and exciting enterprise which was brought to a happy end, thanks to Claudine Lemaire who was the driving force behind it. I would like to pay tribute to her. We studied Germanic philology together at Ghent, she taught for a short time in Brussels, raised her three children and then, after many years, made the mistake of remembering me. I have a bad conscience towards her, because I gave her one tricky job after another. Her first work in the Library coincided with the arrival of the Henry van de Velde archives, the famous *art nouveau* artist of Belgian origin. She drew up the inventory of its five thousand items, but where anybody else would stop Claudine went on. She became secretary to the Henry van de Velde Society, editor of its Journal, which she raised to a high level of contents and design and, finally, she was the good fairy to A.M. Hammacher when he wrote his book on Henry van de Velde.

Then came the inauguration of the new library building in 1969. From the very beginning of my directorship in 1956 I had one fixed idea: to prove to the authorities as well as to the public at large that a library was much more than an expensive building, that it was a lively institution needed by society, which it helped to mould while it was simultaneously a specific expression of the society. I am going to resist the temptation to enumerate the thousand ways by which I tried to reach this avowed aim, and shall only cite the *Memorial* volume, which the Library published on the occasion and of which Claudine Lemaire was the general editor, and also the author of several chapters. The purpose of the Memorial was to show, through a four-centuries-long history of the Library collections and, through an elaborate projection of its future, that the new building was only a visible component of the Library and an additional opportunity to deliver enhanced services to the reader.

Shortly after the Memorial came the already mentioned anthology, published under the title *Le Cercle des Choses*, which is a literal French translation of a Dutch verse by Hadewych "Die Cierkel der Dinghe". Claudine scouted for existing translations, commissioned new ones, conceived the whole volume, wrote chapter introductions and also the general preface which I signed. Fernand Baudin gave it a handsome design, Erasmus Inc. printed it well, misprints included because the first edition was rushed through the press. The book became a modest, but useful and efficient medium for the international diffusion of the medieval poetry from the Low Countries. Let me add for the fun of it that at the opening of the exhibition only the anthology was ready, while the original Dutch catalogue arrived a few days later.

The real breakthrough of the new art book movement in my country was achieved with Roger d'Hulst's *Flemish Tapestries*. To issue it a new publishing firm was founded in Brussels, Arcade. It was based on an old printing plant which renewed its equipment and was able to print letterpress, offset and heliogravure. The signing of the contract between Naessens and Arcade was a real Commedia dell'Arte. In Naessens' beautiful garden the two parties met for hours with me as a not too neutral referee. Sometimes I found myself hiding with Maurits Naessens behind one tree, sometimes with the Arcade people whispering behind another one. I have only a visual recollection of the scene, because the discussions were about financial matters. I actually wonder now why I was present. Probably to remind Maurits Naessens that colour plates are more expensive than black-and-white illustrations and to warn the Arcade that I would not accept the use of worn-out matrixes.

I was never involved so much in the preparation of a book as with the *Flemish Tapestries*. Roger d'Hulst was an old friend, who had been working in the Brussels Fine Art Museum next door to the Library and had become, a couple of years before we started on our magic carpet, professor of art history at Ghent University, the University from which we both graduated. Before returning to the field of high and low warp, I must recall that Roger and I had worked together many years earlier on another book. We translated *L'Eloge de la Main* [4] by Henri Focillon from French into Dutch. Focillon's style is glorious, and hence immensely difficult to translate. We had to do it over again several times, correcting one another all the time and being corrected by others. While we were struggling with vocabulary, syntax and above all style, we induced Roger's friend, Jos Verdeghem, to etch a few plates representing hands. The result was superb. He engraved twenty-six plates with endless variations on the same theme. Jan Van Hoorick had the text set by hand and we were still young enough to be proud of the large in-folio which lay before us.

The copyright of *L'Eloge de la main* was with the Presses Universitaires de France and they accepted our proposal to give them free

---

[4] Last chapter of his *Vie des formes*.

copies of our edition in exchange for the right to publish a Dutch translation. We decided to bring these copies to Paris and this became a most memorable journey. Jos Verdeghem, the artist, had once lived for ten years in Paris mostly among circus people, but that was a long time ago, although his Flemish still had some Parisian accent, if it is at all possible to imagine such a mixture. Jan Van Hoorick, the printer, was also our driver, and Jos Verdeghem drove him mad by wanting to find again the Paris which he had left so long before. It is difficult to explain to an artist in pouring rain, that one-way streets are different for pedestrians than for drivers. Anyhow we delivered the copies and we had a good time, forgetting Focillon's negative opinion of the left hand. Except for a few courtesy copies, Jos Verdeghem got them all and sold them well.

By comparison, *Flemish Tapestries* was no amateur job. Roger d'Hulst was an expert on Flemish seventeenth-century drawings and I needed some time to convince him to write on tapestries. I do not remember why he finally gave in: Maurits Naessens' insistence, Carl De Schutter's professional standards, my enthusiasm for the idea to spend again many evenings together working on Dutch texts, drafted by him and rewritten by me? I still regret that I did not join him, his wife and Carl's staff on a photographic safari to the Spanish churches, cathedrals and monasteries where miles of Flemish tapestries are kept. When the text was ready, when the transparencies were made, a new period of hectic work began for all of us. Carl De Schutter surpassed himself with six-colour offset films, Arcade enlisted the services of the most outstanding Belgian typographer, Fernand Baudin, and I began an uneven fight with French, English and German translations.

With the English we had bad luck. Not many people are available to translate from Dutch into English and we thought we had found the rara avis. Since this proved to be a mistake, it was Frances and Clark Stillman who agreed to revise the translation. Nothing is more frustrating than to be compelled to judge the correctness of a language which is not your own. In Belgium many people translate correctly from French into Dutch. The other way round is not so common. Here again we thought that we had found the right person and here again we were wrong. Finally a staff member of the Library, Roger Brucher, revised the translation and we delivered an acceptable text in due time.

For different reasons I kept my report on the German transla-

tion for the end, although it created a minimum of problems. Kurt
Köster, director of the Deutsche Bibliothek at Frankfurt-am-Main
and professor at the University of the same town, was a most
perfect translator, which means that he even improved the original. Since he had previously translated Johan Huizinga's *Waning of
the Middle Ages*, our text must not have been too difficult for him. I
first met Kurt Köster at a meeting of the Internation Federation of
Library Associations (IFLA) and our relations lasted for over fifteen years.

In many cities of the old and new world we have spent good
hours together, discussing professional matters. It is however extremely pleasant to reminisce and recall that each time he had one
or another medieval problem – and more particularly as it related
to the Low Countries – on his mind. He often took a photograph of
a Flemish miniature out of his pocket and showed me an intriguing
iconographical detail. I also received regularly from him offprints
with the results of his scholarly research. In professional circles of
the IFLA he represented that rich type of librarian who was open to
innovative technology but never at the cost of neglecting his
learned responsibility. It should be stressed that under his directorship the Deutsche Bibliothek was the first in the world to produce a national bibliography by computer, the *Deutsche Bibliographie*. I still remember his critical attitude towards this powerful
instrument, which at the beginning had done so much damage to
library management by sheer misuse. But with a yearly increase of
10% on the thousand pages of bibliographical descriptions which
his library produced, using automated descriptions was the only
way out. Since then he and many others have proved that computers can be put to good use in libraries.

Parallel to his skillful leadership of the Deutsche Bibliothek,
where he has always been able to surround himself with a highly
qualified staff and to establish effective and rewarding links with
other institutions, such as the Zentralstelle für Maschinelle
Dokumentation, he gave a large part of his time to his professorial
responsibility. I hope that the preceding sentence denotes some
jealousy because I have never been able to serve two masters. If the
Bible is right, I have to conclude that library management and
scholarly research were not two masters for Kurt Köster.

Our relations were particularly close during the translation of
Roger d'Hulst's book and he regularly complained to me that the

image of modern Flemish literature in German translation was too biased towards *Heimatliteratur*, and that Flemish authors of world standing like Willem Elsschot and Marnix Gijsen were not well enough known in Germany. In the meanwhile these two authors have been translated more extensively, but it is my personal opinion that Kurt Köster's judgment about the image of the Flemish literature in his country is still correct.

The bibliographical prize of the International League of Antiquarian Booksellers also brought us together from time to time when the meetings of the jury, of which Kurt Köster was a member, were held in Brussels. The year that the prize went to a bibliography in which the Royal Library in Brussels was deeply involved is still vivid in my memory. The book was the life work of the notary J. Peeters-Fontainas from Louvain and was an exhaustive record of all the Spanish-language books printed in the Low Countries before 1800. Who would believe that the author had listed exactly 1417 of these books and that he owned most of them? At the time of publication he was, however, already an old man, and the library offered him the cooperation of a distinguished Hispanicist, Anne-Marie Frédéric. After two years the manuscript was ready as a result of a close cooperation of the two authors and was published in two volumes in 1965. Kurt Köster did not tell me that it had won the prize before the official announcement was made, much too late according to my opinion. J. Peeters-Fontainas left the sum of money which went with the prize to the Royal Library and his bibliography enhanced so much the commercial value of his collection, that this same Library could not afford to buy it when it was offered for sale after his death, the more so in that the Library had half of the books. Not so long ago the collection was auctioned at Sotheby's and the Library bought over a hundred items. In the meanwhile A.M. Frédéric had published a supplement to the bibliography.

From the very beginning of the Deutsche Bibliothek at Frankfurt-am-Main (which was created after the war, because the traditional German book centre, Leipzig, was located in East Germany), it started to collect German *Exil-Literatur*, German publications issued outside Nazi-Germany by authors who had been forced to quit their home country. In 1965 the Deutsche Bibliothek began to circulate an impressive exhibition of a selection of three hundred representative items of its collection of *Exil-*

Literatur of more than eight thousand pieces brought together by
H.W. Eppelsheimer. This exhibition reached the Royal Library in
Brussels in 1967 where it met with an exceptional interest, because
many refugees from the Nazi nightmare passed through Belgium
before our country was also occupied in 1940, one of the most
famous among them being Einstein. That small part of Europe,
where Belgium is situated, having lived for centuries under
foreign rule, has established, since its independence in 1830, a
strong tradition of hospitality for political refugees. As a symbol of
its democratic way of life we added to the Frankfurt exhibition of
Exil-literatur from our own collection two rather striking documents: *Aux proscrits français réfugiés en Belgique* by Victor Hugo in
an autograph manuscript version, and the best known copy of the
Deutsche Brüsseler Zeitung which Karl Marx published here in 1847-
1848. (We hid carefully the newspaper which the Nazis published
during the war under the same title.)

The catalogue of the exhibition was designed by Hermann Zapf,
who was a friend of Kurt Köster and through whom we had got
acquainted. As a result I had organized, in the Library, a Hermann
Zapf exhibition, which was opened by Kurt Köster in 1962 and for
which Hermann Zapf wrote, in his exceptionally elegant calligraphy, a quotation from the Belgian winner of the Nobel prize for
literature, Maurice Maeterlinck. It was pleasant to discover,
through Hermann Zapf, Kurt Köster's and my common interest in
modern typographical design. His library housed the Gesellschaft
für Buchkunst and so it happened that when I received, at the
opening of the Frankfurter Buchmesse in 1973, the First International Book Award, the charter was designed in the library by
Willberg, from whom I still receive each year the catalogue of the
fifty best books.

To conclude these loose recollections of my physical and intellectual encounters with Kurt Köster I would like to give them a
slight theological and philosophical slant. Generally when he came
to Brussels he paid a visit to the Bollandists, where we had a
common friend, Father Maurice Coens (1893-1972). The latter
was a trustee of the Royal Library as a representative of this group
of learned Jesuits. When the Jesuit libraries in Belgium were
secularized, after the French Revolution, their rich collections –
among them the autograph manuscript of Thomas a Kempis'
Imitatio – ended in the Royal Library. As rightful compensation a

Bollandist is traditionally a member of the Board of Trustees of the Library. Father Coens was on the Board for many years until his death in 1972. He was one of the most outstanding experts on medieval manuscripts and as such has been of invaluable assistence to scholars like Kurt Köster. In a different direction I would like to recall my introduction by Kurt Köster to Paul Tillich when he was awarded the Friedenspreis at the opening of the Frankfurter Buchmesse in 1962. His acceptance speech at the St. Paulskirche had an exceptional ethical tone, which was only matched by his human depth. Ethics and humanity are two appropriate words with which to end this portrait of an outstanding librarian and fine scholar like Kurt Köster.

After many years I look back upon the *Flemish Tapestries* as the real beginning of the new art book in my country. Paul Loiseau, director of the Arcade, repeated several times to me that this book virtually made his firm the leading publishing house of art books in Belgium. As such it may be compared to Toulouse Lautrec's *Histoire Naturelle* by Jules Renard with which he started in 1899 the vogue of the "livres de peintres" in France. As *Flemish Tapestries* was the beginning of a still growing series of art books by Arcade, so was Arcade itself the beginning of a flourishing art book industry with several outstanding publishers. Together they have given my country a very favourable reputation in this field, which is generally recognized at the yearly bookfair in Frankfurt. One day the history of this postwar Belgian phenomenon with an international dimension will be written, and in order to make sure that the author does not forget my share I might as well note here myself that I got the ball going.

I should not forget to pay due homage to two predecessors before the first world war in the field of art book publishing. People like Edmond Deman and G. van Oest deserve unlimited credit. The former received it during his lifetime from no less an artist than Stéphane Mallarmé, who broke his contract with his Parisian publisher in order to work with Deman. For obvious reasons books in their time had not yet reached the visual impact which is customary today. The literary quality of the text, its setting without mistakes and its printings on adequate paper were the major criteria of quality. It was still mainly so when G. van Oest began to issue his monographs on Belgian artistic schools, periods and individual painters. The time lag between the two however allowed the latter to be more elaborate in his books, to introduce illustrations and reproductions using techniques which nowadays may look rather primitive but with which striking results were achieved.

Gradually I got less and less involved in the Naessens books. Do I need to look for an explanation? Though the publication of each new book was always a pleasant occasion for a reunion, with each book new problems arose. Generally I was the confidant of the author and most of the time he wanted me to intervene when he was either in conflict with Maurits Naessens or with Paul Loiseau. With Naessens the conflicts were mostly linked to an overlapping of his capitalistic outlook and his egocentrism. With Paul Loiseau the difficulties appeared when he was blind to the niceties of scholarship. The former had to foot the bill and the latter had to meet the deadline. I was sensitive to all parties and I always tried to explain the point of view of the other one. Being between the hammer and the anvil most of the time, it must have eroded my pleasure in contributing to these books. After a number of years, actually in 1965, Maurits Naessens no longer worked with the Arcade and set up his own publishing house, Mercatorfonds, in Antwerp. From time to time I cooperated with both of them on a rather limited scale. At the time of writing they have merged again.

Before closing this chapter I still have to speak about three books, actually one booklet and two books, two big books. In 1973 I published a small book under the title *Cécile Voorkens, 1934-1972*. Cécile Voorkens, who had been Maurits Naessens' secretary, had died a year before at the age of thirty-eight. All the authors, all the artists, all those who had worked with her wanted to contribute to this In Memoriam volume. And everyone expressed the same feeling in different words or drawings or even musical scores. I myself compared her role with Naessens to that of a typographer with a book: a silent presence, a monologue without words, a calculated restraint, and above all an incentive to the others. The way that Maurits Naessens dealt with people would have left many more scars were it not for Cécile Voorkens. That is the reason why I felt so miserable when he said that though he had no objections to the publication of this In Memoriam, he did not want to undertake it. Everybody connected with this book worked free of charge. The colophon reads as follows: "The present group of testimonials has been set in Baskerville 12 point and printed on Arjomari-Prioux paper following a layout by Louis van den Eede. Sem Hartz drew the frontispiece. All thousand copies were contributed by Photogravure De Schutter at Antwerp and by the printshop Van den Bossche at Mechlin to the Mercatorfonds on 7 July 1973. No copies are for sale, but the National Anti-Cancer League can distribute copies to donors." When the booklet was on Maurits Naessens' desk, he wrote me a moving letter.

The second book grew out of an incredible Japanese expedition. It started with a routine commitment in the Royal Library: the celebration of the four hundredth anniversary of the birth of Breughel. I share the opinion that historical anniversaries are non-events, but they are an easy way out to establish a programme of exhibitions, conferences, or other forms of celebration. They are also a useful device to command interest from public authorities, i.e. financial means which otherwise would not be forthcoming.

Breughel's anniversary in 1969 gave us the opportunity to exhibit our fairly complete set of Breughel prints. A curator of the Library's Print Room, Louis Lebeer, had collected notes on these engravings over more than three decades and although he had been retired for a number of years before the show was put up, he wrote a masterly catalogue. For our generation, it was the last word on the subject, mainly through a sharp distinction between original imprints and late or apocryphal reproductions. The director of the Modern Museum of Kamakura, Teiichi Hijikata, happened to see the exhibition in Brussels and proposed to stage it in six Japanese towns. When the exhibition opened in Kamakura I was pleasantly surprised to see a completely different show than the one I had been familiar with in Brussels, and the catalogue was even more strikingly elegant. In Brussels I was proud of both exhibition and catalogue. In Kamakura I could easily admit that both were better. The tour of the exhibition was organized at Teiichi Hijikata's initiative by the Chunichi newspaper, as is common practice in Japan. I always suspect that the post-war international prestige of Japanese civilization is due to the fact that the country has no ministry of culture. Through the splendid organization, more Japanese saw the Breughel prints in six months, than Belgians and others in one hundred years in Brussels.

It would be less than courteous not to mention that not only were the prints taken on a glorious tour, but the Library's director and

his wife were invited to spend as much time as they could afford in
Japanese Japan, not in the cosmopolitan hotels nor in French
restaurants, but with a style of life as close to the domestic one as a
Westerner could enjoy. It naturally started in Nagoya where the
Chunichi Shimbun has its headquarters and the end of the tour
was not the end of the story. On the last day but one, I was invited
by a Japanese publisher, Iwanami Shoten, to a splendid restaurant
without geishas. His proposal was to reprint the whole engraved
work of Breughel in original size and he wondered if Louis Lebeer
and I would be willing to provide a slightly adapted text from the
catalogue. The result is one of these imposing books for which the
Japanese have the production secret. What one says in a language
one does not understand and what one sees elegantly printed in
characters one cannot read must be important. And I was even
paid for my introduction. In that text I have ventured an explanation for the similarity between Breughel and the Japanese prints.
Above all they both speak a universal language, their dominant
quality is purely graphic, and finally they both look from a high
vantage point at a multitude of small human beings. To round off
this recollection I should mention that not so long ago Mercatorfonds published a French and Dutch version of Iwanami Shoten's
Breughel.

   Through Breughel, through International Book Year, through
UNESCO, I became acquainted with some leading Japanese publishers such as Kodansha and Heibonsha, not to mention Iwanami
Shoten. The benefit of these relations is that I have a fairly rep-
resentative collection of new books on old Japan, its culture, its art,
and more particularly its calligraphy. I cherish above all the twenty-eight volume encyclopedia of Oriental calligraphy published by
Heibonsha. Actually, I know the publishers better than the librarians in Japan, although I have visited the Diet Library and the
Japan Library Association a couple of times. The last time I was in
Tokyo in 1974, the president of the Japan Library Association was
Dr. Tatsuo Morito, former minister of education, who was famous
in his country because he successfully resisted too heavy pressure
from the American forces on various issues of national importance. Dr. Tatsuo Morito was not only president of the JLA but also
of the National League of Anglers. That is the reason why I use a
Japanese rod.

   In all fairness I must however add that it is to one of my librarian friends that I owe my unforgettable meeting with the leading calligrapher of his day, Bundo. The very first day of my first visit to Japan, in 1964, I was taken straight from the airport to Bundo's house. I shall never forget the map of the city, in ten volumes I think, which was used to bring me to an unpretentious neighbourhood where I discovered, behind a wall and a door, my first perfect example of a classic Japanese house and garden. I would not say that the many hours, during which I sat uncomfortably on the floor, were marked by a lively discussion and I certainly do not remember one sentence of the conversation. My recollections are purely visual: Mrs. Bundo appearing on her knees in the doorway and from time to time sliding a bottle of whisky or a telephone towards the master on the tatami. Apparently it took Bundo a few hours to get inwardly ready to write, and when we moved to his studio, I remember that rubbing the ink took another endless time. Finally he wrote for me, in a few seconds, a wonderful kakemono. When it was dry, I ventured to ask my interpreter what it meant. After a long inner debate he finally gave me the following answer: I understand the quietness of the moon. For the last fourteen years I have been looking nearly daily at the painting and I am still wondering what the understanding of the quietness of the moon means.

Although I have not yet described the importance which UNESCO's International Book Year 1972 had in my life, I may as well tell here how it ended. Close to Christmas 1972 I was able to present to the director general of UNESCO, René Maheu, the first copy of *The Book: Through Five Thousand Years*, the third and last book I want to mention. The self-imposed deadline – to issue the book before International Book Year was over – looks to me in retrospect both incredible and ridiculous. It nearly cost me a number of long-standing friendships. I would not have dared to sell the idea of such a book to Paul Loiseau, director of Arcade, were it not that I had in the back of my mind the name of Dis Vervliet as its general editor. He marshalled twenty-six authors, some worldwide authorities in their fields and some goodwill contributors, such as Claudine Lemaire, Fernand Baudin or Paul Culot, who took *in extremis* the place of experts who had needed six months, out of the twelve that were available, to decline the offer. Among the first ones I would like to mention Kenneth Gardner from the British Museum, who wrote the chapter on printed

Japanese books and whom I had consulted a few years earlier when the Royal Library bought a collection of books printed in Japan. I wrote, of course, the introduction and conceived it as a kind of sociology of the book, while Ruari McLean contributed an afterword, "The Book as Object," ending with a quotation from a children's book on books: "A book is full of surprises, feelings and learning and what growing up is like and loving and all the really big things there are!"

9. International Book Year and the World at Large

THIS WOULD NOT BE a book by a librarian if, towards the end, it did not remind one of those miscellanea, at the bottom of each classification scheme, with which he has been struggling all his life. In order to simulate some logical sequence I have decided to center my comments around names of some people I have known and the International Book Year. It has been my experience that when one speaks about others it is only a disguise to talk about oneself; oblique self-portraiture as one Shakespeare biographer would have it.

I am tempted to start with the silent librarian to whom I would like to dedicate this book. Generally this type of a librarian is a woman, often with an unusual language ability and always extremely competent. Without her there would be no libraries in the world. She carefully executes day after day the workload which has been assigned to her and, if a large proportion of it must be considered as routine work, she never descends to the level of carrying out her work in a mechanical way. She sits somewhere in the production line anxiously waiting to find – among the pile of books which is being dropped as regularly on her desk as it is taken away – one book, the subject of which has a strong appeal to her or one written in a language about which she cares particularly. With the passing of years and if the library is well run, the pile of books will tend to have a majority of books of particular interest to her or mostly written in her favourite foreign language.

This is a type of librarian who is a modest member of the national library association, although this is not sure at all, and who never attends international meetings unless by sheer accident. Early in my career as a non-silent librarian, I have been instrumental in provoking such accidents with the deliberate purpose of exposing the modest but hardworking librarian to the noise of the international forum. The pretext which I used most was the poor job of interpretation carried out by professional interpreters at a General Council meeting of the International Federation of Library Associations (IFLA) in Toronto in 1967 where some rather heavy responsibility was thrust upon me, due to the illness of the president. As a result of this situation I was involved in all kinds of problems which fortunately do not come to the attention of the bulk of the participants. One of them was that half of the generous grant of the Canadian government to the local organizing committee had to be used to fly in interpreters from the UN headquarters in New York and to pay their per diem. I was deeply shocked when I discovered this imbalance, but I was simply disgusted when I tried to evaluate their performance.

I attended a meeting where all speakers were from the Library of Congress and they presented their new major programme "Shared Cataloguing" to an international audience for the first time. Since I was familiar with this programme I listened to the French interpretation and when the meeting was over I knew less than before it started. I looked at the bewildered faces of my colleagues who had to learn about the programme through this so-called French translation. Not one sentence made any sense when time and again "shared cataloguing" was translated as *"catalogue partagé,"* when it was clear from the most simple definition of the programme that it should have been *"catalogage en coopération."* To translate "union catalogue" as *"catalogue des syndicats"* is also nonsense, but it is at least funny. From that sad experience I drew two conclusions of unequal importance.

The first one was that librarians used more jargon than they were aware of, and I think that this is true of all professions. The real problems are not the obvious technical terms, but the common words with a technical meaning. Besides the already quoted examples, I could add, from French to English, the word *magasin* which should be translated by "stacks" but never is translated that way by professional interpreters. When a French-speaking librarian says that he would never allow his stacks to be open, the interpreter who uses "store" instead of "stack" should at least wonder why the store exists if it never opens, but the professional interpreter never wonders. How often have I tried to have a discussion with them, but they did not care, except when we were talking about automatic translation, computer-produced translations. Then the coffee break became the most lively part of the session. I told them that automatic translation should not yet worry them too much and that they should not yet fear for their jobs, but when I accused them of being automatic interpreters themselves, the conversation generally came to an end. [1]

My second conclusion was that I would propose to the International Federation of Library Associations to use librarian interpreters henceforth. I added that besides avoiding the wasting of money it would bring to our meetings younger librarians, selected from that silent majority which normally would only come to our international meetings when they had reached a high level in the hierarchy. In other words, when they were no longer young. I was not the only member who had come to that conclusion and it passed easily at the board.

Many years before I had a personal experience of the same problem. Actually it was my first real multinational meeting. UNESCO had brought together in Vienna in 1958 the national librarians from Europe. It was the first meeting of this type and it was also the first example of cooperation of western and eastern Europe. I was the youngest participant and was appointed secretary, together with Marie-Thérèse Kleindienst who was the assistant of Julien Cain, director of the Bibliothèque Nationale in Paris, and the oldest librarian present. I have known him for many years, always the oldest while I was, for a certain time at least, the youngest. He considered me a bit like his spiritual son, which meant in fact that I was always supposed to agree with him and to cast my vote the way he did. Among the many unpleasant results of having the responsibility of being secretary at Vienna was the fact that during the three weeks of meeting, Marie-Thérèse Kleindienst and I never went to the Opera, while all the others did, but wrote reports until late at night; and that only, on the very last

---

[1] I happened to be present at the UNESCO meeting in Paris where the Soviet delegation proposed to include Karl Marx in the programme of outstanding personalities who contributed to international cooperation. The Soviet proposal was supported by a delegate from the United Kingdom who said "After all, Marx is buried in London and quite a number of people think that his philosophy is a product of Victorian capitalism." After a couple of minutes the Soviet delegation protested vehemently and the chairman had to interrupt the meeting to discover that "Victorian capitalism" had been translated as "victorious capitalism." Rather typical, I would say.

afternoon and at my special request, did I see a few Flemish drawings from the brilliant Albertina collection, housed in the same building in which we had been meeting during these three long weeks.

The advantages of the job were that Marie-Thérèse Kleindienst, who became secretary general of the Bibliothèque Nationale, and I remained good friends, that I knew immediately the snags of international work, that I got acquainted at once with all my older colleagues, that Vienna was the beginning of many bilateral projects, and finally that I gained first-hand experience of professional interpretation. The meeting was divided into three sections, and at the one which I attended the interpretation was as primitive as the equipment. I was separated from the good-looking interpreter by a small glass partition and when I leaned back a bit I could talk to her. I was sitting between her and the chairman, the speaker having his place on the other side of the chairman. During the first day I had already noticed some awkward mistakes from French into English, but I remained silent. In the afternoon of the second day it was too much and I politely whispered in her earphone that she was wrong. I did it a couple of times and suddenly she was mad at me and asked if I could do a better job. I said yes and she wanted me to prove it. For half an hour or so I combined my work of secretary with that of interpreter. The result was not extremely good, mainly from French into English. Another result was that I took the real interpreter out for dinner. We talked a lot but used only one language. Here lies also the origin of my proposal years later in Canada to ask the librarians to be only one-way interpreters, that is to say from the foreign language into the mother tongue, the other way being too difficult if one is not a professional interpreter. As a result the International Federation of Library Associations has tried for a number of years to work with twenty-four librarian interpreters to cover the four official IFLA languages.

I readily admit that I am biased in my conclusion about this on-going experiment. It was mainly my idea, although Peter Havard-Williams, presently professor of librarianship at Loughborough University of Technology, who carried it out as head of the group of interpreters, had come to the same conclusion in Canada. Actually he was elected a vice-president of IFLA because his implementation had met with general approval. After all I may not be biased, and it may be an objective observation that the result was better than with professional interpreters and that it exposed a group of younger librarians to the mechanisms of international cooperation. The financial considerations should not be overlooked and the savings which it allowed were used for the more direct benefit of professional development.

Often I have tried to find out how other professional organizations faced with the same problems dealt with them, but circumstances have prevented me from looking carefully into the matter. I have, however, sometimes pleaded that national infrastructures, such as congress buildings with equipment for simultaneous interpretation, should include a team of interpreters put at the disposal of organizers of international meetings. It is of course easy to realize that such a solution would have to be based on professional interpreters and would not solve the problem with which I started. I have been somewhat long in this matter of interpretation, but it stands to reason that communication is the main problem of all international meetings, and that a basic understanding is already difficult enough without adding to it the charms of the Tower of Babel. And this brings a last remark to my mind. If one works with colleagues, who are not anonymous persons hidden in a booth behind a dark glass, but human faces becoming more and more familiar year after year, the chances of reaching real communication are greatest.

Vienna 1958, as I already said, was my first exposure to the international forum and hence to the leading librarians in Europe, actually not in Europe alone because the United States and Israël were invited as observers. Curt Wormann from Jerusalem wrote the best critical report on the meeting. Quincy Mumford from the Library of Congress and Brad Rogers from the National Library of Medicine at Bethesda represented the United States, introducing by this double representation the difficulties related to the definition of a national library. Actually, West Germany was also represented, for similar reasons by three librarians: Martin Cremer from the Westdeutsche Bibliothek (at the time still located in Marburg-a/L); Kurt Köster from the Deutsche Bibliothek in Frankfurt-a/M; and Gustav Hofmann from the Bayerische Staatsbibliothek in Munich. The Vienna meeting gave a lot of time to the discussion of a definition of a national library, as can still be read in the official UNESCO report. This report was edited by Maria

Razumowsky from the Austrian national library, who had been our guardian angel while we were in Vienna. Her kindness was only matched by her language ability. I was very fortunate to work with her for a period of six years at the National and University Library Section of IFLA which came out of the Vienna meeting.

Relations were close between IFLA and UNESCO in Vienna, though I was not yet familiar enough with the organizations to realize their importance. Pierre Bourgeois, president of IFLA, chaired the meeting, and said in his introductory speech that the meeting had its origin three years before in Brussels when national librarians had come for the first time to the conclusion that they had specific problems, different from those of other types of libraries. Besides the chairman, the Vienna meeting was dominated by experienced librarians like William Beattie, Leendert Brummel, Julien Cain, Martin Cremer, Laura de Felice Olivieri, Frank Francis, Gustav Hofmann, Kurt Köster, Josef Stummvoll and Uno Willers. I may have a tendency to forget some outstanding names because for one reason or other I did not meet their owners again later.

In the following years Julien Cain was always chairman of the meetings I attended. He was by far older than anybody else and behaved as if everything was due to him. Gradually I learned that he had spent part of the war in the concentration camp at Dachau and this was the reason why he was continued in function long after the normal age of retirement. Even after he had left the Bibliothèque Nationale, he remained active as the director of the Musée Jacquemart-André. I visited him many times either in his official apartment in the Bibliothèque Nationale or in a small cosy flat full of books near the Jacquemart-André or in his delicious summer house at Louveciennes, an hour's drive south of Paris. In that house, more than in the city, one felt the presence of Mrs. Cain, a striking little woman, with a rare combination of ugliness and charm, wearing red socks at an advanced age when youngsters were still dressed like part of the establishment. But above all she was a living anthology of French poetry. I remember very well a time when a visitor had learned, for the purpose, three or four obscure lines from Racine or Rimbaud and she took over when he pretended that his memory failed. I never met another person so impregnated by literature and it did not require many looks around the room and many meals to be convinced that only literature mattered in her life. The one exception, and she was proud about it, were her liqueurs, made with her own fruit thanks to the "alembic which passed in the village once a year."

It belonged to Julien Cain's philosophy of life that he would never prepare a meeting which he had to chair. He always had one or another assistant around and besides he was a master at presiding. When I saw him in earlier years he pretended during the first half hour that he was interested. In later years he fell asleep immediately after he had opened the meeting and given the floor to the first speaker, who was always extremely qualified to handle the topic under consideration, at least according to Julien Cain's introductory remarks. The wonderful part of his performance, however, was that he always awoke at the right time to close the meeting and that his short concluding comments seemed to indicate that he did not miss everything. Once I saw him flabbergasted. It was at one of UNESCO's mishaps. The advisory committee on libraries had been entrusted with an independent evaluation of UNESCO's programme in its field of competence, and in order to avoid any influence from the secretariat, the meeting was not held as usual at the headquarters but in Moscow. The only obvious result of that decision was that nearly the full secretariat of the library division had to be flown in to Moscow and that the members of the committee had never been exposed to any comparable lobbying. This is a passing remark. My main recollection is Julien Cain who awoke at the right time of the closing session, immediately after the rapporteur had read the final report. The chairman looked at the members of the committee and said in French, because he always refused to speak another language "I presume that everybody approves the report." The neighbour on my left, who had not said one word during the whole week, raised his hand and said no, also in French. Julien Cain could not believe his ears, such a thing had never happened to him during the half century that he had been chairing meetings. After a tense silence, he finally asked "But, sir, why?" and then came the most wonderful answer one could imagine: "Because I want to prove to my government that I have been here." That killed Julien Cain and all the others, and I shall not give the name of the country.

At the same meeting my other neighbour did not say much either. She was a brilliant sociologist and principal of a London college. At the very beginning she told me that she knew nothing about libraries. Since at that type of meeting we have always two fields of interest in reserve, either documentation or archives, she admitted a lack of interest in these fields too. Why was she in Moscow for that particular meeting? Those who are somewhat familiar with UNESCO will know the answer. The others will not be too surprized to hear that the distinguished member had a good friend at the headquarters in Paris who had called her a week or so before the meeting and told her that for the geographical and sexual balance of the group, it would be advisable to have a lady from the United Kingdom. But the technical competence? Well, that was not so important, because an independent consultant had written an evaluation and a competent rapporteur was going to carry out the work during the meeting. So, some common sense was enough and I can bear witness to the fact that she had a lot of it.

Once I had another alphabetical neighbour at another UNESCO meeting. I knew nothing about him and the meeting was a large and formal one at the headquarters in Paris. He came in before the morning session began and told me that he had to go to the city and that he would be back at the end of the day and asked if I would be kind enough to tell him what had happened. This lasted for two or three days and then he no longer came in the evening. One morning I told him that I had voted on his behalf. He was very thankful and did not ask how I had cast his vote. So I went on until the end of the meeting. At such meetings the voting procedure is by raising the wooden marker on which the name of one's country is inscribed. Since I had two hands I raised two markers and maybe the size of my country did not warrant two votes, but the width of my own belief certainly did. And after all I did not break the basic rule of voting at the United Nations: one country, one vote. Some time later I visited Barbados to see for myself for which country I had been voting and I came to the conclusion that I had behaved like a good citizen.

It was not yet my intention to leave Paris for Barbados because I still have a typical recollection of Julien Cain to tell. He must have learned to drive his car at the age of seventy and once I sat next to him heading for l'Etoile. After a few minutes I realized that he had a rather personal way of handling Parisian traffic and I decided that this was not only the first but also the last time that I would sit in a car with him behind the driver's wheel. At a certain moment he jumped a red light at the risk of our own and others' lives. We were stopped by a policeman. He opened his left window, took off his hat and said "Julien Cain de l'Institut" and drove on. The policeman looked at me in despair.

Somewhat later I was again driving through Paris, but this time Maurice Piquard, librarian of the Sorbonne, had our fate in his hands and there was no reason to be panic-stricken. Kitty and Frank Francis were also in the car. At a certain moment we were driving through a street called Aulard and Kitty Francis said "What a strange name." Maurice Piquard remarked that he was the well-known historian of the French Revolution, François-Alphonse Aulard, and Frank Francis said to his wife that there was nothing funny about this name, since after all in England they had Francis Bacon.

I used this story to open a book fair which was organized on the occasion of a gastronomical week in Dijon. The setting of the fair was very spiritual since it was in the deconsecrated but beautiful romanesque church of St. Philibert. It was, however, extremely cold in the church and after the Aulard-Bacon introduction I expanded a bit on the relationship of books and wine, dwelling upon the fact that both came from the press, etc. Although the low temperature called for a very short speech, the mayor, who was no longer the famous Canon Kir, but already the brilliant Minister Poujade, replied astutely "There is one major difference between books and wine. Books are cold on the feet, and wine is warm at the heart. Let us leave these books as quickly as possible and have a good glass of Burgundy." Afterwards I looked in vain for the pension where I stayed when I was a one-week student at the University of Dijon in 1940. I still remember the name of that student hostel, *Le gai manoir*.

Josef Stummvoll was not only our Austrian colleague but also our host in Vienna. It was important to have a good host in Vienna in 1958 because life was not easy at all, and the aftermath of war was still present or visible everywhere. When one walked through the streets and saw house after house, pregnant with European history, one could not get rid of the uneasy feeling that Austria's past was too heavy for the country's future. There is something strange about a city like Vienna, which is also its obvious charm – that mixture of imperial grandeur and peasant simplicity. Nothing conveys this feeling better than the old-fashioned titles of the civil servants pronounced in delectable Austrian German.

Our meeting had a formal opening in the renowned baroque reading room of the Austrian national library on the Josefsplatz, a room which serves every purpose except reading, where Josef Stummvoll spoke in six or more languages. I always suspected that he had discovered some obscure national libraries in the outskirts of Europe just to be able to welcome its director in his own language. This is all I remember about the official opening, but my recollections are more vivid regarding the unofficial opening at night in a restaurant on top of the Kahlenberg. A good and long speech was given by mayor Jonas, who was to become president of the Republic, but who was famous at the time for the Viennese Jonas-Grotten (this was the local expression for the pedestrian underpasses, for which mayor Jonas had a particular liking). His speech was brilliantly translated by Kaminkar, the father of Simone Signoret, for whose talent I am prepared to revise my mediocre opinion of most of his colleagues. And after the speech the lights were turned off and from a dark room on the hill we admired the city lights of Vienna in the valley and, of course, a waltz was played by the orchestra. While queuing at the cloakroom when everything was over I wanted to be friendly to the person standing in front of me and I wanted to ask her if she had enjoyed the evening. Not knowing which language to use, I decided to try pidgin French: "*Vous amusée?*" She looked at me a bit surprised and said: "*Non à bibliothèque!*"

Josef Stummvoll left the National Library of Austria for a number of years to become director of the library of the United Nations in New York. I met him there from time to time and I have already told the story of the dedication of the Dag Hammerskjöld Library. The keynote speaker was Uno Willers, director of the Royal Library of Sweden, and a close friend of Dag Hammerskjöld. I remember that among many points in common there was a privileged place for French literature. At a certain moment they both had a French candidate for the Nobel Prize. Hammerskjöld's candidate got it, Willers' nearly. I still see Uno Willers dancing with our Soviet colleague in Vienna, *détente-avant-la-lettre*, and when I met him again it was in Moscow in a wheel chair. His physical helplessness was only matched by his moral courage. For many years he went on directing the Royal Library while he could only move in a wheel chair. In Moscow he came to the IFLA meeting, which coincided with the one hundredth anniversary of

Lenin's birth, to present to the Lenin Library the table on which Lenin had been working regularly at the Royal Library in Stockholm. Such tables of Lenin remind me irreverently of the beds of Napoleon and of the wood of the holy cross. Also of the story of Karl Marx and the reading room of the British Museum, which I have already told.

While Josef Stummvoll was in New York we organized together a glorious exhibition of artistic documents related to Belgian history kept in the National Library of Austria. Each of the 159 items was a visual evocation of an important moment or event in our national history. It would be impossible to open the catalogue without going into a long series of digressions about the Habsburgs or about the Flemish artists who worked for them. Instead I would prefer to dwell upon its front cover which has an exquisite miniature portrait of Marguerita of Austria topped by her motto *Fortvne Infortvne Fort Vne*. My colleagues in Brussels and I picked it out, because for once we had a bilingual motto, that is to say we had a Latin one for the Dutch catalogue *Fortis Fortvna Infortvnat Fortiter Vnam*. It has been a major tragedy of my life, mainly professional, that mottoes, puns, coined phrases, striking sentences could never be used in the two national languages.

The language story which links Josef Stummvoll to the opening of the Brussels exhibition can however be told. He had come to Brussels from New York on the occasion of his home leave and he had decided to travel via Central and South America. When he arrived in Brussels the day before the opening, he told me that he would not only say a few words in French but also in Dutch. Knowing his language ability I was not surprised and was pleased from a local political point of view. He wondered if I would care to listen to his Dutch pronunciation. When I heard him I was amazed and told him politely that he had not been speaking Dutch. "Well," he said to me, "I went for a haircut in Willemstad in Curaçao and the hairdresser and I wrote that short text together." We had a good time when we found out that it was written in Papiamento, which is a rather mathematical mixture of English, Spanish and Dutch. The Dutch speech which he delivered next day was much less fun and instead of writing it I should have left Josef Stummvoll with his poetic version of the historical relations between the southern Low Countries and Austria. I did not have the courage to tell him that I had instituted a bilingual silence at the opening of the exhibitions of the Royal Library, no speeches in either of the two national languages. It is curious how people complain about boring opening speeches, and are greatly disappointed when there are none.

Sometimes I have the feeling that the International Federation of Library Associations, UNESCO, the Internationel Federation for Documentation and the Soviet Union all came into my quiet life at home at the same time, which is not true of course. Before I had to preside over the General Council of IFLA in Moscow in 1970, I had been to the Soviet Union a few times, either with a UNESCO committee or with an IFLA Board. I had even been once with a Belgian friend on private business. He was a typographer and by now the reader will know that I was not uninterested in typography. We had a few copies with us of a reprint of the second book issued in Moscow: *Tchassovnik* (Moscow, Ivan Federov and Petr Timofeev, 1564). For some mysterious reason, the only known copy of the original edition of this book belonged to the Royal Library in Brussels. It was J.S.G. Simmonds, Slavicist and bibliographer from Oxford, who had drawn my attention to the uniqueness of this copy which the Library had sent to him by ordinary mail. My friend was working in a thriving reprint business and we decided to make a reprint of the book with a bibliographic and historical introduction by J.S.G. Simmonds. The reprint was soon ready but we had waited a couple of years for the introduction and the copies we finally took to Moscow were without it. We distributed the copies to the main libraries in Moscow and we took one to the Institute of Marxism-Leninism. This was not exactly a place where interest in liturgical books of the sixteenth century is high, but we had an idea in the back of our mind. We wanted to make a reprint of the *Deutsche Brüsseler Zeitung*, a weekly which Karl Marx published in Brussels in 1847-1848. The most complete copy is at the Royal Library in Brussels, but it still lacks a number of issues. The two other known copies are at the Institute of Social History in Amsterdam and the Institute of Marxism-Leninism in Moscow. Merging the three copies would have given a quasi-complete set that could be used for the reprint. I wanted to secure permission to use the Moscow copy for this purpose. This was granted. I am sure that the 1564 imprint of our Tchassovnik had nothing to do with this agreement, but rather the fact that I came from Belgium. A few years before my visit a well-known Belgian socialist leader,

Camille Huysmans (1871-1968) had given to the Institute the many letters which Lenin had written to him before World War I. In the meantime our project did not materialize. Such failures are always disappointing.

I might as well deal with UNESCO here, because my presidency of IFLA coincided roughly with the years a Soviet staff-member, Oleg Mikhailov, spent at UNESCO as director of the Division of Libraries, Documentation and Archives. I would have been a better president if this coincidence had not existed. We had nothing in common and we were forced to cooperate. I do not want to be unfair to a man I never understood, but with his smiling ignorance he has constantly hurt me. He started each conversation by telling me that he was an engineer, and that he had no interest in libraries (which he was supposed to help in their development). Time and again he repeated to me how wonderful an organization the International Federation for Documentation (FID) was and what a nuisance IFLA was. Although I have tried to avoid identifying UNESCO with Oleg Mikhailov, I must confess that in my opinion an organization which gives leading positions to people of this type is looking for trouble. Such an organization lacks the intellectual integrety to face basic problems which are unavoidable in the world in which we live.

Before Oleg Mikhailov I had known two of his predecessors, Everett Petersen and Carlos Penna. Both of them were as different from one another, as each of them was from Oleg Mikhailov. Though Everett Petersen was an American he had a kind of nonchalance about him which must have been the result of his French environment. Through his wife he lived in a Bourdelle atmosphere and as an international civil servant he was taking life easy. As a rule the American librarians did not like him and they reacted as if he had betrayed their national characteristics. I got along rather well with him because, I guess, he considered me as sufficiently half-way between the Old and the New World, between east and west, between librarian and documentalist, between governmental and nongovernmental associations, an ideal man-in-the-middle with whom he would not have too much trouble. It was also the time when another American librarian was director-general of UNESCO, Luther Evans, whom I had met briefly while he was still Librarian of Congress. In Paris I had no direct contact with him and I heard rumours that his term of office was tinted sombrely by the McCarthy era. Luther Evans came over from Paris to Brussels to give a speech at the opening session of the 1955 congress of the International Federation of Library Associations. I remember that he nearly insulted his audience by blaming the librarians for spending too much money on their buildings. To have said that in Brussels, a few months after the cornerstone of the new building of the national library had been laid, should have sounded prophetic to those who were going to be responsible for an awfully expensive building. For me it was my first, and limited, contact with both UNESCO and the International Federation of Library Associations, since I was in the rather dubious position of waiting for my appointment.

Carlos Penna was a proselyte, sometimes a dangerous one, who kept himself alive at UNESCO because he was a Latin American. He had one single idea and a good one at that: library planning. If one agreed with him on the importance of library planning one immediately became an outstanding librarian. Much to his credit I would say that he forced quite a number of librarians to broaden their horizon, to consider themselves a part, but not the most important part, of the educational process, to talk in terms of cost/benefit and to go beyond mere shop talk. I had easy and difficult moments with him. One had to reserve the serious problems for after the siesta. In Buenos Aires we had a good time. He felt at home and introduced me to all aspects of local life. There I only had a good-will speech to make on the occasion of the seventy-fifth anniversary of the International Federation for Documentation. I still regret that I did not have the presence of mind to conclude my speech by saying that, after all, the so-called technical assistance which the rich countries were offering to the poor ones would never amount to anything like the gift of the potato which was received by Europe from Latin America four hundred years before.

With the successor of Oleg Mikhailov we remain in Latin America, since it was the Brazilian Celia Zaher who took over. *La passionaria* of documentation, as she was called in the corridors of UNESCO. She talked too much and did not listen enough. I told her this repeatedly, but to no avail. She devoted too much of her time to that kind of internal fighting of which international governmental organizations have the secret. Elsewhere I have referred to this empire building. When the fight with Adam

Wysocki was hottest and she was doomed to lose it, I sided with her. Not because I wanted to be gallant, but because she occupied a position in UNESCO where she should have been the spokesperson – must one say it that way? – of the library community. If Oleg Mikhailov had still been there I would have taken sides with him. This reminds me of the origin of the big fight within UNESCO. I sensed it when UNISIST was mentioned for the first time at the International Advisory Committee on Libraries, Documentation and Archives of which I was an old member. I asked Oleg Mikhailov how he reacted to the UNISIST initiative taken illogically outside his division. "That is very simple," he said, "On Sunday, Adam and I go to the Bois de Boulogne, we play a game of *pétanque* and we empty a bottle of vodka." I did not laugh, realizing that a lot of time and money was going to be lost in sterile fights. A year later Adam told me "No Bois de Boulogne, no *pétanque* and no vodka any more."

Somewhere in the background of my relations with UNESCO, more particularly during the Mikhailov era, lingered the image of the International Federation for Documentation. An effort can and should be made to look objectively at organizations and institutions, but personal attitudes very often exclude rational explanations. Allegiance to one or another organization inevitably results in irrational sympathies and antipathies among people representing those organizations. It is quite normal that I single out Helmut Arntz who was my opposite number all the time in the International Federation for Documentation. He was a German who spoke twice as many languages and twice as much as I did. Strangely enough he seemed to be proud to be no documentalist, and often repeated to me and others that he was responsible for publications of the Federal Republic of Germany in more than twenty different languages, a job for which he was freed from a university. He lived on the Rhine in "Burg Arntz," a *fin-de-siècle* villa which bore his family's name. I once attended a *Sektprobe*, a tasting of German champagne in his house, because he was president of the German wine tasters. I was a rather dry participant because I was afraid to miss the plane which was to take me to Canada the next morning. Later he repeated the tasting in my home on the occasion of a board meeting of the International Federation of Library Associations and it was an enjoyable introduction to the discussions where good wine, to smooth the path, would not be available. Looking at our numerous meetings on the four continents I must confess that the sites changed all the time, but that the contents of the arguments seemed to be part of the luggage which we took with us. It once occurred to me, in the middle of a sentence, that both of us were wearing the same tie as at the previous time when we were voicing the same opinions. This proves that the rationale of progress is not very rational. Neither of us could help that circumstances had given a queer slant to our relations. After all, Brussels was my home town and, much more than I, he was the spokesman for those professional ideas, to start with his own organization FID and all it stands for, which were born in the shadow of my library. One day the circle may be closed when the International Federation for Documentation will have as its president the director of the Royal Library of Belgium. And if he should be a man born in Brussels it would be even better!

While measuring the similarities and the differences between FID and IFLA, my attention was drawn by Hermann Fussler from the University of Chicago to the doctoral thesis written by W. Boyd Rayward on *The Universe of Information: The Work of Paul Otlet for Documentation and International Organization*. I had some difficulty in finding a copy, but I finally got one. What a strange publication: Belgian subject treated by an American author, printed in the Soviet Union and distributed from Holland! Let me immediately say that the author has done an outstanding job and that his subject was worth the trouble he took to analyze and document it in such a detailed way. This will remain the definitive work on Paul Otlet, the pioneer in the field of international organization, documentation and information of a generation which lived in the dreamworld of eternal peace, notwithstanding that the first world war had scattered its ideals. It is pathetic to see how stubbornly Paul Otlet, Henri La Fontaine – Nobel Prize for Peace in 1913! – and their associates tried to rebuild their perfect society in spite of the grim realities of the surrounding world. Fortunately Rayward's text does not confirm the naïve paragraph of his preface where he hopes that the failure of Otlet's visionary zeal will be replaced by the success of UNESCO's computer. It is sad that a good book should be sent into the world in such a shape. It is "published for the International Federation for Documentation (FID) by All-Union Institute for Scientific and Technical Information (VINITI)." As usual poor paper, poor printing, poor illustrations, but a very low price, as with all Soviet books; in this case, 2R.14k. At what rate of exchange FID Headquarters in The Hague reckon the rouble I do not know, but I had to pay $ 15. for the book! This is too steep, even with the free leaflet of Errata included. A dozen errata are listed, but a dozen on each page would be more accurate. Never were misprints so expensive. I do not know Boyd Rayward personally, but he must be very unhappy to see what happened to his excellent work. And if for one reason or another he is not, he should be.

International Book Year (IBY) exposed me to a completely different world, one where I felt among kindred spirits. It brought back to me once more the priority of persons over organizations and even UNESCO took on a fairer face. I was ready to accept any commitment because IBY provided me, as a librarian, with an opportunity to try to convince the other representatives of the book profession that librarians were people with a broad scope of vision and did not limit themselves to cataloguing technicalities. Earlier I had already been able to follow a similar line with educationists, when I worked with Carlos V. Penna on problems of library planning and actually repeating a previous experience when I had been involved in library building with architects and designers.

IBY started in a strange way for me. Late in February 1970, I flew from Erevan, Armenia, to Milan, Italy, to attend the first informal planning meeting of IBY. I had been invited, through the cultural agreement between the Soviet Union and Belgium to visit the USSR in wintertime to see places with which I was not yet familiar. Vilnius, west of Moscow, and Erevan, south, were picked out. In both places my Russian interpreter was not of great use and most toasts had to be translated twice. This was not of much importance, and even less when the words were spoken after glasses of vodka in Lithuania and of cognac in Armenia. In the University Library of Vilnius I had a particular interest in the private library of Joachim Lelewel which was kept there, apparently in its original set-up. When Lelewel was a political refugee in Belgium he worked for more than a quarter of a century as a numismatist and historian in the Coin Room of the Royal Library. Some of the manuscript tools which he devised, such as the first inventory of the coin collection of the city of Brussels, have not yet been completely superseded. Two visual memories of Vilnius remained with me for many years:

the huge reconstructed ghetto and the dominant Gothic of the historic buildings. An old encounter, which I had completely forgotten, came back to my mind while I was walking in the cold snow of Vilnius. During my first trip to the United States, twenty years earlier, I visited a large and famous printing plant in Chicago, the Lakeside Press. A young printer, standing next to his press, said rather abruptly to me "You are from Europe?" "Yes." "Europe is hell and America is paradise." "Well, I said, it is not as simple as that. . . ." "Listen, I am from Lithuania, my father was killed by the Germans and my mother by the Russians." He brought his press to full speed and the noise took care of the rest of the conversation.

It is a long distance from Vilnius to Erevan in all respects. My first morning in Armenia started with breakfast in the rare books reading room of the national library. It did not start early and it lasted late. The Armenian table was set as for a banquet, with wine and cognac. Fourteen people were present and after two toasts of cognac I understood that another twelve were ahead. At the fourth I said to my interpreter that I wanted to propose the next one. He tried to protest but I got up, feeling that I was still able to say what I wanted. My interpreter – who was only an intermediary because his Russian still had to be translated into Armenian – whispered in my ear that my toast had a couple of inaccuracies. I told him that it was not of the slightest importance and pressed him to translate. What I finally said in Armenian I shall never know, but the *tamada* was very pleased and breakfast with toasts went on for the better part of the morning.

My recollections of the few days I spent in Armenia remain rather vague. It seems to me that each time I saw a library it was sandwiched between two meals. All that I still see are vertical rows of books and horizontal layers of food. More food on the table when the meal was over than before it started. Some meals were served in farms where women promised to improve their local library work, while they were pouring wine or cognac, and men were busy outside with the fire and the kebab. I remember, or at least I think I remember, that in one of these farms it was enough to recline backwards from the chair to land on a kind of bed, which ran along three of the four walls.

My memory singles out two libraries: a children's library and the Matenaradan. The children's library had nothing exceptional except that I was welcomed by a group of very young pioneers who were singing revolutionary songs, I imagine, in my honour. I was coming straight from one of my memorable meals – no way to tell whether it was lunch or dinner – and at the end of the two long rows of young pioneers, with their white shirts and red scarves, between which I passed, shaking hands on the left and smiling on the right, I discovered a table with bottles of champagne. That was too much and I felt for the youngest pioneer who had so much trouble with the bottle that he spilled half of the champagne on the ground. Since then, wrongly or rightly, I have associated Soviet children's libraries with champagne offered by pioneers.

The Matenaradan is another story and I was so much impressed by this unique centre for the study of Armenian civilization that I strongly advised my Iranian friends to copy it for their proposed Persian centre. There was a monumental entrance to a large reading room where original Armenian manuscripts could be studied in ideal circumstances because a large and up-to-date reference library was available. The collection of precious books is kept in stacks hewn in the rock and I understand that the fifteen thousand items represent half of the Armenian manuscripts still in existence, the other half being scattered with the Armenians in the diaspora. I was shown some striking examples of Armenian book illumination and was told that the colophons are more picturesque than in the western manuscripts.

Every morning when I left the hotel I saw Mount Ararat and it did not take long before I realized that every Armenian was ready to cross the border and to fight a new war against the Turks, were it not for the Soviet government which prevented it. I also talked French to a few Armenians who had spent their youth in Lyon, France, and who had been induced by the Soviet authorities to start a new life in their homeland after the war. These conversations were not devoid of some nostalgia, and I was a big disappointment to them when I could not tell how the Armenian quarter of Lyon fared in the sixties. I knew something about early printing in Lyon in the sixteenth century but it did not restore my standing. I should not end my visit to Erevan in too serious a vein, even though I have forgotten almost all the thousand Radio Erevan jokes which were told to me. (One which I had forgotten, but heard again recently – Q: Could the United States turn communist? A: Yes, but who would then sell corn to the Soviet Union?) Upon arrival one of my hosts said that it was a pity that I had not come one week earlier because I could have met Marc Aryan. Who was Marc Aryan, I asked myself, was he a famous poet, painter, or composer whom I should know? I had not the slightest idea. When I was shown somewhat later a stadium where Marc Aryan had attracted twenty thousand people I excluded the poet and the painter, but still had no clue. Once I was back home I confessed my ignorance about Marc Aryan and my son asked with contempt if I really did not know him, Marc Aryan, the most popular Belgian crooner and of Armenian origin.

In Armenia one of my hosts was Nathalia Tyulina who had written a thesis on *Byron in Russia*. The day after I left her I met Robert Escarpit who had written a thesis on *Byron in France*. This occurred at the first meeting of International Book Year which took place at the Villa Serbelloni, on Lake Como, where a paper-free, off-the-record, and brain-storming session was going to keep very different bookmen together for a week. All who have had the privilege to attend a meeting at the Villa Serbelloni, which belongs to the Rockefeller Foundation, know that it is one of the most congenial places one can imagine. Meetings at the Villa are small and last normally from Tuesday through Friday, short enough to make the participants jealous of the writers-in-residence at the Villa who can stay there for several weeks. My good friend Kees Reedijk, director of the Royal Library in the Hague, was one such lucky man who could edit in this gracious place the Lyell lectures on *Erasmus and his Printers*, which he had given at Oxford.

Viewed in retrospect this planning meeting must have been very good since IBY became a generally acclaimed venture. The quality of the work at the Villa was set by a background paper prepared for IFLA by Wim Koops, a librarian with experience as a publisher. Another reason for the positive aspects of IBY is the leadership Julian Behrstock gave to the whole enterprise. Although he was a UNESCO official, cooperation with him is one of my most pleasant recollections. He could strike the right balance in his dealings with nongovernmental organizations. He was also very clever in using them to carry out assignments which would create political problems if dealt with at the governmental level. He gave me my share of them. The many discussions I had with Vladimir Naidenov, from the State Committee of the Press in Moscow, on copyright, censorship, pornography, etc. were more exciting than pleasant. He was an outstanding debater, who always had the last word by quoting an old Russian saying. I still suspect him of having invented on the spot quite a number of such old Russian proverbs.

The only drawback I could discover, later in the Villa meeting, was the lack of interest from the people responsible for the physical problems related to book production. Although the famed typographer John Dreyfus was present at the Villa and made an excellent contribution to the meeting, later on there were practically no contributions from printers, papermakers, typefounders, engravers, etc. Indirectly the International Typographical Association was instrumental in securing the cooperation of Michel Olyffe, who designed the IBY logo, which was soon to conquer the whole world. The worst absence was that of the papermakers. Even those who have only a superficial experience of the literacy problems in the developing world know that the lack of paper supply blocks most of the progress. Relapse into illiteracy is nearly always caused by the absence of reading material. Tropical wood being generally inadequate for paperpulp, international cooperation is vital in this field. That IBY could not enhance this cooperation is its major failure.

In my eyes Julian Behrstock had only one weakness. He preferred publishers to librarians, and he actually blamed the poor librarians for being well organized as compared to the rich publishers who were poorly organized. Through him I made the acquaintance of Ted Waller, a New York publisher, who had been active in the American Library Association as a link between publishers and librarians. The renowned *Freedom to Read* manifesto is one of the results of this cooperation. A footnote to my association with Ted Waller is the lecture I gave at his suggestion at the Las Vegas meeting of the American Library Association in 1973 on "Reading in the Next Decade." It is a shame to mention in the same context IBY and Las Vegas.

Fortunately, committee meetings of International Book Year were held in more decent cities. I have already mentioned initial and informal meetings in the small village of Bellagio on Lake Como and the official and dull meeting in the huge Union Palace of Moscow. Julian Behrstock and his UNESCO colleague Jean Millerioux had the good idea to suggest that we should meet in the home cities of the various members of the Committee. At the invitation of Dr. O.G. Prachner, president of the International Community of Booksellers Associations, we had a very pleasant meeting in Vienna, while Ted Waller, representing the publishers in our midst, brought us to New York from where we issued the *Mohonk Statement* which I think will remain as one of the better texts inspired by International Book Year. At Shoichi Noma's suggestion we had a meeting and lecture programme in Tokyo where we could familiarize ourselves with the tremendous achievements of our Japanese colleagues in the whole of the East, going from children's books in various languages to the creation of typographical alphabets. There is no reason to mention various meetings at UNESCO headquarters in Paris or in Brussels, where I was the host and where nothing special happened, except that we got, *du bout des lèvres,* grudgingly, the Soviet agreement on an IBY Manifesto, notwithstanding a serious argument about the book versus the good book. I was so happy with this Soviet agreement that I immediately ordered a calligraphic version of the statement. Later in the year the King gave a party in honour of International Book Year for the hundreds of delegates which the Book Fair had brought to Brussels, but I had to miss it because the International Federation of Library Associations had once more taken me out of the country. Since the IBY Committee had not yet visited all the members in their home base when the International Book Year was over we transformed our Planning and Organizing Committee into a Support Committee and we happily met at Cardenas Nanetti's invitation in Bogota, Columbia.

I would have liked to spend more time in Columbia because Latin America is a weak spot in my knowledge of the world. I have already mentioned a short visit to Argentina and after Bogota I went on a tourist tour to Guatemala to see the early Maya monuments after I had seen the later ones in Yucatan. When I first arrived in Mexico City I was taken on a tour by Armando M. Sandoval with whom I had been sitting earlier in a UNESCO committee. Sandoval had just been appointed director of the University Library and I told him I knew this Library well from the outside because photographs of its beautiful murals had been used by the Belgian airlines to publicize its schedule to Mexico. "Yes," he sighed, "it may be from the outside one of the most beautiful libraries of the world, but from the inside certainly one of the worst." Later I heard that he had resigned shortly after he had taken over.

I have two other recollections of my Mexican trip. Still in Mexico

City I was taken by the owner of a chain of department stores to one of those fashionable houses which had to be abandoned for safety reasons because the city was gradually sinking. It was rather mysterious in such a house with dim light and full of cobwebs, behind which I could see some paintings hanging slantwise on the walls. The owner was proud of his Belgian origin and of the quality of his Flemish paintings. As a tribute to his country of origin he wanted to present the collection, which also included a couple of illuminated manuscripts, to the city of Bruges. I gave a carefully balanced opinion on the paintings, protesting my lack of competence, but since it was only one point of view among the several he was soliciting, I encouraged him to stick to his idea and his paintings are now part of the collection of the Bruges museum.

From Oaxaca my wife and I shared a taxi with an American couple to go to the ruins of Monte Albán. This was a rather strange ride where the scenery did not seem to interest either the American travellers or us. I had the feeling that the husband was not unfamiliar to me and I tried to listen to the conversation he had with his wife. Although my wife and I spoke Dutch he did not seem to be totally uninterested in what we were saying to each other. When we reached our destination he said to me, "Mr. Liebaers, I presume," and I said "Mr. Kristeller, I presume." We were of course both right, and he took a galley proof from his pocket with an article on a manuscript from the Royal Library. Believe it or not, but three weeks later I ran into him again on the campus of Columbia University. This reminds me that three times I met abroad by accident my compatriot Herman Bouchery, curator of the Plantin Moretus Museum in Antwerp before he became professor of Renaissance Latin at Ghent University. The last time this happened was at the church of Brou not long before his death. On this occasion we discovered the explanation of our identical first name: our fathers shared an enthusiasts' admiration for the Dutch revolutionary poet Herman Gorter (1864-1927). Although Herman Bouchery was an outstanding bookman, his story had made me forget International Book Year.

How Dina Malhotra, the successful publisher in Delhi of the first Hindi bestseller, managed to get the Committee to India I do not know since I was no longer a member. I have, however, recollections of my various visits to India and of my meetings with Dina in Delhi. He gave me a beautiful Sarasvathi painted on linen. This goddess of wisdom had been with me since I learned from Mal-colm S. Adiseshiah, then assistant director-general of UNESCO, that in some parts of India people open a book once a year to spread saffran over the page to honour Saravathi puja. I have tried over and over again to desanctify the book, to replace the saffran by the alphabet, to open the book daily, to say that the Bhagavad-gita is all right, but that a telephone directory should not be scorned. The choice is very often, in many parts of the world, between God and hunger, or food and nuisance. Those stupid Westerners who want to live and moreover want others to live like Easterners, always bring Peter Ustinov to my mind, who said that it is fun to be poor when you are rich. [2]

I once even paid an unexpected visit to Dina Malhotra. My plane had been delayed at the airport of Delhi, where it was awfully hot. I was booked for Kabul from where I wanted to proceed to Bamian to see the rupicolous Buddhas on the Silk Road, and although my Afghan plane was on the tarmac we had to wait for more than thirty hours because the airport of destination was snowed in. I finally gave up, joined a genuine Indian party at Dina's home and never made Kabul. I went straight to Tehran and what happened to me there has already been told.

Before I visited India for the first time I had already been introduced to the subcontinent by my colleague and friend Kesh, B.S. Keshavan, former director of the National Library in Calcutta and afterwards director of the Indian Documentation Centre in Delhi. He was one of those brilliant Oxford graduates, quoting his classics in English and in German while spreading his deeply rooted religious wisdom over his audience. Although he induced me to visit his country, he was absent the first time I arrived in Delhi, because he had already left for a UNESCO meeting in Manila, which he was going to chair and where I was going to join him as an expert (together with Rudy Rogers, at the time Assistant Librarian of Congress). By accident I arrived in Delhi on National Day and the first thing I saw on the ground was a beautifully painted elephant. Kesh had never told me that all elephants were beauti-fully painted in India. It did not take me long to see why. The Belgian ambassador took me to the parade and I was very much impressed by the dark-skinned bagpipers wearing kilts. This first

[2] A few months ago I met Peter Ustinov and I asked him if this was a true quotation. He answered that he was not sure but that it was good enough to be by him.

visit to Delhi, on my way to Manila, expanded my horizon beyond
Europe and the United States. The more so that after the Manila
meeting I went unexpectedly to Japan, and being there I decided
that I might as well go home via the United States to complete my
first world tour.

In Manila, I arrived at night, and having spent the whole day in a
plane, I went out for a walk. It did not last long and next morning
at the opening briefing I understood very well why men were
advised not to walk alone at night in the streets of Manila. Rudy
Rogers and I fully agreed on two points in our Pilippino experience: all girls were beautiful and our friend Kesh talked too much
as chairman. When we happened to pass, in the street, a young
woman who was not beautiful we could not take our eyes off her
because it was so unexpected. Kesh domineered heavily over his
Asian colleagues, many of them even having difficulty in making
themselves understood in English. Rudy and I told him to restrain
himself somewhat and he was genuinely and sadly surprised at our
remarks. As chairman he once went around the table with the
question: "How many books are published yearly in your country?" The first librarian could not answer the question. I am not
going to give the name of the country though it is not difficult to
find out since at UNESCO one always sits in alphabetical order even
in a part of the world where the alphabet has still to be invented.
Kesh said "Well, think it over, I only want a rough estimate, one
hundred or one thousand, and I shall come back to you at the end
of the round." At that time the man said, still after some hesitation
"twenty," and this is why technical assistance is so awfully difficult
and disappointing. I was surprised to see my old friend Curt
Wormann from Jerusalem in Manila. I told him that I did not
know that he was an Asian. "Neither did I," was his answer.
UNESCO had to cut the world into parts, in one way or another, and
that is why the best national librarian of my generation, trained in
Leipzig, was sitting in Manila at the same table as the one who did
not know how many books were printed in his country.

The meeting was also attended by two Japanese colleagues from
the Diet Library in Tokyo. I told them that I was considering a
return trip via their country, where I had never been. Next morning they told me they had called Tokyo and had reserved a room
for me at the International House of Japan and they asked me if I
had any special wishes. Surprised, I said – just to say something –

calligraphy. Next morning they told me that they had called Tokyo and had made an appointment with a calligrapher (see p. 185). At this stage I had no choice but to go home via Japan. I was happy to leave the Philippines. I did not like the country at all and I promised myself never to go back, but I went back and did not regret it. That time I met the director of the National Museum. Not long before she had been appointed, (a political appointee as one would have it) she had been elected Miss Universe, and the better part of the collection for which she was responsible was photographs of her when she was initiated in the rites of a remote mountain tribe. Who says that museums are dead places? Still during the same trip, when I had to make a stopover in Hawaii, I made a similar promise not to visit that island a second time, but I went back again without regretting it. The first time I saw only Waikiki Beach and the second time the University. That very year the month of February had thirty days for me and the other passengers who crossed the international date line eastbound.

My second visit to India was the most serious one and had been prepared by Kesh. It was another UNESCO meeting which had brought me to Ceylon, not yet called Sri Lanka, and when the work was over I joined my wife in Madras from where we started a five-weeks' tour of the country. In Colombo, I had met D.R. Kalia whom I was going to see again in Calcutta, where he succeeded Kesh as director of the National Library. I heard later that he had to take up his post under the protection of the army. They did not like one another as was true of most Indians whom I knew. This observation has very often intrigued me, because I was not the only foreigner to make it. Individually they all had a lot of charm and I understand very well British nostalgia for India, but I would venture as an explanation that belonging to a certain caste made them so proud that lack of modesty was not their least obvious weakness. They knew everything so well, they were so sure of themselves and the gods were always with them.

When we drove back from our first trip to the shore temples near Madras, Kesh, my wife and I were caught in a street riot. Kids shouted, threw stones, jumped on our car and I did not understand what it was all about. Kesh told us that they were shouting "Hindi down" and that the whole trouble was a language issue. Coming from Belgium I felt immediately at ease and we arrived safely at the hotel. The explanation which Kesh gave us afterwards was that our visit coincided with the twentieth anniversary of the country's independence and that Delhi wanted to drop English as an associate language, as written into the constitution, and impose Hindi as a national language. The Tamil people won the battle and I was fully on their side. Kesh was a good guide in the inexplicable language situation of the country. He was, among many other things, the proud publisher of the first volume of the national bibliography using twelve different languages, I think. I should remember the figure better because I saw Kesh very often, in and outside India, walking around with the heavy red volume under his arm.

In the state of Mysore I was an official guest and after the introduction Kesh left. The first day we had a working breakfast with the chief-minister S. Nijalingappa who had just been elected chairman of the Congress party and was leaving for Delhi. He told us that, to have a chance to succeed at the national level in such a vast country, one had to tackle the problems with an *idée fixe*. Some had tried it with fertilizers, some with family planning, and he had decided that his way would be water, a fuller use of the available water. I never saw him again but I heard that it did not take long before he was at cross purposes with Indira Gandhi. At the end of the breakfast he began to talk to us with great excitement about the forthcoming Khedda. We did not know what a Khedda was, but he made it quite clear to us that it was the capture of a herd of wild elephants, celebrated all over the world as the big event of Mysore. It took place every seven or eight years. This however would be the last one and it was organized as a contribution of India to the International Year of Tourism. If we happened to be in his state three weeks later, it would be a pleasure for him to have us as his guests. Since we would not be, we forgot all about it. How great was our surprise when we received three weeks later, late at night in our hotel room in Bombay, where we were waiting to fly home next day, a telephone call telling us that the invitation was still standing and that if we decided to fly back to Bangalore the next day a car would meet us at the airport to take us to the Khedda. We attended the Khedda after we had spent the night in a guesthouse which was still as British as it could be: tea in bed, newspaper, perfect service and unexceptional food. The Khedda is a sight for the gods, as the "National Geographic" put it, covering with striking photographs and an excellent text the setting, the wild elephants, the tame elephants, the elephant drivers and us.

During the three weeks which separated us from the first meeting with S. Nijalingappa and the actual Khedda, I had been a guest of the Indian Council for Cultural Relations, and had given a series of lectures, one of which started at 6 AM under a tree at the school of the national professor of library science, Ranganathan. The wise man from India had many admirers in the West, but I was not one of them. He may have been an outstanding theorist but the actual library situation in his country was appalling before, during and after his reign. I visited many libraries and saw not one that could be considered satisfactory. My only good recollection was from a university library, where above the entrance of a reading room an inscription was written in an alphabet that I could not decipher and which meant, "Let no harm come to those who work with these books." I visited more temples than libraries and I did not see one house of the gods that did not appeal to me. If one's thoughts move from temples to libraries it is not hard to guess where wisdom lies.

Still in Mysore we spent Christmas eve in a national park where we were housed in a small, primitive and ugly cabin. The food was very poor and the cook explained that it was because he was drunk and that he was drunk because he was a Christian from Goa. We had not asked for an explanation. On arrival before sunset we were put on the back of a tame elephant to watch wild animals. Unfortunately we did not see many. The next morning before sunrise the curator of the park took us in his jeep. Except for a few wild elephants, which in fact we could only hear, the result was as disappointing as the ride on the back of the elephant, but for the black panther that jumped in front of the jeep and disappeared immediately in the bushes at the very moment that we were entering the curator's garden. He had not seen one for many years.

We saw the Taj Mahal at sunset on 31 December and again at sunrise on 1 January 1968. Dare I say that the Taj is too perfect for my taste, even the lettering on both sides of the main entrance? This does not mean that I prefer the heartbreaking scenes on the banks of the Ganges in Benares. Between these two extremes the choice is easy, but as long as the Taj Mahal belongs to the cosmopolitan jet-set and the Ganges to the local people there is something rotten in the kingdom of the Mahatma.

10. Recollections as IFLA President

TORONTO 1967, Moscow 1970, Liverpool 1971, Budapest 1972, Grenoble 1973 and Washington 1974: there are the cities and the dates of General Councils of the International Federation of Library Associations (IFLA) where I had the honour and the pleasure to preside. In Toronto, it was by accident because the president, Sir Frank Francis, was ill. I arrived innocently at the airport to learn that I had to take over in my capacity of first vice-president. I was scared to death. What worried me most was the fact that I had to read out the opening address which Sir Frank had prepared, and I knew from previous meetings that it was written in an elegant style full of subtle quotations from the most outstanding English authors. It was Shakespeare who was my most certain enemy. Even before reading the president's text I was sure I would meet Shakespeare after a couple of paragraphs, because once Sir Frank had told me – I think it was on a bus trip to Plovdiv – that you always could quote Shakespeare in any circumstance. Fortunately I felt relieved when Foster Mohrhardt, another vice-president, agreed to read Sir Frank's paper. It pleases me to be able to introduce here immediately the name of Foster Mohrhardt who has meant most to me in my IFLA years. He has been the connecting link between the New and the Old World. I would also add between the old and the new IFLA. For me he is also the one who allowed me to merge professional and personal relations: a librarian and a friend. Over the years I made many friends among my colleagues and I owe it to Foster's inspiring kindness. My only regret is that circumstances prevented him from becoming president of IFLA. He would have been outstanding, just as he was a good ALA president in his home country. Writing now nearly four years after my retirement as president, I would like to pronounce in the same breath the name of another vice-president, another potential president of IFLA, another former president of ALA: Robert Vosper, another dear friend.

Moscow was my first regular meeting as president. I look back to it with mixed feelings. It came too soon after the Frankfurt meeting in 1968, where in the middle of the General Council, the news reached us of the Soviet invasion of Czechoslovakia. The day before this happened the Board had decided to nominate me as president and that, in the meanwhile, I would only have a very light responsibility, more particularly taking care of international goodwill relations. As a result I spent the better part of the following night running back and forth between the hotels where the Soviet delegation and the Czechoslovak librarians stayed. The two groups were sad, silent and bewildered. They couldn't make up their minds whether to stay or to leave. I asked them to take no decision under the stress of the first hours. Next morning all participants met in the large hall of the university library and inevitably political discussions overshadowed professional matters. A relief fund was organized to help the Czechoslovak colleagues, which they actually did not need at the time. Measures were taken for the physical protection of the Soviet delegation, which appeared to be not completely useless. I remained the link between the antagonistic parties. Both, however, agreed to stay and to participate in the meetings. Near the end of the Conference, the German hosts had organized a reception in the Goethe Haus. The weather was mild, it was full moon, the music in the garden was wonderful, the Rhine wine was delicious and I brought the two groups of librarians together to shake hands. It was a moment of hope, which did not last.

Next day at the closing business meeting, the tension was great and nobody cared about rare books, catalogues or other bibliographical matters. A proposal was passed to postpone the 1969 meeting in Moscow, which had been approved the year before in Toronto. At this critical moment in the history of IFLA, a small group of Danish librarians took it upon themselves, on the spot, to invite us to Copenhagen in 1969. This was a relief indeed.

I want to add a footnote. A couple of months after the Frankfurt meeting, in October 1968, I went to Prague and to Bratislava. This trip had been planned before the events of August. In Brno I had dinner with a group of librarians in a restaurant which was a former prison. Food and wine were excellent, and those members of the Czech group who had been in Frankfurt thanked me for the assistance I had given them during those difficult days. In February 1970, I went to Erevan, as I have already noted in the previous chapter. In the capital of Armenia, I had breakfast in the reading room of the rare books department of the National Library. Food and cognac were excellent and those members of the Soviet group who had been in Frankfurt thanked me for the assistance I had given them during those difficult days. Brno and Erevan, a restaurant full of librarians and a library full of food, but in the two cases human beings and for me, once more, that absolute certainty that libraries can only develop in peace. Our profession is irrevocably linked to peace. In too many opening addresses as president I had to refer to this truth because war was always raging in some part of the world.

Being elected at Copenhagen, taking over in Moscow and ending in Washington seems now to me to be rather symbolic of my way of looking at international cooperation. Like the Danes, my natural environment is a small democracy with a constitutional monarch at the top. I firmly believe that an individual who comes from a small country and to whom personal freedom is a sacred privilege has many advantages on the international scene. Certainly when the organization one is serving is only concerned with professional matters and is working with an obsolete constitution. In Copenhagen the elections were still a joke, in Washington they began to look serious. By the way, my successor is a Dane. I am not sure that if this trend towards formalism continues the Federation will be improved. Later I may be blamed for having been the first over-serious president of IFLA.

I hope that my predecessor agrees with me that together we cover a transition period in the development of IFLA. He inherited what I would call a "Bourgeois Club," not referring to the social status of the directors of national libraries but to Pierre Bourgeois who was for many years president (the longest term of any president) and director of the Swiss national library at Bern. After his death I published an obituary and some Swiss librarians protested against the profile I had drawn. In retrospect I think they were right, but at the time I was so full of the new IFLA matters that I failed to see that the weaknesses of Pierre Bourgeois caught my attention too much and his good qualities too little. The IFLA I received from Sir Frank still had a number of Bourgeois features, in fact the IFLA I handed over to Preben Kirkegård still had too many. I am however no longer sure, as I was during my presidency, that we had to eradicate them drastically.

Starting in Moscow it seems to me appropriate to analyze the cooperation with the Soviet librarians and those of the other socialist countries. The Soviet Union joined formally in 1959. That is four years after I attended my first IFLA meeting. I have a vague recollection of V.I. Shunkov, director of the Library of Social Sciences in Moscow, as a distinguished scholar and a shy man. Margarita Ivanovna Rudomino was my real introduction to Soviet librarianship and she opened the Soviet Union to IFLA. Over the years we became good friends. I had the privilege to attend the fiftieth anniversary of the Library of Foreign Literature in Moscow which she herself had founded in 1921. This was a unique event in librarianship and I was proud to congratulate her on the service she had rendered to international cooperation. I read the following message in the usual way: one sentence in French, followed by a Russian translation, and so on. If you are familiar with your interpreter this exercise gives you the feeling that you understand Russian. Unfortunately this feeling vanishes with the last sentence . . . : "The international library community would be poorer were it not for the Library of Foreign Literature in Moscow. The international vocation of the library which we celebrate today is written in its foundation charter. Hence it is quite normal that for your friends abroad, Margarita Ivanovna, this library symbolizes the link between them and their Soviet colleagues. In a celebration like this, one easily mixes the institution and its head, and why not, pushing this confusion to its limits, when today's director was yesterday's founder. Margarita Ivanovna, my dear colleague, my good friend, in your person I thank your colleagues and your authorities for the radiant importance you have given to the profession which brings us here together today. If I had to summarize your contributions in one sentence I would say that you opened Soviet librarianship to the world and international librarianship to the Soviet Union. This is a major contribution to understanding among people and to our profession which can only develop in peace. In the name of IFLA – of which you are also a vice-president – it is my privilege to hand you this etching by

Margot Weemaes representing a dove of peace, which will keep alive the memory of this beautiful day, which is also the zenith of your brilliant career."

I often travelled alone in the Soviet Union, though individual tourism is not exactly what Intourist stands for. I sometimes had to formally join a Belgian tourist party to secure a bed for myself in one of those huge Soviet hotels. I do not like Intourist, because they always treat you as a dirty capitalist. I tried to explain to the ladies who run the organization that outside the Soviet Union I was no dirty capitalist. I failed completely and could only convey a vague idea that I was a bourgeois propagandist. My main argument with Intourist was when I went to Moscow to prepare the General IFLA Council of 1970. I wanted to include Leningrad in the Conference and they wanted to keep it out. We had exactly the same motives but we did not say so. The trip to Leningrad was much cheaper when it was included in the Conference and the existence of Intourist is to bring into the country as much hard currency as possible. The situation was rather antagonistic. At a certain moment I remember that I said a bit too roughly that the ladies were tougher than the toughest American businessmen. I finally won the battle by an ignominious act of pure blackmail. After three hours of discussion, one of the ladies made the mistake of saying that she did not have enough planes to transfer eight hundred people from Moscow to Leningrad in one night. I said, "All right, a fact is stronger than a Lord Mayor and I shall publish this information in the Western press."

Notwithstanding Intourist, nowithstanding the regime, notwithstanding bureaucracy and statistics, I like the Russians, though it is not easy to like someone through an interpreter. I fortunately have met a number of Russians with whom I could talk directly in a Western language I knew. In 1972 my contacts were most intensive through International Book Year of which I was the chairman, and which was a Soviet initiative proposed to and accepted by UNESCO. Since the State runs the whole country, publishers, booksellers and librarians are civil servants and this makes quite a difference as compared to Western countries, where the different representatives of the book industry made a special effort, during International Book Year, to understand one another. However the official UNESCO Book Year conference in Moscow in 1972 was one of the most frustrating meetings I ever attended. Not one of the basic issues of the still divided book world was discussed. On the one side we heard a series of laudatory Soviet speeches about the situation in the host country, on the other side were platitudes by visitors from abroad. I left the meeting with the unpleasant feeling that in the eyes of Soviet officialdom we, the others, were all crypto-pornographers.

It was early in my presidency that IFLA was kicked out of UNESCO because it had members in South Africa. The International Federation for Documentation (FID) was not kicked out although its member in South Africa was a government institution. I was not at all jealous of FID. I just had to accept that UNESCO had no backbone, no moral criteria, no intellectual power. Nobody is more opposed to apartheid than I am. But UNESCO's anti-apartheid policy was a fundamental mistake, because it severed the black and liberal people in the country from unbiased sources of information. We finally had to ask for the resignation of our members in South Africa in order to rejoin UNESCO. We could not afford to stay outside UNESCO, because it stands for the international community of education, science and culture of which IFLA aspired to be an important part.

UNESCO mainly represents that international community in the developing countries and the real cooperation between IFLA and the third world actually started when I was in charge. I have taken the involvement of new countries in international library matters very seriously. I devoted a lot of my time to this difficult problem. I have travelled extensively in those countries, I listened carefully to their librarians, and I even have the impression that it was not all in vain. But all this does not offset the feeling that I stabbed in the back my colleagues of that university library in Cape Town where the faculty had courageously put a plaque at the entrance hall: "This University lost its Academic Freedom on 26 July 1960 and recovered it in. . . . " (The original text is in Latin and I imagine that it was to avoid a choice between English and Afrikaans.) It is too easy to shout loudly against apartheid in a cosy UNESCO room in Paris. And after South Africa, came China, and after China, Israel. What next? It is one of the conclusions of my IFLA experience, that the international community needs strong non-governmental organizations to keep the governmental organizations within the limits of their responsibility, to build a harmonious community of people as opposed to the divided world of states.

Liverpool, where I chaired my second General IFLA Council, will remain for me the breakthrough of developing countries within IFLA. After long negotiations with UNESCO we were finally able to organize a pre-session seminar for librarians from those countries. Travel expenses and accommodation were provided for English-speaking librarians by UNESCO, the British Council and the Commonwealth Foundation. The Liverpool experiment set the tone for the following years and it also created new problems with which IFLA is still struggling. It was however worthwile to be faced with specific problems of cooperation with librarians from developing countries. This is no place to repeat what I so often said publicly and wrote about those problems. I just want to emphasize once more that there are no basic differences between librarians from industrialized and developing countries. Each conversation with a colleague from Asia or Africa started with the same words "In my country library development has a low priority," and my answer was also the same each time "In my country also"; just as among American or European librarians it is only a small minority which is interested in international cooperation. There is, however, one big distinction to be made. The uninterested Americans or Europeans stay at home, while the uninterested Asians, Africans, Arabs or Latin Americans are always on the move, travelling mostly on UNESCO money. Over the years a real jet set of developing-country librarians has developed, whose only international interest is to attend a meeting (or its opening and closing sessions) in Paris or New York and to forget about it as soon as they get home – where their only concern is to get ready for the next trip. I could quote names, but this would not be fair because the responsibility lies not with them. Those who create false problems in the field of international cooperation are the local authorities and the international governmental organizations which pick out the wrong people. This being said, it is marvellous to remember some of my friends of the third world, who crossed language and other barriers, to work closely with us. I learned a lot from them, foremost to be modest in the face of reality.

The succeeding pre-session seminars struggled with the language problem. All participants had to be at least bilingual. An international language is an indispensable key to international cooperation. A good knowledge of such a language, let's say English for an Indian or Spanish for a Columbian, is however, no sufficient warrant of real library development. Parallel to the international communication is the local language. In recent years most new countries have developed their vernacular languages and this is certainly of the utmost importance for raising the average level of development in order to avoid having a trained élite turned into a self-conscious ghetto. President Senghor of Senegal is an outstanding example of a fighter on two fronts. While being a creative artist in French, he used the International Book Year momentum of 1972 to decree officially six national languages in his country. Let the world, the country, the city, the village become as bilingual as possible. Peace will profit.

I would like to come back a last time to the pre-session seminars. They were essentially a means to bring librarians from developing countries to the regular sessions of the General Council of IFLA. And looking in retrospect, a successful means. UNESCO was always very serious about the themes of these pre-session seminars. I couldn't have cared less. Once the theme was agreed upon we tried to do our best, but the ultimate purpose was to expose these new librarians to the problems of international cooperation. I still remember vividly that for the first time we invited the participants in the pre-session seminar at Liverpool to attend a meeting of the Consultative Committee of IFLA. Some of them were quite shocked, discovering that international cooperation had so many weaknesses. It is my firm belief that such a shock is less harmful than all the blah-blah about the generosity of the rich for the poor.

It would be a lack of courtesy and an example of false modesty not to mention that a few months before the Liverpool meeting, to be exact on 9 July 1971, I received a doctorate honoris causa from the University of Liverpool for service rendered to scholarly and international librarianship. I felt rather in good company, remembering that Sir Anthony Panizzi started his British career as professor of Italian in Liverpool before becoming the famous librarian of the British Museum. Among those who were awarded a degree at the same time as myself I remember Sir Alistair Pilkington from Liverpool, for his invention of floating glass. He told me that he feared only one name in the world "Glaverbel," the Belgian glass trust. A few years later he had no reason any more to fear this name because the firm dropped from one crisis into another. Sir Ludwig Guttmann, the founder of the Olympic Games for handicapped people, thanked the university authorities brilliantly on behalf of the recipients.

At the dinner which closed the ceremony my neighbour was the wife of the bishop and she questioned me about the linguistic difficulties at the University of Louvain and if it was true that the holdings of the library had been split up blindly according to even and uneven numbers. Shamefully I answered in the affirmative and did not add that, if consulted, I would strongly have advised against it. Actually my opinion was asked by Brussels University which split also, but in much better spirit and at about the same time. Good advice was simple indeed. The one who leaves – either Dutch speaking in Brussels or French speaking at Louvain – starts from scratch and after half a dozen years of hard labour he wins, because he does not have to deal with a large proportion of dead material which is a nuisance to any library. I also remember the Brussels sprouts at the dinner, which may have been served in my honour. In the meanwhile the Parisian restaurant, *La Tour d'Argent,* where my colleagues from the jury of the Plateau Beaubourg had dinner that same evening, lingered in my mind. Brussels sprouts and the splitting up of the Louvain library, neither of which I liked, have been following me for many years during my peregrinations around the world.

1972 saw us all together in Budapest, the beautiful city on the Danube with a strange mixture of socialist regime and remnants of the old Austro-Hungarian empire. Like Moscow, like Liverpool, a new experience. For me the most bookish year of my whole life. The theme of the General Council was "Books for All" and was to become IFLA's major contribution to International Book Year (IBY). At Budapest the main papers were given by non-librarians and they have been published under the title "Reading in a Changing World." I wrote the introduction to this book almost four years after the lectures were given, and it gave me the wonderful opportunity to catch again the spirit of IBY. From a more particularly IFLA point of view, Budapest saw the beginning of a broad improvement of its work as a whole. Before I became president the wise decision had been taken to have at each General Council a main theme (for instance, in Toronto "Library Service for a Nation Covering a Large Geographical Area," in Moscow "Lenin and Libraries," in Washington "National and International Library Planning"). Before Budapest, however, the main theme was only dealt with at the opening session, where two or three relevant papers were read. After Budapest, sections and commitees began to deal also with the main theme from their particular angle. Alongside a newly set up Programme Development Group (PDG), chaired by Kees Reedijk, director of the Royal Library in The Hague, began to give a real backbone to the IFLA structure. This started the long process of overall restructure which was finalized at Lausanne in 1976. I am proud that I backed PDG from the outset and I do believe that it was the driving force which gradually allowed IFLA to speak for the whole international library community.

Besides PDG I would not hesitate to claim a certain share in setting up an effective publication programme for IFLA. For many years I had been a witness, generally a passive one and sometimes an active one, of well-intentioned efforts to establish a publishing policy within the Federation. As early as 1963 I did my share in the writing of Leendert Brummel's *Libraries in the World*. Quite a number of faithful IFLA members voiced brilliant ideas about books we ought to issue, but unfortunately action did not follow suggestion. However, one day the miracle happened and in 1972 IFLA started a publishing programme which is flourishing today. If I try to explain this miracle in retrospect I would cite three reasons, in declining order of importance: Wim Koops, Klaus Saur and me. The first one, who is currently the director of the University Library at Groningen, Netherlands, had long experience in the publishing business. It made of him, at least theoretically, the ideal editor of our publications. But practically he had two qualifications which were much more important and which account for the success of the whole venture: he had a legal training and he was unique in the fact that he admirably blended warm seriousness with dry wit. The second, Klaus Saur, director of Verlag Dokumentation at München, was the ideal commercial partner for Wim Koops, to become IFLA's publisher. They strike a queer balance between agreement and disagreement, but new items on IFLA's publication list appeared always when the Federation needed and wanted them. This is a rare compliment. The difference between these two angles is a rather serious one, which I can illustrate with an *ad hoc* example: Wim Koops will have checked and rechecked any text before sending it to Klaus Saur, while the latter will have printed and distributed it before reading it. They are both equally useful. I mentioned myself as the third partner in the game, but I must frankly admit that not much space is left for me. I guess it is just a human weakness of someone, who considers himself first and foremost to be a bookmaker (literally speaking). that when volume after volume of the series IFLA Publications and issue after issue of the IFLA Journal reach his desk he thinks he somehow had a finger in the pie.

From Budapest to Grenoble means for me from IBY to UBC. Universal Bibliographic Control. IBY remained of course after Budapest and UBC was already with us before Grenoble, but the charisma should be linked to the name of those two cities. I suppose that twenty-five years from now I shall be called the UBC president of IFLA. Right now I do not yet see a reason to be ashamed. In my opinion IFLA had badly needed a major programme for a number of years. It is open to argument whether IFLA needed a major programme because it had come to maturity or, on the contrary, that a major programme brought IFLA to maturity. I have no strong personal opinion, but I am slightly inclined to believe in the causal effect of UBC. I am not going to dwell on this topic because Dorothy Anderson writes better on these matters than I could pretend to do and actually has published, in the IFLA Series, a whole book on the subject. I refuse to check whether she or I wrote the introduction. It is, anyhow, signed by me. I only had to invent the acronym, which happened probably during a sleepless night way back in 1967. All the rest existed: years of steady work by IFLA's Cataloguing Committee, able and devoted leaders like Hugh Chaplin and Dorothy Anderson, computer progress in cataloguing, financial assistance from the Council on Library Resources, awareness in developing countries and, finally, UNESCO backing. The future of IFLA's UBC programme looks bright and it will not be long before everyone will realize that this programme contributes to the development of each individual library, large or small, old or new, rich or poor. Our flagship, as the current president of IFLA says.

My connection with IFLA has been a happy one. This does not mean that I had no difficult moments. I already mentioned the apartheid affair. But at Grenoble I had my saddest IFLA experience on a personal level. It would be easy to omit it from these recollections. But it would leave me with the feeling of a lack of courage. The role I played during the Board meeting of 26 August 1973, in asking for Preben Kirkegård's resignation as treasurer was not an enviable one. Preben and I were old friends, we had travelled together in many parts of the world, I lectured at his school in Copenhagen, we shared a common interest in book design, we visited one another's families, we appreciated good company and we had many common friends in and outside IFLA circles. Both to apologize to Preben and to pay tribute to our friendship I shall not withhold the Grenoble crisis in our relations.

It began innocently a couple of years earlier when I found myself saying repeatedly "I have been elected president, but I appointed myself secretary and treasurer". Anthony Thompson had been appointed secretary under my predecessor. We had nothing in common and it has been from the beginning to the end a *dialogue de sourds*. He wanted to remain a faithful personal secretary to the president, and I was convinced that what the Federation needed was a general secretary as independent of the president as possible. Margreet Wijnstroom has given me the chance to prove that I was right as soon as she was appointed secretary general.

The difference of opinion with Preben Kirkegård was on a completely different level, although if I try to get to the root of the problem it may amount to the same basic misunderstanding. In all my life I have only been capable of one loyalty and for a number of years this loyalty has been IFLA and the corollary was that I expected the same radical and exclusive attitude from the other officers. This was of course a mistake but it did not occur to me. It should not have escaped my attention because I was aware that I inherited this harshness from my father, though tempered, at least in my opinion, by the sweetness of my mother. My father was so often unjust to me that I promised to myself never to be unjust to anybody else. I do not think that I have been unjust to Preben, but I came close to it. I wanted a strong and powerful IFLA and I wanted it my way. The finances were a permanent headache. Stupid of me to think that one day there could come an end to such a situation. But I wanted to be able to spend more money, to force sections and committees to broaden the scope of their activities and to enhance the quality of their programmes. Finally I blamed Preben for not bringing in himself the three quarters of our budget which we spent over our dues income. I did it by letter first and later we agreed to bring it before the Board. This was a sad meeting where everybody felt miserable. Preben explained his position with his usual enigmatic dignity. I did not always fully understand his argument and after several painful hours he resigned. The next Board meeting happened to be in Tokyo and I was constantly reminded of an empty chair after the eight years that Preben had spent on the Board. One year later I backed him to become my successor as president. Two footnotes: when Preben took over in 1966 as treasurer from Pierre Bourgeois, the former president who afterwards became our very unorthodox treasurer, there was also an abrupt crisis in their personal relations. I guess Preben wanted to have it his own way. When Anthony Thompson resigned as secretary, Preben published a laudatory article in *Libri*, after he had made sure I had no objections. I add these casual footnotes as a kind of self-defence. I might also add that just after the sad Board meeting at Grenoble I was elected an honorary vice-president of the British Library Association. For once I had no feeling for the humour of my friends from the other side of the Channel.

For a couple of years IFLA had assumed such an importance in my professional work that I had the growing feeling that I had begun to neglect my own library in Brussels. I am absolutely incapable of organizing my life in compartments, of drawing dividing lines. Because international problems received all my attention, I lost interest in local library matters. To be honest, I must add that I derived much more satisfaction from the international role I found myself playing, than from quarrels at home with a bureaucratic authority. The Council on Library Resources (CLR) most generously gave me an opportunity to devote nearly all my time to international library development by appointing me consultant to its international programme. I took a year's leave of absence from the Royal Library and began my work in Washington at the CLR. I spent rewarding months with the Council, which I already knew well, as can be inferred from the preceding pages. During my stay with the Council I travelled a lot outside the United States, but also in the United States, mainly to places with which I was less familiar. I had decided to update Wilhelm Munthe's excellent book on *American Librarianship from a European Angle* published in 1939. The scene had changed so much since the thirties, the world had become so much larger, that the more I learned the more I became aware that it was impossible to update the book and that a new one was needed. I had collected enough material to allow myself to consider making an application to be appointed writer-in-residence at the Villa Serbelloni, at Bellagio, sometime in the middle of 1974. Through recommendations of Gordon Ray, Bob Vosper, Kees Reedijk and Louis Wright I was accepted, and was preparing my notes and myself for the Villa, where I had already attended a five day meeting in 1970 to prepare International Book Year. [1]

Circumstances however were going to decide otherwise. On 12 October 1973, I was presented with the first International Book Prize Award at the Opening of the Frankfurt Book Fair. Chancellor Brandt did not read the paper which had been distributed in advance, but said – I quote and translate from memory – "Once again war is threatening the world and I am not going to speak about books. . . . " How right he was. Next day I went back home and the King of the Belgians asked me if I would consider working for him. For thirty years I had been a happy librarian, first inside my country and later outside, and in my inner horizon there was no profile of a royal palace. Once the surprise of the proposal was over, I humbly accepted. The Council on Library Resources allowed me to leave on 31 December 1973, four months before the end of my contract. I resigned as president of IFLA at the Brussels Board Meeting of 18 December 1973, and my resignation was accepted by the Board "to become officially effective at the conclusion of the Washington General Council in November 1974." Although I could not give much of my time to IFLA during the last months of my presidency, I was happy to stay till the Washington meeting and to quit my beloved Federation in a country with which I have had a love affair for over a quarter of a century.

Recently I have gone over these relations on the occasion of a lecture I gave at the ALA Centennial Conference in Chicago. [2] To do it again here would give me a feeling of plagiarizing myself and we have all learned at school that this is the worst form of plagiarism. Though I am no longer sure that it is true, I shall not do it. It is awfully difficult for me to avoid quoting such American librarians as Verner Clapp, Bob Vosper, Foster Mohrhardt, David Clift, Jack Dalton, Rudy Rogers and so many others with whom I

---

[1] This and the preceding reference to the Villa were written long before I went back to Bellagio as a writer-in-residence in order to correct the manuscript of this book. It is tempting to underscore once more what a unique place this is with the best of America and Italy blended. Dropped by nature at "the point which divides the winds" which blow over lake Como, but built by men at the point where mind and heart meet, which is close to the dream assigned to it by Pliny the Younger, the local genius.

[2] Basically chapter 3.

had different but always inspiring associations over the years. Fascinating sounds to my ears are also names like Library of Congress, New York Public Library, Pierpont Morgan Library, Newberry Library, Yale and Harvard Libraries, and so many others. Let me just note here, what I did not do in my Chicago paper, that I would have left the profession more than a quarter of a century ago, if I had not been exposed to American librarianship. My early experience at home had left me with a feeling of obsolete narrow-mindedness, with a world of gentlemen and spinsters who had built a huge wall of books between themselves and the world at large. On the ship which brought me home after my first American trip in 1951, I promised myself that I would try to make my library a part of the surrounding world and to use the books to build bridges. At the time this was not very clear in my mind, but vague feelings belong to youth.

The dividing book wall must have taken a precise meaning at that time. It was also the beginning of my interest in IFLA. I never missed a General Council since 1956, I was chairman of the section of national and university libraries from 1959 till 1964, I was coopted as a Board member in Rome in 1964 (at the Palazzo Barberini under *Venus and Adonis* by Titian) and I became a vice-president in Helsinki in 1965, first vice-president in 1967 in Toronto, president in 1969 in Copenhagen, and honorary president in Washington in 1974. It is undoubtedly with a feeling of gratitude for the confidence of the membership that I write down these dates. Behind these dates I see many faces of human beings and as I said on quitting in Washington before the largest audience IFLA ever had, "it is you who made me like my work for IFLA." My daughter and my son-in-law were in that audience. I was happy and proud that they were repeating, in their own field, my American adventure of a quarter of a century ago.

Poets like to use in their verses the names of cities, and a simple geographical name receives, through their talent, a transcendental dimension. To conclude I would like to imitate the poets and list a series of proper names, which for one reason or another I was not able to mention in this chapter and which belong to people whom I still meet very often in my mind when library matters are being overshadowed by human feelings. I first considered listing pell-mell all names of which I thought spontaneously, but an army of friendly profiles was assaulting me and so I decided rather arbi-

trarily to limit myself to a few names beginning with "P." I always
had a weak spot in my heart for the letter "p," because it is the first
letter of papyrus, parchment and paper. So, with an apology to all
the other letters of the alphabet and the names they would introduce, I salute Ke-Long Park, Geneviève Patte, Laïna Peep, Carlos
Penna, Everett Petersen, Günther Pflug, Maurice Piquard, Roger
Pierrot, Angela Popescu, Branka Popovic, Gerhard Pommasl, and
Minna Poznanskaya.

Name Index